This wonderful book is both recognizab[...]
are given here is not simply another bool[...]
for living in and with meaning, Christi[...]
ing. Wherever we are, here and now is t[...]
because this here and now is where God has chosen [...]

The Most Revd Rowan Williams

Precious few are the books that accomplish what this masterfully practical and inspiring book accomplishes. Nor do they do so with such grace, depth and unflinching insight. While this book serves as a practical rule of life to guide the Nazareth Community in the heart of London, it is at the same time a trellis of life where the buds and blossoms of our beseeching find stability in silence, the beauty of the stranger and a door wide open for all who feel they have no place to call home. Those who tread the pathless path of contemplation will be grateful to be in Richard Carter's debt for the gift of this remarkable book.

Martin Laird OSA, author of An Ocean of Light

Reading The City is my Monastery I felt that I was being invited to walk with Richard Carter in many different places, to pause as he reflected with love and with wonder on the people and events around him, to share his joy or indignation, to understand how to begin to construct a prayerful community that lives fully in the world – and, above all, to see through his eyes that God is in every one of us. This is a book that moved me deeply and will surely strengthen and give heart to many. It is an autobiography of poetry and prayer. A primer on how to build a community of still spirituality in a busy city. Above all, a powerful poetic meditation on meeting God every day on the streets and in the people of London.

Neil MacGregor, founding director of the Humboldt Forum in Berlin, director of the British Museum 2002–15

The City is my Monastery is beautiful, inspiring, humble and attractive. I think this is the beginning of something special. It is so deeply soaked in loving attention, and that is what makes it so infectious.

The Revd Sam Wells, Vicar of St Martin-in-the-Fields

For those of us who seek to minister from a still centre and nurture our faith in a hectic world this book is a generous gift. The City is My Monastery is rich and moving reading which warmed my spirit and encouraged me to stay.

The Rt Revd Sarah Mullally, Bishop of London

This entrancing book – part lectio, part prayer, part autobiography in frag-ments – is designed to show all those who are called to a life in deepening union with Christ how they can find their 'monastery' wherever they are. In Richard Carter's case, this has led to the foundation of a new form of religious life at St Martin-in-the-Fields, amid the immigrants, homeless and desperate who find a refuge there. This is a life-changing book, and needs to be read as it is written – as a prayer.

Sarah Coakley, Norris-Hulse Professor Emerita, University of Cambridge

Prayer is as natural as breathing. To be human is to pray, yet most of us feel inadequate about our praying. All of us can learn and grow in the company of those who are passionate and experienced teachers of prayer. Richard Carter is such a person – a natural teacher who is deeply committed to a life of prayer. His vocation was nurtured in the UK and grown in the beauty of Pacific islands in the company of a remarkable religious community. Now he has the most extraordinarily fruitful ministry at St Martin-in-the-Fields where the city has become his monastery. He prays with and for all sorts of people to whom he is as attentive as he is to God. This book is a wonderful mix of his inward reflections and an unusually practical guide about how to pray and deepen our love of God, one another and the wonderful creation in which we find ourselves. There are treasures on every page: wisdom gathered, practised and shared. This book is so readable it could be a quick read, but linger and use it slowly over the months and years. This is a guide to life.

The Rt Revd Nicholas Holtam, Bishop of Salisbury

In the centre of the city, with all its bustle and violence, Richard Carter's book, simple and filled with poetry, opens up for us a place of peace and community, in which the God whom we falteringly seek is discovered as eagerly rushing towards us.

Father Timothy Radcliffe OP

There is something for everybody in this very readable kaleidoscope of life at its most real, in a flow of poetry, stories and guidance on prayer. By turns funny, touching, heartbreaking, shocking, it stops us in the tracks of our complacency, revealing that even within much of the human suffering that goes on behind the scenes in our society there is still the presence of pure gold: God present in everybody, especially at the heart of the big city, beckoning us to see with new eyes and be changed. This is one of those books that can be a lifetime's companion, holding before us what we are here for: *Life.*

Father George Guiver, Community of the Resurrection

A beautiful and inspiring book that invites us to make space in the middle of the city, to make time in the middle of a busy day, to make peace between us across our differences. Richard Carter has written a book not of abstract theory but of lived experience and practice. It will inspire urban and rural dwellers alike, who want to become more deeply still in a distracted and fractious world.

Revd Lucy Winkett, Rector of St James's Church, Piccadilly

THE CITY IS MY
MONASTERY

A Contemporary
Rule of Life

RICHARD CARTER

PARACLETE PRESS
BREWSTER, MASSACHUSETTS

   Library of Congress Cataloging-in-Publication Data
Names: Carter, Richard, 1959- author.
Title: The city is my monastery : a contemporary rule of life / Richard
   Carter.
Description: Brewster, Massachusetts : Paraclete Press, 2020. | Summary:
   "Carter tells the story of the Nazareth Community in the heart of
   London, where members gather to seek God in contemplation, to
   acknowledge their dependence on God's grace, and to learn to live openly
   and generously with all"-- Provided by publisher.
Identifiers: LCCN 2020017405 (print) | LCCN 2020017406 (ebook) | ISBN
   9781640605824 (trade paperback) | ISBN 9781640605831 (epub) | ISBN
   9781640605848 (pdf)
Subjects: LCSH: Nazareth Community (St. Martin-in-the-Fields (Church :
   Westminster, London, England)) | St. Martin-in-the-Fields (Church :
   Westminster, London, England) | Christian communities--England--London.
   | Spiritual life--Christianity. | London (England)--Church history. |
   Christian life--Anglican authors.
Classification: LCC BX5186.N39 C37 2020 (print) | LCC BX5186.N39 (ebook)
   | DDC 283/.4213--dc23
LC record available at https://lccn.loc.gov/2020017405
LC ebook record available at https://lccn.loc.gov/2020017406

10 9 8 7 6 5 4 3 2 1

Published by Paraclete Press
Brewster, Massachusetts
www.paracletepress.com

Printed in the United States of America

In Memory of Fr Simon Holden CR
the monk who helped me to see that the
city was my monastery

And for Ebenezer Okrah and all those who
each day show us the way to Nazareth

On 3 October 2013, an unmarked vessel carrying 500 migrants, mainly from Eritrea and Somalia, sank off the coast of the Italian island of Lampedusa. It is thought that 360 people drowned and 150 were rescued by the Italian Coastguard. Searching for a way to bring comfort, Mr Tuccio, a local carpenter, collected wood from the wrecked boat and made simple crosses for the survivors to wear. The British Museum commissioned Mr Tuccio to make a cross for their collection as a symbol of the beginning of the twenty-first century. Mr Tuccio also sent a Lampedusa Cross to St Martin-in-the-Fields as a sign of our own outreach to refugees, asylum seekers and those with no recourse to public funds. When we began the Nazareth Community, Mr Tuccio made crosses for each of our members as a sign of our community and God's love revealed to us in the suffering of the cross: a call to be with God and neighbour where we are now.

Contents

Foreword

SAMUEL WELLS

Ever since Antony, often described as the first monk, left the
city in the third century to live an ascetic life in the desert of
Egypt, those seeking a holy life have been more inclined to
head away from the city than towards it. And so it was that
when I waved Richard Carter off for a month's reflection in
January 2017, knowing he was going to Dorset and recognizing he was looking for the next step in deepening his walk
with God, I was expecting him to come back with the same
conclusion as Antony. But he didn't. He said, 'The city is my
monastery – St Martin's is my monastery.'

Now for anyone at St Martin-in-the-Fields, surprise is a
daily occurrence. You can't stay around St Martin's for long
without believing in a God of Surprises. But Richard's revelatory moment did surprise me, for two reasons. One was that
it was clear Richard's vision for a deeper, holier life involved
one thing more than anything else: silence. And St Martin's,
as Richard describes vividly and completely accurately in this
book, is seldom if ever silent. The siren, the busker, the troubled
and the protester together fill most unforgiving minutes. The
other was that Richard may be a person at home in silence,
but he's certainly not a solitary. He's one of the most gregar-
ious people I've ever met – a magnet drawing towards him a
community of faithful and forsaken, wondrous and woolly. So
the question was, 'If this is your monastery, who are the other
monks?'

In many ways, this book is Richard's answer to these two
surprises. For here he describes in illuminating detail the ways

he has come to build a spirituality in the heart of this huge, grand and complex city, and the people who have become his companions. From February to November 2017, Richard discussed with me, and experimented with others, as he explored what eventually became the seven pillars of community outlined in this book. What you will read in these pages are the ingredients that we realized, by the end of 2017, had become an embryonic community. We thought it would number perhaps a dozen. In fact, on the day of its birth, 18 March, 2018, it numbered 49; and six months later another nine members joined, making it 58. What's the secret?

Its character is very close to Richard's own character, manifest in these pages. Rooted in profound faith, and a constant longing to make that faith take flesh in practices of daily humility and holiness. Passionate in seeking connection with other human beings, not just people like himself, but whoever God sends his way. Genuinely expectant of seeing the face of Christ in each stranger. Faithful in approaching prayer just as carefully as in building a relationship – listening, being still, staying receptive – hanging out, communicating in actions more than words that 'you're worth it'. Searching through poetry and prose, art and drama, for a way to express the deepest and daily experiences that touch the heart and the soul. And regularly rewarded by revelations of grace: having made room in mind and spirit and life to be hospitable to the Spirit, knowing Christ to be most commonly present in the least of these, receiving such visitations almost habitually.

What this book describes is immersion in the ways of the Spirit – an infectious immersion that draws others to trust, to hope, to try, to persevere. There's discipline, routine and regularity; but these are suffused with imagination, hunger, desire, longing; and the whole is surrounded with irony, humour, self-deprecation, that seeks the pearl of great price, yet doesn't take itself too seriously. This isn't a definitive handbook, for all that the contents page might suggest. This is a series of memories, dreams and reflections, whose cumulative effect is to make one set the book aside and plunge into this life oneself. It's an appetizer that draws one into an experiment.

When you love someone, you notice things about them: the way they speak, the mannerisms they repeat, the habits they embody, the phrases they use. Your attention discloses the depth of your joy in them. This is a book about what it means to love God. It's full of the same depth of attention and observation, care and devotion, such that no one who finishes reading it can fail to be wiser and more acute in perceiving how God lives and moves and suffuses our being. When we love someone, we simply want to be with them. What we do together isn't especially important: what's important is the being with. This, then, is a book about what it means to be with God – and not in an abstract, idealized way, but in a very earthy, honest, practical and tangible way. It's a book to inspire us to be with God together – as a community, a community that shares desire, passion, longing, depth, but also irony and humour.

One of the best-known stories about the Desert Fathers, of whom St Antony was the first, goes like this:

Abba Lot went to Abba Joseph and said to him, 'Abba, as far as I can I say my little office, I fast a little, I pray and meditate, I live in peace as far as I can, I purify my thoughts. What else can I do?' Then the old man stood up and stretched his hands toward heaven. His fingers became like ten lamps of fire and he said to him, 'If you will, you can become all flame.'

This book is like that story. It's not about replicating every experience related here or even inhabiting every single habit commended here. It's about being caught up in the infectious holiness of God, and inspired by these narratives and these poems, prayers and promises to believe that you too can be suffused with the Spirit, not alone, but in community, and the city can become your monastery too. If you think it's simple, you haven't tried it. If you think it's impossible, you're trying too hard. 'Not I,' said St Paul, 'but the grace of Christ in me.' There's no better feeling in the world. May you know that feeling today. And always.

Acknowledgements

I have been writing and reflecting upon this rule of life for the last three years, but I think I have been discovering this way of life as long as I can remember. It is inspired by many people, some of whom I would like to acknowledge here.

I would like to thank the whole of St Martin-in-the-Fields for its breadth and diversity and its challenge. It is an incredible place to work where every day is new. It is a church I love deeply, which has shown me the face of Christ in countless ways. It continues to be a privilege to serve and learn from this community 'at the heart and on the edge'. I would like particularly to thank our vicar, Sam Wells, who has written the Foreword to this book – for his insight, encouragement, challenge and support in the formation and life of the Nazareth Community. I am grateful to all the members of our clergy team, past and present, especially Katherine Hedderly and her husband, Loren Mrkusic, who have been such caring companions on the way. I would also like to thank all those who serve this church, too many to mention, in so many generous incarnational ways.

I would like to acknowledge the Melanesian Brotherhood, the community I served for 15 years, and which formed me in their 'true way of service'. This community is such an example of brave humility and what it means to live the gospel. They will always hold my heart.

I would like to thank my family for all they have taught me about loving both God and neighbour. My father Tony Carter, who died in 1999, showed me the beauty of the Anglican Church with its generosity and grace; my mother Sally who created a home with an open door and taught me to do the same; and all the members of my family – Tim, Jenny, Joe, George, Matthew, Siobhan, Molly, Jack, Andrew and Helen (who have contributed the wonderful drawings and prints which have so enhanced this book), Francis, Alice and Daniel. Daniel has once again read all the drafts of this book several times and helped prepare it for publication with the patience of a true saint. They themselves are a community of unconditional love.

I am also very grateful for some dear friends: Jerry Eggleston, who first read some of my prayers, reflections and poems, and encouraged me to continue and get these published. She has listened to many of the stories contained here and heard and understood, she sees the wonder of even the smallest created thing; Catherine Duce, who lived this community life with me, read the draft and helped me to discover this way of life, even praying in the park come wind and rain; Robert Pfeiffer, who read so carefully and offered helpful advice as did Jessica Kingsly; Elizabeth Garsten, who read the first draft and believed in it and has always encouraged me to write; Juliette Hulme, who has been such a faithful friend and priest on this journey; Annie Blaber, who gave me the generous hospitality of a wonderful place to write some of this book, and delicious meals and good company after a day's writing; Vicky Howard, a member of the Nazareth Community who contributed her prints with Andrew Carter and Helen Ireland mentioned above; Jamie, who prayed for me; the Society of St Francis, for continuing to inspire this vision in me; and Rowan Williams, who has embodied in his ministry so much of what I have tried to capture here and who has written the afterword to this book.

I would like to thank Christine Smith and all at Canterbury Press for their enthusiastic encouragement and help in publishing this book. I would also like to thank SPCK for permission to include part of my chapter 'My Neighbour in Trafalgar Square' from *Who is my Neighbour: The Global and Personal Challenge* (edited by Richard Carter and Samuel Wells, 2018).

Finally, may I thank all those who appear in the pages of this book either named or anonymously. I believe that the Word was made flesh and continues to be revealed in silence, in service, in sacrament, in Scripture, in sharing, in Sabbath time and in staying with – and most of all, in each one of you. I hope I have done you justice in these pages. Thank you to all the members of the Nazareth Community and our Sunday International Group – you have shown me a life-giving way. May the city truly be our monastery where the presence of God is always found.

Introduction

Andrew Carter

The city is my monastery

We plan the holiday in advance
But the holy day is today
The monks knew the ancient wisdom of giving each part of
the day to God
So that they tasted the height, breadth and depth of
God's presence
The coming of the light, the hopes and struggles of the day,
the intensity of noon,
the shadows of evening bringing the toil to an end,
food and refreshment, the silence and darkness of the night
But we no longer notice the movements of the sun
We do not see the sky just the screen
We have used the remote and become remote
We who have no time for God

Have become time's prisoners
We have pulled the curtains on the sun and moon and have
    closed the windows so that we no longer smell the rain or
    breathe the air of the changing seasons
We have been given this treasure beyond price and yet we
    scarcely notice it.

Our monastery is here and now
Where you are today
The person you are speaking with
The room you are sitting in
The street where you are walking
The action you are doing now
This is your monastery
This is your prayer
Eternity is now
The city is our monastery.

In each person there is a portion of solitude which no
    human intimacy can ever fill
Yet you are never alone
Let yourself be plummeted to the depths
And you will see that in your heart of hearts
In the place where no two people are alike
Christ is waiting for you
And what you never dared hope for springs to life.[1]

At the beginning of 2017 I left London for a month to stay in a Franciscan community in order to try to discern the will of God in my life. I longed, as perhaps many long, to get away, to rediscover silence and through prayer the presence of God. I needed time to listen again. It's easy in our lives to lose that reflective space – we do not abandon it willingly, but we can so easily be distracted and fragmented in the rush and anxiety of living and coping.

I love London, with all its energy and creativity. It feels alive to me. I felt I had come home to this city after living in different parts of the world. I have lived in the centre of this city for twelve years and I feel I belong. I love its diversity. Outside my front door you can meet people from every walk of life and every part of the world. I do not often experience loneliness here because there is always too much going on. Wonderful things – art, history, churches, cathedrals, drama, music, food, sport, parks, ponds, a wonderful river, with north bank and south bank – and of course people. This is the United Kingdom I believe in, a people of every age, language, island and race – infinite in uniqueness. And St Martin-in-the-Fields, where I am a priest, is the most wonderfully alive church, where no two days are the same. When you open the door, humanity flows in. What more could I ask for in ministry than to meet Christ in such diversity? And yet I hungered for not only this breadth of experience but also depth: a still point, an intimacy with God. I had known this contemplative stillness before, but now it often got lost in the rush and the stress of this city that never stops.

Before coming to St Martin's, I had lived a life of great simplicity as a member of the Melanesian Brotherhood in the Solomon Islands in the South Pacific. This is a Community of Anglican Brothers who take renewable vows of poverty, chastity and obedience for five years. Stripped of many of the material appendages of the West, I had learnt to become atten-tive to the wonder of God: the day, the night, the heat, the rain, the vastness of the sea, the reality of death, the fellowship of my community. Now in the middle of London it sometimes felt I had lost something beyond price – lost that sense of God's transcendence, the sense of a space higher, broader and deeper than I could imagine. In my life in Melanesia I had been con-stantly aware of the mystery of life and God present in all things. Present when we planted the gardens, knowing we would be dependent on what we grew; present as we set out to sea in canoes or boats; present in floods and cyclones and the heat that dried up the land and made you pray for the rains to come again. In London, I felt I had lost connectedness. Every moment of the day was filled with stuff from the time I woke up to the time I went to sleep. And although I loved so much of what I did, I felt that if I slowed down, all the plates I was trying to spin at the same time would come crashing down around me. What I was missing was the experience of being attentive to the love of God, and being recharged by it. I was no longer awake to a world alive with miracles. Although I loved London, there was also within me a call to retreat, to rediscover God at the very centre of my life, to move back again from head to heart. Perhaps like St Antony, I thought, I should leave the city behind again and try to rediscover a simpler, more prayerful way of living.

So, as part of my discernment, I spent January at Hilfield Friary in the middle of Dorset. One of the first things I noticed was the darkness at night, thick darkness where you could not see your own hand in front of your face. How different after the constant, 24-hour street life of Trafalgar Square. And I discovered silence again. At this community I spent time in silence, time in prayer, time receiving and offering the sacrament of Eucharist, time working with others in the kitchen and gardens, time serving and helping, and time reading. I even learnt to lay a hedge. These elements have always been part of the religious life. It felt like an oasis and a sanctuary. I have always loved the pattern and the rhythm of the religious life. It is healing. This friary at Hilfield has always felt like a spiritual home for me. When I was young, I remember kneeling at the altar in the darkness of its simple converted barn of a chapel with my father, the St Damiano cross, which spoke to Francis, suspended in front of me. It was one of my earliest experiences of the beauty of prayer. Since then, all of my life it has been a place of return for me, which has held the chapters of my life together, and I have loved this place and the many Brothers I have known who live this life with humanity and humility.

Yet there was a surprise in this. Here in the quiet, I listened and again and again felt the same call. Not to retreat and escape the city, but to return to it. I felt that the voice of God within me was saying: 'The city is your monastery.' Or perhaps even more distinctly, 'St Martin's is your monastery.' At this present time this is the place of need: those open doors, opening on to Trafalgar Square through which the needs of the modern world come in and also flow out. It is here in the centre of the city that you must continue to seek God. And you will continue to find God in the many faces of Christ of those who are all made in his image. Do not flee the city. Rather return to it. Stay. Seek the wellspring in the place where the water is needed by so many. And find the wellspring where it has always been, *within* those who need it most, indeed within your own greatest need. It was a distinct call to stability in a city which is so transient, indeed a call within my own life which has often seemed transient too. Stability in a place where change is so fast and, particularly among the vulnerable, where there is a sense that while everything and everyone else is part of a process that moves on, they are somehow left behind in limbo.

God's call is mysterious; it comes in the darkness of faith. It is so fine, so subtle, that it is only within the deepest silence within us that we can hear it. And yet nothing is so decisive and overpowering for anyone on this earth, nothing surer or stronger. This call is uninterrupted. God is always calling us. But there are distinctive moments of this call, moments that leave a permanent mark on us – moments that we never forget and which set the course and patterns of our life.[2]

The city, more than ever, is in need of God's love. This city is God's, just as much as the hills and valleys. Perhaps even more so, for it is filled to bursting with those made in God's image, and among them many in poverty in whom we are told Christ is especially present. St Martin-in-the-Fields discovered its narrative in the horror of the First World War – it became the place of belonging, the place that the dispossessed could call home, the place they learnt again of the love of God after the horror of the trenches. Now in the crisis our world faces, a crisis of identity and belonging, a crisis where once again people both fear the violence in our midst and want to turn inwards and return to a national identity that does not exist, is it not now more than ever that we must reimagine the kingdom of God – a kingdom truly worth living for? It is now that the church with the open door for all is needed, a place of discovery and hope, offering prayers for our city and nation: a church at the heart and on the edge.

I sense within myself, more than ever, not the need to do more, but actually to be stiller. The need for the monastic values in the centre of the city – for sacred space, for people to come and replenish tired, stressful or simply busy lives. To provide space for silence. To become an oasis of the Spirit. Not simply to be managers organizing resources and events, but those who seek God: to be men and women of contemplation and prayer, who know their utter dependence on God's grace; those who believe that God is incarnated in our lives and whose vocation is to make a place and a space for that presence.

How can I or others do this? How can we do it without being depleted or running dry like those water mains which burst so that the water runs frothy and grey down the gutters and is wasted? The good news is that we do not do this. We simply prepare the space for God to be with us. We create a sacred space, a Nazareth in the centre of the city – the pattern that allows us to be present. Discipline is not a prison to be feared. It is a deeper listening. It is the creation of a form, structure and exercise that allows for the roots to go down and the branches to grow. If we keep on digging up our roots how will we grow? Or to use another image – our spiritual discipline is like the banks of a river. It is not for its own sake. Banks without the river would be pointless, but the banks are there to allow the river of God's love to flow.

What is this discipline? Well, in the words of St Benedict it is 'a school of love'. It is learning to listen again with 'the ear of the heart'.[3]

It will actually involve not doing more, but doing less, but each element with more attentiveness and joy.
It will involve letting go of some of those elements of your life that you do not need. A turning off of the stuff that is dragging you away from where you want to be. Literally a turning off at some times of the mobile, the computer, the television, the agendas and habits that are depleting you.

It will involve a slower and more attentive way of living,
    and practising the things that bring consolation, hope and
    thanksgiving.
You will find that the cure to your sense of meaningless and
    loneliness is solitude.

So what was my own deepest longing? I had lived for 15 years
as a member of the Melanesian Brotherhood in the South
Pacific. I knew the deep rhythms and beauty of the religious
way of life as well as its struggles and difficulties. But how
could the wisdom of that life be embodied in the midst of a
busy city? And the more I prayed, the more I heard this calling:

Live more prayerfully
Live more holistically
Live slower
Live more gently with others and with self
Live with more space for silence and solitude
Live generously and hospitably
Live with an attentiveness to God, to creation and
    to neighbour
Live with a greater recognition of God in all things
Learn from the community of others
Rediscover a poverty of spirit that lets go of ambition and
    self-interest and look for Christ where he was found
    during his life – on the edge among the lost
Rediscover the gift of peace at the very centre of all that
    you do.

I needed to discover the simple disciplines that can enable a
community to grow: an obedience, a listening, a life-giving rule
of life. I discerned that the way forward was to write down a
'rule of life' for a community living in the midst of the city.
This was the community, at that stage yet to be formed, which
now has become known as the Nazareth Community. But I
could not sit down and write a rule of life cold, as it were. I
had to pray it into being. Neither would it be a rule with the
connotation of something prescribed or fixed – rather I was

seeking to discern a pattern of life, a means of becoming, a life-giving way. I was seeking not a rule to create guilt but one through which the Spirit could flourish and bloom where it was planted. It would need to be a contemporary rule of life, one that recognized the demands of the modern world and yet held fast to a sustainable discipline. I have been praying this pattern of life into being for many years, perhaps all of my life, and these reflections are punctuated with the prayers I have written during this time and the people who have become my prayers. I hope all those who read this will participate in this experiment in being with God and others.

What I have written is a spiritual journal of discovery, fragments of a conversation with God, myself and others. You will find many different voices, the hope and the despair, the light and the shadow, the beauty of life and the fear. You will find poetry, prayer, narrative, the voice of the preacher, the longing of a lover, the despair of the lost, the hope and doubt of the disciple, and the narratives of a witness. My hope and prayer is that you too will discover Nazareth – the time, place and pattern within your own life to seek God; that you too will find God with you in your park, or on the street, in the church, or in the face of those you meet, in the ordinary and extra-ordinary, in the moments of revelation and in the struggle, on the altar, or in the call of the one whose poverty makes you turn away – in the inscape of your life and the life all around you. I have not written a set of rules. Rather in response to this city and through the gifts this city has given me I have tried to weave a cloak that like St Martin I can share. For I know I have shared the cloak of many others.

When John Bell writes a hymn, he says he lets it be sung by the community for a few years before it becomes a hymn written down for others. I think this rule of life is the same. It has to be taken up and prayed and lived. The rules of life, the good ones, are not a list of regulations, but spring from the prayer of the heart. Brother Roger at Taizé spent three years praying alone in Taizé before the first Brothers came to join him. We should not underestimate the working of that Spirit. We do not form Nazareth Communities, God does. Communities are gifts. So

both this book and the Nazareth Community has been prayed
and lived into being.

What do you seek?

When a Taizé Brother makes his life commitment he is asked
this question: 'Beloved Brother, what are you asking for?'

To which he answers: 'The mercy of God and the community of my Brothers.'

I have always thought that to be the most beautiful of
requests. What more could one ask in life than for the mercy
of God and the community of one's brothers and sisters. If we
were to lose mercy, we would have lost everything. The mercy
of God is the source of compassion. It is the reservoir of God's
unconditional love for you that makes the future possible.
All community life is based on this mercy. 'Lord Jesus Christ,
Son of God, have mercy on me, a sinner.' This is the Jesus
Prayer that holds life together; as essential as one's heartbeat.
For those seeking a life together, Christ's mercy is the most
essential request. Will you allow yourself to be challenged by
that most ultimate love, to forgive not seven times but seventy
times seven – forgive out of the very depths of your own need
of God's mercy?

So perhaps all of us should begin with that question.
What do you seek? At the beginning of any call to Christian
community, this is the most searching of questions. Seeking is
not about simply abandoning, rather it is about discovering.
All of us will have a long list of things that we might dream
of leaving behind: loneliness, stress, overeating, resentment,
greed, jealousy, alienation from the lifestyles we live, relationships that have gone wrong and now fester within: it will not
need much imagination to add to the list of the things that
weigh you down. But what is it that you seek? Here is the list I
made – gathered from the blessings of life.

What do I seek?

The mercy of God.
The community of my sisters and brothers.
'Seven whole days not one in seven I will praise thee.'
A deeper sense of connectedness with God at the very centre
of self.
Time for my neighbour and the discovery of who my
neighbour is.
A deeper attentiveness to creation and God's presence in
all things.
To embrace the holiness of my present state. To do ordinary
things extraordinarily well. To bloom where we are
planted. (Francis de Sales)
A path with heart: 'Take heart, it is I, do not be afraid.'
(Mark 6.50)
To live not faster or more eclectically but with more space
to find the gaps and inhabit the spaces.
A compassionate generosity, where, like the miracle of the
loaves and fish, the scarcity of the gifts we each offer in
humility, can become the signs of the abundance of God's
coming kingdom.
To discover within my own neighbourhoods the presence of
Christ.
A community where we are more than the sum of our parts
and celebrate the gifts that each person brings, together
withstanding the cynicism, despair and destructiveness of
our time.
A community that tries to 'live Jesus' allowing Jesus to walk
once again – incarnated in the flesh and blood of our own
lives. (Francis de Sales)
To rediscover a greater poverty of spirit, not a poverty
that is oppressive, but one which lives the joy of the
Beatitudes.
To participate in God's justice, a justice that challenges
discrimination and structures of oppression and fear and
empowers each individual to become the witness of God's
grace.

To let go of dualistic thinking with its competition
   and defence of private territory and to enter into the
   contemplative unity of the Trinity.
To discover in Christ a new hope and laughter, where the
   journey, and the companions, and the conversations on
   that journey are as important as the final destination.
To practise the little relational values: gentleness, humility,
   kindness, patience, charity, cordiality, hospitality,
   mildness, simplicity, forbearance towards one's
   neighbour, service to others, listening, friendliness,
   respect, tolerance of imperfections including one's own.
   (Francis de Sales)
Remembering that 'nothing is so strong as gentleness and
   nothing so gentle as real strength'. (Francis de Sales)
'Heart speaks to heart.' We learn not by argument but by
   relationships of truth. (Francis de Sales)
To incarnate these values in the places where we live and
   work so that we do not abandon these qualities in the
   process of reaching our goals. Rather the way we live
   now is our goal.
Follow blessing rather than curse and recrimination.
The discipline we seek is not a set of rules to confine us but
   a pattern of life to set us free. We want to live the gospel.
   O Lord, give us grace.

Why Nazareth?

Nazareth is the place of formation. We know very little of what
happened at Nazareth, but we see the man. We see the result
of all that grew and was nurtured within him and was to be
revealed in his ministry, death and resurrection. In Nazareth,
Jesus lived his message before he spoke it. His message was
his life. If we are to be the disciples of Christ, we also need a
Nazareth time: the time to let the seed that Christ sows find
good soil and grow in us.

What is the theological significance of the hidden 90 per cent – the thirty-odd years Jesus spent in Nazareth? Those Nazareth years demonstrate, in their obscurity as much as their sheer duration, in their simplicity as much as their large majority, God's fundamental purpose to be with us – not primarily to rescue us, or even empower us, but simply to be with us, to share our existence, to enjoy our hopes and fears, our delights and griefs, our triumphs and disasters. This is the way incarnation echoes creation and anticipates heaven: Jesus simply relishes life with us and bewilders and disarms us with his patience, his gentleness, his presence and his attention.[4]

Perhaps we have all had the sneaking hope that our Christian faith will help us escape our present life, not stay in it and with it. But suppose God's calling is that we should also be with – with others, with Jesus, with his patience, his gentleness, his presence and his attention? The Nazareth Community is an experiment in being with. Being with in a way we have perhaps been with before, like those disciples on the road to Emmaus, but not fully recognized that being with until the guest has departed. Nazareth is about creating the opportunity to be with in a more intentional way: creating opportunities to be present with God and one another. That sounds difficult, until one realizes that actually Christ has been present all along but we have not noticed. Creating a Nazareth Community is actually about recognizing that Nazareth is not a different place. It is here and now. Here in the centre of the city or wherever you are present.

Charles de Foucauld said that if the contemplative life were possible only behind monastery walls or in the silence of the desert, we should give a little monastery and a tract of desert to everyone working hard to survive in a bustling city. He did not renounce contemplation; far from it, he had decided that the place the contemplative life needed to be lived was on the streets. 'Oh Jesus, a monastery like your house at Nazareth, in which to live hidden as you did when you came among us.'[5] Contemplation on the streets, that is our task – a fusion of the two greatest commandments: 'Love God with all your heart, soul and strength, and love your neighbour as yourself.'

Sam Wells summarizes this Nazareth calling in the following way:

The Nazareth Manifesto: Being with God

1 Our calling is to imitate the way God is.
2 Our clue to how to imitate God is to follow the way God is with us in Christ.
3 Our first awareness is the abundance of God and our own scarcity – together with our gratitude that we have been given so many ways to transform our scarcity into God's abundance.
4 It is a miracle of grace that God meets our scarcity through the abundance we discover in those apparently more exposed to scarcity than ourselves.
5 A community seeking regeneration has already within it most of what it needs for its own transformation.
6 We do not configure situations as problems needing solutions.
7 We cannot understand, listen to, be taught by or receive grace from people unless we inhabit their world which we see as valuable for its own sake.
8 There is no goal beyond restored relationship: reconciliation is the gospel.
9 The centre of ministry is worship (being with God); and the centre of mission is being with the disadvantaged and receiving abundance from them.
10 Being with is both the method and goal of social engagement.[6]

What is the pattern or structure of this life together? The Nazareth Community was formed by being with God and by being with one another:

With Silence
With Service
With Scripture
With Sacrament
With Sharing
With Sabbath
Staying With.

Remember this life is with us already, it is just that we have not realized it yet or recognized the treasure in our midst.

Notes

1 Brother Roger of Taizé, *The Sources of Taizé*, GIA Publications Inc., 2000, p. 11.

2 Carlo Carretto, *Letters from the Desert*, Darton, Longman & Todd, 1972, from the Introduction, p. xi.

3 *The Rule of St Benedict*, Prologue.

4 Samuel Wells, *A Nazareth Manifesto*, Wiley Blackwell, 2015, p. 24.

5 Charles de Foucauld, quoted by Carretto, *Letters from the Desert*, p. 72.

6 Wells, *A Nazareth Manifesto*, pp. 27–31.

I

With Silence

Andrew Carter

Teach me, my God and King,
In all things thee to see,
And what I do in anything,
To do it as for thee.

George Herbert

Silence

It is silence that offers space for our lives
Too big and complex to be contained or explained by
  any words
It is the silence of God that gives a home
to all the hopes, the fears, the fragments, the layers, the
  tangents, the tangles and the tearings
And in the silence God holds us, all of us, and tells us
'You are mine.'
The light, the dark, the shadow,
the sun, the rain, the wind,
the rainbows of our lives
We seek to discover the silence of our God
at the very centre of all that we are
The living centre
that makes the fullness of our humanity possible
Silence is the only language spacious enough to include
  everything.

I remember when I first went to the Taizé Community in France. On the Saturday night, people gathered from all over the world to hear Brother Roger speak. There were earphones that you could use so that his words would be simultaneously translated into the many different languages of those who had gathered. Brother Roger got up to speak and came slowly towards the microphone to deliver his message. 'I have nothing to say,' he said, 'let us keep silence, for God will speak in the silence much better than me.' It was one of the shortest addresses I have ever heard but actually one of the few I have always remembered.

Why keep silence?

We know it brings relaxation and a sense of peace. We have heard that the rediscovery of mindfulness is good for wellbeing. It counteracts the stress of the modern world. It helps us to be more centred and attentive. Practise it and see. Remember the description of creation in which God's Spirit hovers over the chaos and brings forth life in the world. This inner sea is our meeting place with God who hovers over the waters of our chaos within and without – who breathes life into us and pulls our partners from our very side and breathes life into them too. God does not want us to be alone. This silence is the time when God breathes the breath of life into you – breathes into your body his love for you – and brings forth from your body love for others and for all creation. This silence is God's gift of love to you.

Why sit with God in silence?
Sit as you would sit at the bedside of someone you love
   in hospital
Not knowing the answers but longing to heal.

Sit as you would hold the hand of the elderly person you love
Who could not tell you the reason or the purpose or the day
   but knows the touch.

Sit as if floating in the sea and looking up at the sky
Realizing that it is in the struggle and the thrashing that
   you drown
And in the stillness your body can ride the waves.

Sit as if you are held by the person you love
Your contours meeting and dissolving
Breathing the same breath
Sensing their warmth like the kiss of first sunshine.

Sit as if you are holding a child in your arms
Filled with both tenderness and the longing to protect.

Sit, for you are waiting for the sparrows to land,
come close,
dodge,
explore
and then take off in the miracle of flight.

Sit, listening to the fall of the rain
The wonderful soft drumming upon your roof
And dripping from the eaves of your dwelling
Rain watering dry land
Quenching
Nourishing thirsty soil.

What is the sound of silence?

When you are silent you will hear
The sound of creation,
like the song of birds,
or wind in the trees,
or rain upon your roof
The cry of the world and the sound of compassion's gasp.

The sound of God's Word as soft as dew falling on a soft
  sponge
The sound of God's presence, like the warmth of a new fire
  crackling in the hearth
The sound of the human heart beating and the flow of the
  blood of your body
The sound of resurrection and the smell of the sea
The sound of eternity and seeing that eternity in a person's
  face.

What are the fruits of silence?

Silent eyes behold and give thanks
Silent ears hear the music of all creation
A silent body is like a swept room, clean, uncluttered,
  spacious
Silent hands are open hands ready both to give and receive
A silent mind is free of me and mine, of jealousies, hates,
  hurts, threats and aversions
A silent heart is full of gratitude, forgiveness and compassion

A silent intellect is attentive and free of dogma, fixations,
 prejudice and agendas
Silence embraces life beyond self
Knowing that the dwelling place of Christ is within all of us
This is the silence that discovers the Word made flesh
And lives in the kingdom of heaven.

Andrew Carter

I

Seek in your day a space for solitude and silence – a time to be with God

Remember those words of George Herbert's hymn, 'Seven whole days, not one in seven, I will praise thee. In my heart, though not in heaven, I will raise thee.' We don't need a special day or place. We don't need to go into holy mode before we begin to pray. Prayer doesn't have to wait until Sunday. St Paul called us to pray at all times. It is so easy to become forgetful of God.

As St Augustine put it, we are 'called home from the noise that is around us to the joys that are silent. Why do we rush about searching for God who is already here at home with us? If only we would be with God.'[1] Silent contemplative space is the ground in which everything else is nurtured and grows. It is the ground of our being. And to discover it again is like a seed that has died discovering the soil and growing.

I say discovering *again* because actually it is not about grasping a new thing, it is about realizing the ground of your being, something that has always been there but which you had not

5

recognized or had filled with the clutter of your life. Discovering silence is about less not more. It is the kernel breaking open – and being open and naked before God, the immensity of the universe, the enormity of eternity. It is then that the new shoot emerges. As tender and as vulnerable as new birth. That sounds frightening and it can be, but we do not go into this silent land alone. We go with God. Christ's presence never forsakes us. It is in the silence that you will discover that.

It is difficult to describe this experience in systematic language any more than one could describe to a person how to swim when they are on dry land. The only way is to enter the water. When I was a Melanesian Brother, I began each day with silence. Very early in the morning while it was still dark, I would wake up and wash under the outside tap and dress in the silence and the dark. We had no electricity. Without artificial light, I found I became aware and awake to the beauty of the night. I could find my way across the grass and down the coral path with bare feet to the chapel and there sit breathing in the stillness and the silence as slowly, in the half-half-light the whole community gathered and the first light of morning began to filter through the window. I would sit for an hour in silence soaking it up before Morning Prayer began. These mornings are some of the most beautiful moments of my life. I remember experiencing them like soft rain on a thirsty land. At night too after Compline at 9.00 p.m., it was as though the whole community became enveloped in a silence, like velvet – like a seed held in God's hand. In religious life we called this 'the Great Silence', which was not broken until after the First Office of the following day. How would I describe it? Like finding a depth, a harmony, which is both within and beyond.

In London, I thirsted for that silence. This is a city where the noise never stops. The sounds of traffic, the sirens, the shouts, the busker's songs, the sounds of reversing lorries and emptying bottle banks, and arguments and snatched mobile phone conversations. You are in the midst of all this. But do not be depleted by the noise. Do not let it invade you or distract you from the silence of God. Rather, we need consciously to create opportunities to become aware once again of the God with us.

We do not seek silence to escape from the world. Rather, we seek silence to rediscover our humanity and a world infused by God. Neither do we seek silence to escape others but to find them.

With God

Perhaps you are unused to silence,
fear the gaps and the emptiness and the memories of
    abandonment within,
so you fill it
You have not realized that we are not alone
You are with God
Delight in that.

You must make a space for this meeting
Strip away the clutter of your life
You need to be still; you need to be open
For in this meeting you need to let the sky in,
the light in, the earth in, let prayer in
for those you love,
for those you hurt for,
long for,
hope for
Let them in
Carry them within your prayers
Hold them all within your heart
The heart you have opened to the mercy of God.

Breathe in the wind
Breathe in the mercy of God
Breathe in the person you long to love
In and out – the breath of life God gave to you
Let your heart be filled by that breath.

Notice the clouds of fear and anxiety which still come and go
Sometimes they will fill you with the darkness of the storms
    they carry

But do not hold on to them
Rather let them flow through you
In this place of mercy, you are not the cloud
You are the sky
The cloud comes, the cloud goes
But you stay
Your heart, unconfined – as broad, as deep, as high, as
    eternal as God's love for you.

Into the silent world

Into the space beyond the clutter
Into the depths of your heart
As though lowering a bucket to draw fresh water
Like the discovery of the well crystal-clear below the ground
Or becoming the wellspring.

Or like oxygen in the blood of your body
This life flowing through your limbs
Like walking into a shower of light
The warmth replenishing you through the pores of your skin
Like being unwound
Like being healed
Like being loved
At the very centre of your existence.

Stillness

We are always moving
So we don't see
Always talking
So we don't hear
Or we hear in snatches, or bites
But we do not listen to the heights or depths.

You actually have to stop to see
To be still to notice
How often we walk through rather than being with
Walk past without offering time or space
Take the photo without realizing that the true camera is our
    inner eye
We think we have to catch up with the world
Actually, we have to be still enough to let the world catch
    up with us
And meet us in the still place
Our lives can be like fast trains rushing through a station
So fast you cannot read the signs
Only a flash of colour and blur of people and place
No time to notice
Or see the signs of God.

Here and now
Stop
Be in the moment
Lest you miss it and let your mind and body race on
To further racing.

When the clouds open

There are moments when the clouds open
and the inner and the outer become one
And I am here and now and breathing deep
and standing straight
and still
Then the God beyond me is within me
And the within me is beyond me
As close as my breath of life
and yet greater than the wind
This going up, this coming down
This breathing in
This breathing out
This God.

Andrew Carter

II

Develop a simple practice of contemplative prayer

The practice of silence involves a discipline that we will slowly learn together. There is a contemplative practice that helps those who seek silence. Just as a runner needs to exercise so does the one who seeks the silence of contemplative prayer. The Nazareth Community learn this practice together.

1 The most important thing to do is to create the space for silence and to keep to that time.
2 Our posture will also be important as we sit in silence. A simple rule is to sit in alignment – imagining the flow of God's Spirit from the crown of our head to the base of our spine. As straight as you can, but not rigid. Imagine yourself like a reed, straight and yet flexible to the wind of the Spirit. Imagine the warmth of that channel of grace flowing down through your spine, to the toes of your feet and through your shoulders to the tips of your fingers releasing all the knots of tension. Notice the softness of your body. You may find a prayer stool, or prayer cushion, or straight-backed chair helpful to keep this sense of alignment.
3 Become aware of your breathing – a simple breathing in, holding the breath and breathing out. A steady and deep breathing arising from the depths of your diaphragm – filling you. A natural, deep breath, rhythmic and relaxed. Breathe in – one, two, three.
Hold – one, two, three.

Out – one, two, three, four.

Feel your whole diaphragm expanding. Notice the breath as you breathe in, dissolving the tension and loosening and untangling those knots of stress you carry within your body.

4 Now take a word or a phrase of prayer – as though you were floating it on that breath, receiving that word, holding that word and sharing that word as you breathe it out. In and out. Keep returning to that word as your mind wanders. The word is like an anchor which holds you in that still place. This word is your own. It is a word or phrase which will grow with you – a word of God made flesh. Some people use a single word of Christ's like 'Maranatha'. Others use a phrase like 'Peace, be still, do you not know that I am with you?' Others may use a repeated prayer, the best-known being the Jesus Prayer:

'Lord Jesus Christ
Son of God
Have mercy on me, a sinner.'

5 Each time thoughts start bubbling up into your mind, return to your prayer word. The prayer word simply holds things in place like a breakwater, which prevents the beach being churned up by the sea and swept away. The prayer word provides a stability that prevents your inner stillness from being swept away. Do not worry if your thoughts wander. There is no right or wrong in this. Just keep returning to your word or prayer.

Sitting with God

Imagine a stable door
It swings in
And it swings out
As it swings in, the Spirit is your guest
As it swings out, the Spirit is God's gift you are offering to
   the world
This door is your breath
Breathing in and breathing out

Receiving the breath of life
Sharing the breath of life
In
and out.

Breathing in, I receive Christ's peace
Breathing out, I smile.

Breathing in, I know Christ is with me
Breathing out, I know Christ is with you.

Breathing in, I know I am accepted
Breathing out, I smile.

Breathing in, I know I am forgiven
Breathing out, I share that forgiveness.

Breathing in, I know the gift of life
Breathing out, I share the gift of life.

Breathing in, I am present now
Breathing out, you are present with me.

Breathing in, I love you
Breathing out, I know you love me.

Breathing in, I smile
Breathing out, I share that joy.[2]

Imagine you are sitting in the beam of God's love

From the crown of your head, to the base of your spine,
to the soles of your feet,
to the tips of your fingers
Warmed
Replenished
Overflowing.

Imagine you are being anointed with holy oil
Poured onto the crown of your head
The warmth of the oil
Its fragrance
Its liquid golden warmth
Flowing down your face
Your neck
Your arms
Your hands
Your fingers
Your chest
Your stomach
The intimate parts of your body
Your thighs
Your legs
Your feet
Your toes
All of you
Your whole body is anointed by God
Made in God's image
Chosen by God.

Imagine you are the seed held in God's hand

Imagine the gentle closing of that hand
The place of darkness, the place of unknowing
The place where you fear death
But also the place of new life
The soil where the seed will break open, where the roots
    will grow down
And where the new shoot will begin to seek the light
You are that seed
Imagine God's loving and longing for the world
Imagine the dwelling place for God's loving and caring
    and sharing
Is your own flesh.

Praying the Jesus Prayer

All of the gospel is here
This prayer can be your anchor
It is Christ's gift of mercy, his gift of grace
Pray it in the depths of the night,
at your waking,
in your need and in your fear,
in your living and loving
Let it be the prayer of your breathing.

Lord

Above all and greater than all
A word of honour and recognition of the wonder and
    the mystery
Our honest humility before our God
An attitude of open obedience.

Jesus

The name of the promise offered
The name of the life received
The name above all names
The name is Saviour
My Saviour
Our Saviour
The Saviour of the world.

Christ

The chosen one
The anointed one
The one who has chosen and anointed us
The beloved of God

The one who loves us
And says that we too are the beloved of God.

Son of God

Held in the mystery of relationship
God from God
Light from Light
Calling you to become his son or daughter.

Have mercy

The tender mercy from on high
A mercy which is pure gift
Undeserved, not earnt
Offered in love and acceptance
Unconditional
Broad, high, deep
Eternal
Unfathomable
For you
and to be shared by you.

On me

Me sitting here, lying here, standing here, walking here
Me, small, ordinary, one among millions
Frail, mortal, uncertain
Open handed before you.

A sinner

Aware of my deep incompleteness
My falling short

The failures that haunt me
The wounds I have caused
The pain I carry with me
The memories of that which cannot be undone
I come to my senses
I am naked before you
Can you embrace me?
Forgive me?
Heal me?
Raise me?
You who are still watching and waiting
And run to meet me
And hold me
And clothe me with the robe of your love and joy
And prepare a table for me
And are with me all the days of my life
So that I may dwell in your house forever.

Letting go of words completely

Perhaps there will come a time when you will want to let go
    of words completely
And simply be held by the silence
Less words – more silence
Less explanation – more stillness
Less answer – more unknowing
More height and depth, breadth and beauty – more
    magnitude.

I have come simply to sit with you
Knowing not where you are taking me
Only knowing a freedom that beckons
And a love that I long for.

Praying in silence in the church

How blessed I am to come into this sacred place
Before London fully wakes
And feel the space of this building opening me
And beyond the east window the light
Here I sweep away the debris and the clutter
And open my dormant soul
to the wonder of the warmth of God
Here the alienated parts of me,
the distracted mind,
the aches and pains of my bones,
the tight tensions and tangles,
the wounds that still fester,
and the wanderings of my mind
Can find a way back
Beyond the wreckage and the waste
To the eternity in our midst
Where the restless 'I' stills
And defragments
And rests in you.

Andrew Carter

Become aware of your distractions

You will discover that silence is far from silent. There will be many distractions which well up in your mind – memories and anxieties, thoughts, moods, irritability, fear – there will be struggles with our inner demons. These are often like inner videos that constantly play on a loop. At first it can seem quite an ordeal. 'When we turn within to seek inner peace, we meet inner chaos instead of peace.'[3] It is important that we do not give up but learn to keep to our practice humbly and simply. 'Peace will indeed come, but it will be the fruit, not of pushing away distractions, but of meeting thoughts and feelings with stillness instead of commentary.'[4] Evagrius, the fourth-century monk and solitary, teaches that we cannot suppress thought, but we can turn the tables on all this chatter and observe without commenting: 'Let him keep careful watch over his thoughts. Let him observe their intensity, their periods of decline and follow them in their rise and fall. Let him note well the complexity of his thoughts ... [and] the demons which cause them.'[5] This is the skill we must learn. We learn to recognize our distractions. To name our fears rather than be swept up in them. Many of these distractions may take the shape of the narrative we tell ourselves about ourselves. By recognizing that narrative, we can stand back from it, for example: 'That is the story of rejection that I have been telling myself for years or this is pride, or that old wound, or anger, or hurt, or grief or guilt, or longing, resurfacing. Today I choose to recognize the narrative but to let it go.'

In this contemplative prayer we begin to see with greater clarity the patterns of the distractions which come into our minds. 'We move from being the victim of what is happening to being a witness to what is happening.'[6] Each time we find our thinking swept away, we return to the prayer word or phrase like an anchor. We move towards a greater silence that is uncluttered and luminous and spacious, and calm; 'We learn that these distractions are no big deal: they are like weather – good weather, bad weather, boring weather'[7] but beyond the weather there is a majesty, an eternity, a peace beyond our understanding. 'It is very liberating to realize that what goes on in our heads, indeed the entire mindstream, does not have the final word on who we are.'[8]

We bring into our silence our present mood and context. A question I often ask the group before we begin a time of silence is to recognize in themselves the weather they are bringing with them. If we imagine that our meditation is like sitting in the open on a mountain, '[the] mountain does not determine what sort of weather is happening but witnesses all the weather that comes and goes'.[9] This weather is the inner thoughts, moods, feelings that we bring. We are bringing all of that into God's presence. But that weather is not God's presence. Distraction is like the turbulence a plane goes through before it flies above it, or the surface waves before we discover the depths or wonder of the ocean. In our meditation, we are not seeking a feeling or a mood however sweet, we are seeking Christ's presence in the midst of our lives. The only way I can describe this presence is love. When we love someone, we are still subject to hopes and fears, highs and lows, overwhelming beauty but also irritation, anxiety and every other mood. These distractions are no big deal. Because the love is deeper and beyond all of that. It is what holds you in the presence of love and brings you back again and again and ready to surrender all that you have for that love. When we truly love, we move beyond words into the presence of what is eternal – what actually can never be taken away even by death. Words fail at this point, but if you forced me to explain what is happening within us it is that in this silence we are letting go of all the distractions in order to see Christ's love face to face.

Face to face

Here in stillness
Here as you breathe in deeply
Let the presence of God unknot you
And fill your longing
Like the beauty of rain quenching a parched land
Like the sunlight's warming brightness after the dampness
    of the shadow
Like the tenderness of love's touch after the brittleness of
    loneliness
Like a flower opening imperceptibly

Like a bird landing and coming close, unafraid, because in
　your stillness you are with him
Like a shower of rain washing away caked dust
Like the discovery of beauty when you thought it had
　gone away
Like the moon reflecting a luminous light
Like seeing the stars again when you thought they no longer
　shone
Feel again the truth of God's life flowing in and out
Untangling you from the inside out
Like love unseen, unheard, undeserved, expanding your heart
Broadening your world
Christ rising in you
The tomb becoming the place of resurrection.

Recognize the diversion

Each distraction is like a diversion leading you into the side
　streets and cul-de-sacs of your neighbourhood
They may help you to discover the locality of your prayer
Just recognize this as your neighbourhood – part of your
　environment and context
Recognize too that these diversions can also lose you
becoming the maze with no centre
Or the GPS that leads you where you do not intend to go
Into a labyrinth of back roads so that you no longer know
which way you are facing or going
Instead recognize the diversion
and the wrong turn
Come back to the path, the practice – the simple route you
　have learnt by heart
Turn off the GPS and look and see
Attentive to the road
Trusting your deepest intuition of right and wrong
Use the road you know to take you to where you want to be
Always attentive to the getting there

Let the path become so much part of you that it is no longer
  just in your head
But in your bodily memory
Like a bird returning from a foreign land
Beyond the struggle you will find the thermals that lift you
  above the walls and fences
And show you the way through the spaces and the gaps
to the sea.

**'Come to me all that are heavy laden and I will refresh
  you
For my yoke is easy and my burden is light'**

Sooner or later in your silence you will be aware of the
  burdens you carry and the fears you cannot escape
Sometimes it seems as if the silence gives space for these
  anxieties to arise
Once we renounce the busyness that keeps the lid on things
  it's as if all the memories arise bubbling up from the
  depths of our minds
Backing up like a blocked drain
So that sometimes it is this silence itself that we fear
Have not all at some stage sought a place of peace away
  from the rush of the world only to discover that the
  disturbance, the rush, the fear is within us?

Jesus quite simply tells us to put our attention elsewhere
He tells us to look at the birds of the sky or the flowers of
  the field
So look at them
Do we make our burdens lighter by letting them oppress us?
Somehow we have to learn to fly again like the sparrows
Their swooping, dodging, landings and darting take-offs –
  their freedom
Why let your spirit be so weighed down?
Can you add one day to your life by worrying – is it not the
  worry that is in fact depleting you?

It is your head that is teaching you a message of fear
   and failure – locking you into a grief for the past, an
   avoidance of the present and a despair for the future
The birds of the air, the flowers of the field reveal life now
Life so fleeting and so miraculous that you will miss it if you
   stay in your head
Like visiting the sea and staying in the car
Like a room with the curtains drawn
Like visiting a foreign land and staying in the airport lounge
   or international hotel room
Imagine in your silence Peter in prison and the doors opening
Imagine the padlocks breaking
Imagine the courage it needs to walk out of your cell and
   into the air
Imagine Christ walking with you now

Naming distractions

In the silence of your prayer you will often begin to recognize
that your distractions have common themes that keep recur-
ring and disturbing you. It helps to recognize these themes
and to name them. Imagine these distractions like waves in the
sea – they come, they go; what we must learn to do is to ride
these waves, not be sunk and churned up by them. Sometimes
these waves seem very fierce, like demons threatening to drown
us in our search for God. Recognizing these themes allows us
to let them go without identification with these thoughts or
allowing them to constantly sink us or tangle us up in their
undercurrents. Remember the image of clouds in the sky. The
clouds come; the clouds pass; we are not the cloud; we are the
sky. Sometimes the cloud feels so dark that it needs to shed its
load. And so the cloud pours out its rain. This is like the grief
within us that must be shed. The tears and sorrow dispersing
the weight of the cloud. Remember we are not the cloud nor
the rain. We hold this within; we let it go; the cloud dissolves;
we are the sky.

What then are these distractions that may constantly recur?

- The if only mind – if only I had not done this or had done it that way. If only that had not happened. If only I had ...
- The wanting mind – if I had this, then my life would be different. The wanting can be for a person, a possession, property, money, security, love.
- The not wanting mind – I don't want to do this, to live like this, to have to deal with this situation, this person, this problem, this life.
- The planning mind – constantly trying to order and control all I have to do, today, this week, next month, forever!
- The sexual mind and body – in which our desires and our bodies long for another or remember intimacy or sexual experiences or remember traumatic moments of the past.
- The suffering mind – forever clenching, forever wanting us to move from compassion, tenderness and non-judgement to self-pity or guilt, or blame or to trap us in victimhood. Why do I have to suffer? Why is life so unfair?
- The fearful mind – my brother, before a very big job at work or stressful day used to call it 'the fear'. 'How are you?' 'I have "the fear"', he would say. Many of us carry the fear – a fear within – a fear of failing, of not being able to cope, a fear of making a mess, a fear of being shown as lacking, a fear of humiliation. We often experience this fear deep in our guts. One of the greatest fears is that of rejection. Some of these fears go right back to our childhood and are wounds that we carry with us and which in silence we are tempted to relive. Recognize the fear – yes, that is my fear replaying its loop. Let it go. Ride this wave, do not let yourself be pulled down into it but breathe the air of God's love for you.
- The tired or apathetic mind – undermines your practice of silence. What is the point of this? Your body is aching and painful; you feel bored and unfocused. The tired mind constantly tempts you to give up your practice.
- The day-dreaming mind – constantly takes you away from the here and now into memories and random thoughts and pictures like an ever-changing kaleidoscope.

Recognize that having these distractions is part of our humanity. It is what it means to be alive. Our practice of silence recognizes these reoccurring themes, not to condemn us, but in order to lead us into the place of forgiveness, truth and self-acceptance where we can be at peace and present now. By naming the distraction, allow yourself to be distanced from it. You will find that certain memories return with great regularity. Learn to recognize these frequent rewinds – 'Oh yes, that's that memory of rejection that I've been experiencing since my childhood.'

One method of meditation which has really helped me is to imagine Christ present in the distraction. Imagine him in the very place of your struggle. Knocking on the door of your playback. Walking in. Imagine yourself passing the burden or the weight of that cross you are carrying to him or sharing it with him. Imagine him whispering to you. What does he say?

Imagine God's Spirit hovering over the chaos of your mind and through his word and his love for you bringing order and creation, separating the waters of chaos from the new life he brings forth.

In his teaching on meditation, Jack Kornfield compares this recognition of distraction to the training of a puppy. Imagine a young puppy dog by your side. You love this puppy. Each time the puppy wanders off, you gently bring it back to your side. It wanders off; you bring it back; you gently stroke it again; it stays a bit longer but then wanders off to chew something; you gently bring it back. You do not get angry; you do not hit the dog when it wanders; you just patiently and constantly bring it back to you until the puppy learns the trust, peace and joy of being close at your side. The puppy will thus learn the freedom of obedience.[10]

The practice of contemplative prayer in the face of distraction

Sit here in the midst of the world
With all its present pain and madness
You are not the sponge soaking up the carbon emissions
Rather you are the channel of God's peace
Let that peace arise from within you
Deeper than the sea of your own need or desire
Let that peace be a purity
A swept room
A tidied house
A simple order
An inner spaciousness
A forgiven merciful place
Released from clawing need
Let go of the castles you have dug for yourself in the
    churned sand
Be washed flat by the beauty of the incoming waves
Let God's goodness in
Like a sparkling incoming tide
Smoothing the sand
And leaving its sheen of silver
Now you have cleared your near distance of the debris of
    your mind
See the expanse
Where heaven and earth meet
And all, all from east to west
From north to south
Is filled with light.

Andrew Carter

IV

Seek natural spaces for your prayer

In London we are blessed with the most beautiful parks. If you go out into the parks, you will find that they are used by all sorts of people involved in many activities – running, or jogging, or walking dogs, or doing exercises or yoga or Tai Chi. Every week we have been praying in the park – practising our silent prayer as slowly we watch the light and seasons change all around us. It is the most beautiful thing to do. In the Nazareth Community as part of our spiritual practice we try to spend an hour of silence in a park or garden each week. It is often good, I have found, to come back to the same place so that you can be attentive to the silent changes and rhythm of the days, seasons and year – noticing how this same space undergoes the rhythm of change. I am reminded of those David Hockney pictures where he has filmed and photographed the same piece of woodland at different times of the year.

Prayer in the park

I step outside
There is nothing here
I find an ordinary place
Wet grass
Grey sky
A path
A row of park benches
Rain falling
And I wait for God to open my heart and nourish me as he
    nourishes all creation
The joggers jog
Some effortlessly gliding
Others with plodding gait carrying heavier loads
A woman with a purple umbrella

A dog almost behaving comes to smell and lick
The dog walker scouts with a plastic bag
A man in high visibility yellow with pincers picks litter
A young Indian with a child in a pushchair looking devoted
All of life here.

And I pray in the park
And the day opens
A church bell chimes
Two swans begin a noisy take-off and then abort
Large drops of rain splosh
A wind comes filling the trees
Filling me.

The ordinary opens
To reveal a life
A life that is always there
If only we have the space to see
I am a prayer in the park.

Beholding

Early morning but the sun is out
The sky is blue with white clouds filled with the sunshine
The trees are full of rain
So that every branch glistens with pearl drops of light
Silhouettes of trees with the beauty and intricacy of their
    lattice work of branches and twigs
Against the sky
The stiller you become the more you see
You can talk through a landscape and not hear it
You can navigate a path without seeing it
You actually need to be with a landscape
To inhabit it
To dwell in it
To let it speak
To live with it
It's not about doing it

Or walking it
Or completing it
It's about breathing it in
Assimilating it through the pores of your skin
Every sense awake
A deeper conversation
A deeper life
This beholding.

Become aware of God's time

One of the beautiful things about praying outside is that you
enter into God's time.

It is a soft damp morning
The geese have come away from the lake to peck at the
    spongy grass
A squirrel dashes across the open space
An elderly portly pigeon waddles over with nodding head
The park is busy with life
The stiller you are, the closer the world of God comes
It's as though the frantic chases away the still truth.

I look at the trees, their shape, their grandeur
The way they slowly follow the rhythm of the year
Their rooted huge trunks unmoving
They will be here long after I am gone
And they speak
Give back time to the earth
Give back space to God
See the life of God in all things.

Your flutter, your clutter, your frantically beating wings
do not lead to take off
Stay by the lake
Like this stately tree
God does not rush on unheeding
Allow for the change of seasons in your branches

The geese have gone back to the lake now, but this tree
  stands firm.

Time rushes on and we scarcely realize the passing days in
  our efforts to keep up
But nature has an inner clock
A deeper rhythm that knows the time of year without words
In the last week I can see the change
Last week a few yellowing leaves
Now a carpet of crisp golds and browns
And the greens of summer almost gone
We too must become present to the deeper rhythms of
  our lives
Notice our autumn dying
Our winter waiting cold and fallow
Our spring awakening
Our summer warmth and flourishing
Open our lives to the seasons of God
Falling
Dying
Germinating
Bursting forth
Opening
Rising
Revealing
Bearing
Offering.

Behold
Lest you miss God's life within
His miracles unfolding.

Andrew Carter

Pray the shape of the day into being

We often think that our busy lives are the reality and prayer the escape. When we set out on this journey of contemplative silence, we discover it is the other way round. Often it is our busyness which is the escape from reality – the blindness that prevents us from inhabiting or recognizing the simple truths of our lives and the mysteries that surround us. The Church has always had a practice of what they call 'praying the hours' – so that each part of the day is given back to God. The church bell ringing for the start of a service, or the ringing of the angelus at midday would be the moment of interruption recalling us to the mystery of God and reminding us of heaven and earth and that our own plans and projects are not the centre of the universe.

Dawn

My soul is still
I have washed and shaved
Cleaned my teeth
And drunk a glass of water
Outside the house I can feel the cold of morning around my
    neck and ears
All around me the day is grey
But in truth there is no such thing as grey when you look
    more carefully
There is so much light and shadow
The sky dissolves into sky blue at its edges and there are
    streaks of cloud tinged with the orange warmth of
    sunrise
No one is out
The day is very still
And at this hour it feels mine

Like a pause before the onslaught of morning traffic
A chance to pause too and to be for this moment as still as
   the day.

The rush of day

There is a fear of being left behind or being late
And so we run faster
And our souls leak
We pass many along the way, but we cannot converse
   because we fear stopping
Lest we never catch up with expectation.

Stop
Turn off the engine of compulsion.

At first it may feel like sinking
So that one's natural instinct will be to resist
Or the panic which leads to drowning
But face the stillness
Face the stopping
Face your God
No flailing
Just floating
A stillness in mind and body
Allowing for an unclenching
Facing the one who walks on water
And calls you to come and join him and do the same.

Afternoon

Return again and again
How quickly we can become separated from the source of
   our being
And lose ourselves in a far-away country
All you are searching for is in you here and now

Find the gap in the dialogue
The space in the crowdedness of your mind
The silence that your anxiety wants to invade
And enter into the presence of God
Like a swimmer entering a pool
Whatever the weather – the pool is still there.

Early evening

I sit beside the Serpentine
I am proud to live in this city of many cultures
How breathtaking this life of ours
Tonight, as the sky is streaked with the setting sun
I see those passing me silhouetted against the backdrop of
    park, lake and sky
Carrying so many places and stories in their bodies
How can we wish this difference harm?
How is it that we fail to celebrate the wonder and beauty of
    such manifold uniqueness?
This sky and land and water is ours, all of ours
It is the gift of God
Let me not possess it or hold it or steal it
Let me simply be amazed by a world that is not mine
And enriched by the humanity of a world I marvel at but do
    not own.

Night

I return home at 11.00 p.m. tonight
The air seems thick with fumes
The streets have quietened a little and those out for the
    evening are making their way home
Some rushing, others staggering for their last trains
The busker is out
Always look on the bright side of life blown on an upturned
    traffic cone

as it has been most nights for the last three years
I return – yes, another long day
With another stretching out before me tomorrow
Time seems in short supply
How I long to be without agenda
Without the list of to-dos
Without the fear of not fulfilling obligations
Night seems too short
And I am so wound up that the spring needs to uncoil
The heart needs stillness
I have returned home
But not returned to you
Be with me to help me face the demons of the night.

The dark before the dawn

The transition between night and morning is so brief
One moment enveloped in soft darkness
The next moment the noise and urgency of the day
We often talk of longing for the light
But there are also times of cherishing the stillness of the
    darkness
That quiet time before the dawn
You cannot go back
But can you carry that stillness with you?
A soft darkness as pregnant as earth
with the hope of becoming
A soft intimacy.

I get up, look out into the street through the window
Appreciate the stillness of the room
And a city hushed before the onslaught
The pavements washed with rain
My soul still softened by sleep
I pray for the day ahead.

'It was the lark, the herald of the morn,
No nightingale. Look, love, what envious streaks
Do lace the severing clouds in yonder east.
Night's candles are burnt out, and jocund day
Stands tiptoe on the misty mountain tops.
I must be gone and live, or stay and die.'[11]

Dawn in the park

My prayer words have ceased
And the day itself has become my prayer
The morning sun breaking into shimmers on the surface of
    the lake
Ducks silently cruising
Runners in their fluorescent pinks and lime greens
An early morning father with a pushchair pushing the most
    precious life he knows, perhaps this child has not slept,
    but sleeps now
Sounds of cars and motorbikes mixed with the cry of geese
    and the coo of pigeons
My prayer is all of this
My prayer word is this gust of wind
This light, these trees, those back-lit rooftops
This man on the bench
This lolloping runner
This diversity, this manifold life
This freedom before the city intensifies
And we get caught up in the machine with its rush and
    intensity and carbon dioxide
And breathe in its grease
Here like the swans the take-off begins from the lake of
    stillness
The slow motion before the frantic flapping to be airborne
The swans lumber into the air with straining necks, beating
    wings and churned water
I smile inwardly
Taste the joy of life

The stillness of morning before the industrial lawnmowers
   whirl
and crunch as their blades hit stone.

God's time

Two prayers I prayed in very different parts of the world:

O Lord Jesus Christ,
when we wake each day to the sound of the bell,
when we kneel in silence and speak to you in prayer,
when we come to the altar and receive your body in our
   hands,
when we study your word and try to understand,
when we wash our clothes with our hands in a bucket of
   water,
when we stir up a fire and blow it into flames,
when we ride on the truck with dust in our eyes,
when we are burnt by the sun as, two by two, we walk the
   roads,
when we stand in the mud of our garden,
when we brush the copra plantation and the sweat runs down,
when we cook food in the smoke of the kitchen,
when we are hungry and share together the fruits you provide,
when we are tired and dirty and swim in the river,
when night comes and the oil lamps are lit:
O let us be filled in all these things with love for you,
let us never forget that you are always with us
and all our lives belong to you. Amen.

(Melanesian Brotherhood, Tabalia, Solomon Islands)

O Lord Jesus Christ
When I wake in the early morning hearing the shouts in the
   street
As I motivate myself to get out of the comfort of my bed
When I stand under the warmth of my shower, then shave
   and dress

When I search for my keys
And come downstairs, to open the door
and carefully step over the pool of urine on the steps
When I walk towards the church and see some of those
who have been in the night shelter or slept on the streets
gathering and calling out to me in friendship
When they help me open the heavy iron gates
And then come into the church to sleep
When I light the candles and they burn on the altar
As I sit in front of the east window blazing with light
When others join in psalms and prayer
When the Scripture is read
When the day intensifies
With meetings and coffee and the rush of emails
As I sit or stand and my mobile pings and the phone rings
And inbox increases by the minute
As I stand behind the altar
And welcome all who have come to this meeting with Christ
And share bread and wine
And shake hands
Then meet and talk
And reflect upon the Scriptures
And hear insights and hope and need, and despair and joy
    and longing
And all of life's amazing originality and diversity
As I shop
As I stumble up the stairs
And take off shoes
And cook and eat
Flopping in front of the 10.00 p.m. news
Hearing the sirens in the street and lonely trumpeter still
    busking
And the sound of text messages still arriving on my phone
As I prepare to sleep
And lie down with thanksgiving
With my head pounding
And a prayer on my lips to still my mind
O let me be filled in all these things with love for you

Let us never forget that you are always with us
And all our lives belong to you. Amen.

(St Martin-in-the-Fields, Trafalgar Square, London)

Andrew Carter

Praying while walking

Once we have begun to let prayer enter into us and filter into
our very flesh and blood, then we begin to pray wherever we
are. Our prayer becomes our response and compassion for the
world.

Many of us experience the need for space and yet we don't
know how to find it
And so our space is crowded out by the fillers that leave us
more depleted
The news on the hour, ever repeated,
the endless inbox
The fictions that can occupy our soul and take us hostage
'For most of my life I have been worrying about things that
never happen'
The addictions which imprison
The conversations which lead nowhere
The unforgiven resentment that festers
The relationship or disagreement that feels like an unhealed
wound
The sin that still haunts you
The enemy within
The crowded mind
The occupied heart
The trapped life.

Each day we need to find space to walk with God

'Follow me,' he says
To look
To hear
To touch
To breathe in
To catch the scent of God's season.

So open your door and go in search of space

Let your walking become your prayer
Let your breathing in and out become your gift and your
offering
Look up and out
Feel the earth

Taste the rain
The shiver of the cold
The warmth of the sun
The gust of wind unbalancing you
See the sky
The shape and movement of the clouds
The position of the sun
The movement of the trees
The colour, the shape, the light, the shadow of the leaves
    and branches
Watch for the messengers of grace, they will come when you
    are least expecting.

See the people you pass

The lives they carry
The stories in their faces
The fragments of conversation you catch
The relationships of those walking together
The pain of some you pass like a cry of longing in your
    own heart
Or the intimacy
And the laughter
And the colour and the youth and age and their differing
    heights and breadths
Imagine the choosing of the clothes they are wearing
See the person
Notice the beauty of this diversity
The depth and the richness and mystery of our humanity
The beauty and uniqueness of each face
Let this humanity also be your prayer
The understandable and the incomprehensible
Each and every person made in the image of God
Each person known by the Creator
Each person loved by the Creator.

Be filled with compassion
Look upon creation with the eyes of a loving father or mother
Let this walking be your offering
Let this walking be your prayer.

Andrew Carter

VII

Praying together and praying alone

We may begin by praying alone. But we very quickly realize that prayer not only connects us with God but also with others. Just as when we sing other voices enrich the harmony, so too when we pray. There is a huge strength and benefit derived from praying together with a group. Even when praying silently, it is often so much better to pray with others rather than alone. Jesus said: 'When two or three (or more) are gathered in my name I am present in the midst.' Praying together helps us observe the discipline of the practice. It prevents us taking the shortcuts, which we are tempted to take when alone. It is like the difference between preparing food for yourself or preparing food to eat with others. But much more than that, there is a solidarity in this common prayer of silence, as though each of those praying deepens the prayer – becomes another seam within the common prayer. The silence of one builds upon the silence of another, lifts the prayer of the other to God. It is like an orchestra of silence in which each of those praying becomes an instrument creating a greater harmony.

Praying together strengthens you

Like a choir enriches a single voice
You can share the tune
Or create harmonies that thicken the sound with beauty
Highlight the peaks
Deepen the mystery of the valleys
and lead you into paths that alone you would not have
    noticed
Like the song of different birds greeting the dawn
Sharing the breath of God
Sharing a rhythm and a pattern greater than your own
And knowing within and beyond you their prayer
    upholding your own
Deepening the silence
Deepening the space with presence
Holding the distraction at bay
Sharing the struggle
Celebrating the wonder in a way that you can only celebrate
    when there are others there to witness
Together we enter the heartbeat of God
God's call to another country
A common home
Knowing that your prayer
Is my prayer
Is creation's prayer
Is God's prayer.

Praying together deepens the silence

Helps form the pattern and the discipline that silence needs
Protects the boundaries of this space,
so that it does not become encroached upon by other
    pressing needs
We pray not with words
We pray with presence

At the mosque I have seen how they pray shoulder to
  shoulder
Each individual taking up the same movement, the same
  kneeling and prostration
So that the lines have rhythm and movement of a wave in
  the sea
Prayer is not private property – it is our prayer, our God
  praying in us
And your prayer is part of your neighbour's prayer
Like a silent orchestra
Each one of us offering our own prayer and presence to this
  symphony of humility,
offering and thanksgiving
We hold each other in and to this common pattern
We pray generously
We pray mercifully, not just for ourselves but for those who
  pray with us
We create the depth of the silence for each other
We lift one another silently into God's presence.

**Pray alone in the knowledge that others are praying
with you**

Many of us, even in a city, fear loneliness
But solitude can be a life-giving thing
A time of spaciousness and luminosity.

When you have cleared the space for silence
It is then that you need the discipline
It is easy for empty space to become derelict space
Littered with the packaging of distraction
The quick takeaways
Like bad television, or texts and mobiles, and cups of coffee
  or flitting between magazines and papers, unfinished
  tasks and mess
Like a bird tempted to feed on plastics
Sacred space needs regularity and discipline

You do not clear the space simply to clutter it again
Keep this time sacred
Hold the time
Keep it focused
Centred
Still
Resist the temptation to cut short
Pray in harmony though apart
Held together by the unseen chain of God's love.

In our Nazareth Community we know that although we may not be physically present in the same space, others will at certain times each week be praying with us. This solidarity is palpable. But we will also need our own discipline. Like a runner, the more time we give and the more disciplined our practice, the more our body becomes in tune with this practice.

Andrew Carter

Make a time of creative encounter

The city provides so much opportunity for creative and sacred encounter. Its art and museums, its theatre, dance and music, its sport and recreation, its lecture programmes, its places of historical interest and the beauty of its architecture. Its places of worship. This city is a place of such fascinating cultural diversity, history and life. Part of discovering God is the discovery of the riches of the place we live. This does not always have to be at great expense. There are such riches to be found in walking the Thames footpath, or visiting the British Museum, or discovering a part of the city you have not explored before. One of the rules of life of our community is each week to make space or the time for a creative encounter. Perhaps as simple as a visit to see a painting or exhibition, or a church you have not yet visited. Or maybe it will be sitting down and listening to a piece of music that needs time to hear. Or perhaps reading a book that has been recommended and is waiting to be read. You will know what is life-giving for you. Perhaps music or theatre or dance or birdsong or painting or knitting, or running or walking or cooking or libraries or buildings or art. Take time to look carefully at what you see. Take time to focus on what you love doing. These encounters feed us. They can replenish our spirit and help us discover and deepen the relationship between ourselves and our world. They awaken our wonder. Put these times into your diary. They are as essential as recharging your mobile. More so, they can recharge your soul.

In his famous book *Ways of Seeing*, John Berger writes:

Seeing comes before words. The child looks and recognizes before it can speak. But there is also another sense in which seeing comes before words. It is seeing which establishes our place in the surrounding world; we explain the world with words, but words can never undo the fact that we are surrounded by it. The relation between what we see and what we know is never settled ... We never look at just one thing; we are always looking at the relation between things and ourselves. Our vision is continually active, continually holding things in a circle around itself, constituting what is present to us as we are.[12]

Art is prayer

I had not realized before, but art is a meditation
Because it is a deeper way of looking at the world
A way of seeing both light and shadow
Of observing the detail that escapes the glazed eye

And all the while seeing it through the context of your own
    life and the context of the artist
Seeing is reciprocal
It is seeing the relationship between things and the
    relationship with you
The proportion, the colour, the shape, the light, the energy,
    the narrative, the life evoked
It is seeing how lines intersect and spaces open up
It is recognizing horizons
The sky above
The earth beneath
The still water in the foreground
It is seeing the tiers of life
It is standing and gazing
No longer my head in the focus but the panorama of life in
    which I too am part
For I am the seer
It is breaking through the diatribe and seeing
Creation with all its seams of wonder.

'Do not speak or comment too much,'

the Melanesian Brothers used to say,
'or you may end up repeating yourself or telling false stories.'
Move into the silence beyond the words
Composers know that silence, for it allows you to hear the
    music
Prayer knows that silence for it knows it is not the words
    that bring healing
but the One who is beyond our words
The dramatist knows that it is the pause that often speaks
    louder than words and like an iceberg most of the subtext
    lies beneath the surface
The actor knows that the audience will only hear the words
    if he can convey the silence in which they float
Art is not just eye noise or eye clutter, it is the ability to
    distil and allow for us to notice

The great artist does not need an explanation for his art, for
the art itself is its explanation
When you go for a walk if you talk too much you will not see
If you only take photos, you will not know the picture taken
in your own heart
There was an explorer who used to give those he was
guiding a note before the journey began
'I know that the view from the mountains is beautiful.'

Andrew Carter

Spend time praying for this city

We who have stepped over the sleeping bag on our doorstep
And smelt the despair that does heads in
We who have seen the tower block burn
And the photos on the wall of the missing
We who have heard the scream of tyres and turned around
fearfully
Who have heard sirens and wondered who?
Who have seen trapped poverty and a system which does
not seem to respond
We who have turned away not because we do not care but
because we have cared too much
We who have seen the mental anguish and heard the shout
and known that there is no one to listen
And we who do not have the space left to hear this cry

We who have heard the news of incomprehensible violence
and felt hearts break within us
We have been called to pray for this city.

To express our love for its diversity and energy
To pray for a greater justice to address its brutal inequalities
And most of all to pray for its people –
Who drive its buses and trains and land its planes
Who clean its streets and stock its shelves
Police it, and drive its fire engines and ambulances and staff
its hospitals
Who serve in its shops or banks or businesses,
or wait at its tables or clean its offices,
and mend roads in the night or build houses or dig out
fatbergs from our sewers,
or mend its traffic lights,
or take away our rubbish,
or care for our elderly with compassion when we can't
Who sing, who dance, who play guitars or violins, or
breakdance in the square, who paint, who perform in our
theatres, or play in our concert halls,
who score goals and hit boundaries, or run in the London
Marathon,
or build the roof of the aquatic centre
We pray for all those who worship in its churches, cathedrals,
mosques, temples, synagogues and prayer spaces
We pray for our city,
for the people who populate it from every part of the world
and who bring their extraordinary gifts
We hold this city in our love and prayers.

Andrew Carter

Examen

The Examen is a method of reviewing your day in the presence of God. It's actually an attitude more than a method, a time set aside for thankful reflection on where God is in your everyday life. It has seven steps, which most people take more or less in order, and it usually takes fifteen to twenty minutes per day. Here it is in a nutshell:

1 Ask God for light. I want to look at my day with God's eyes, not merely my own.
2 Give thanks. The day I have just lived is a gift from God. Be grateful for it.
3 Review the day. I carefully look back on the day just completed, being guided by the Holy Spirit.
4 I discern those moments of desolation – face up to what is wrong – in my life and in me.
5 I discern the moments of God's blessing and consolation.
6 Look towards the day to come. I ask where I need God in the day to come.
7 I ask for a special grace.

Remember the grace may be very small, seemingly insignificant. But this simple grace may change the meaning of the whole day.

Andrew Carter

The practice of silence

Try to keep an hour of silence. Try to keep it regularly. A time each day is best.

Begin as simply as possible:

> O Lord you are my God
> I will seek you early.

And then the words of the Lord's Prayer.

End your silence simply:

> Repeating the words of the Lord's Prayer.
> Giving thanks for the day and those praying with you.
> 'We lift our hearts and lives to you O Lord in praise and
>   thanksgiving.'

Silence grows in you. Martin Laird's book *Into the Silent Land* is a wonderful guide to the practice of silence. He writes that 'we enter the land of silence by the silence of surrender'.[13] And there is no map to that silence because we have surrendered our control as we enter this sacred stillness – we have entered the place where we have humbly set aside our knowing to enter the place of unknowing. 'Our unknowing goes deeper into God than our knowing goes. Seasoned familiarity with God, yet complete incomprehension of God moved Augustine to call this deeper dimension of awareness "learned ignorance".'[14] This contemplative practice does not determine what will happen, but it allows space for God to be present to us. Laird writes that a gardener does not actually grow plants but practises methods of preparation and nurture that allow for a growth which is beyond the gardener's control. In this silence we are seeking not a means of rationalizing or explaining but dwelling within the love of God.

You must descend from your head to your heart. At present your thoughts of God are in your head. And God Himself is, as it were, outside you, and so your prayer and other spiritual exercises remain exterior. Whilst you are still in your head, thoughts will not easily be subdued but will always be whirling about, like snow in winter, or clouds of mosquitoes in the summer ... at the time of prayer the attention must be within – in the heart ... this is the starting point of prayer.[15]

For some, one hour may be too long so you are free to adapt the practice to fit the rhythm of your own life. Less may be more. In the Nazareth Community, we have set hours of prayer where we come together at St Martin's. Others remember these times in their homes or wherever they are. Though everyone may not be in the same space, there will be the knowledge that at these times our community is united in prayer. Communion with others and communion with God are realizations of the same centre. And this centre is everywhere. 'God is that reality whose centre is everywhere and whose circumference is nowhere'.[16]

Silence is recognizing more in less

'You were within me but I was outside myself'[17]
Silence is not about doing more it is about subtracting,
taking off,
until you are left with the essence of all that you are
and realizing
that in this nakedness
stripped down
there is no longer anything that separates
you from yourself
and yourself from God.

Andrew Carter

XII

Keep a notebook, journal or sketchbook of your reflections and discoveries

One of the best ways of responding to God in silence or after the silence is over is to write. This writing is not composition. It is writing from the sense of the prayer within you. Let the words flow out as you would a spontaneous prayer. It is a life-giving thing to do because your words can capture or help recall the insight, the experience or the grace. It's like an artist would use a sketchbook and indeed it is, it is the sketchbook of the response of your soul. In fact, some of those in the community have recorded their journey in sketches and drawings rather than words. I have found no struggle in this process of writing; it is just simply letting the prayer within you find expression. Later, you can return to what you have written and find a reminder of God's presence or wisdom that it would have been so easy to forget. St Ignatius tells us to store up moments of consolation which can help you through those times of spiritual dryness – this notebook can help you record and remember those moments and also the times when you faced desolation and struggle. Your words not only will reflect upon your life, they will begin to inform your life. While it is important to be honest and record the true movement of your heart, as in prayer, try even in times of darkness always to look for the blessing. For we aim to seek God, who is present even in darkness and despair.

I have always felt this notebook to be a special thing. I choose a book different from other books, with a cover or binding that distinguishes it, not too big, so that I can carry it with me in my jacket pocket when I go to sit in silence or to pray. I do not use it for other things – like shopping lists or phone numbers. It is a precious thing and I am anxious if I mislay it – for it is as though it is carrying in its pages the messages of my soul.

As we move onwards into the next chapter of this book many of the insights, descriptions and memories are the records from these notebooks scribbled down over many years.

Notes

1 St Augustine, *On the Trinity*, VIII, 7, 11.

2 After the meditations of Thich Nhat Hanh.

3 Martin Laird, *Into the Silent Land: The Practice of Contemplation*, Darton, Longman & Todd, 2006, p. 79.

4 Ibid., p. 79.

5 Ibid., p. 82.

6 Ibid., p. 81.

7 Ibid., p 89.

8 Ibid., p. 93.

9 Ibid., p 86.

10 Jack Kornfield, *Meditation for Beginners*, Sounds True, 2015; Audio Book. I am particularly indebted to Jack Kornfield for his wise teaching on meditation.

11 William Shakespeare, *Romeo and Juliet*, Act III, Scene V.

12 John Berger, *Ways of Seeing*, Penguin Books, 1972, p. 7.

13 Laird, *Into the Silent Land*, p. 3.

14 Ibid., p. 25.

15 Theophan the Recluse quoted in ibid., pp. 27–8.

16 An ancient description of God that goes back to Hermes Trismegistus and is famously cited by Blaise Pascal.

17 St Augustine, *Confessions*, Book 10, Chapter 27.

2

With Service

Andrew Carter

An essential gift of our community is service: service offered, and service received. This is the service which arises spontaneously from compassion and friendship. It is not about an apron put on to dole out charity. It is about the reciprocity of true *caritas*; it is about the mutual gift of our humanity. What is it that we give? We give what is alive in ourselves – our hopes, our talents, our joy, our friendship, our creativity, and in giving generously we receive back a hundredfold.

I hope in the first chapter of this book I have captured a sense of the silence and stillness that is the ground of all that now follows. This chapter looks at service, but I am very aware that the familiar language of service is inadequate to describe what is essentially a chapter about how we encounter God through sharing the life of others. Parts of this chapter will be painful reading, for when we share in the life of Christ, we also become more and more aware of the pain of the cross in the lives of those we meet and within our own lives too. The temptation is to see ourselves as victim or liberator. Part of our journey of discipleship is to realize that we too are often the betrayers of Christ's love and service, just as those first disciples were. But like those disciples, it is also a journey in which we become witnesses. There is also a movement beyond that of witness; it is when we discover that we can, through the Holy Spirit, become Christ's body – his hands, his feet, his heart. Ours is a call to live the gospel with our lives. How does this transformation take place? It is when we realize that God accepts us as we are. I am accepted. I accept others, just as they are.

We are changed by those we meet

Christ opens us up to see the world beyond through
   others' eyes
Real compassion is born
When the dominant 'I'
Becomes 'us'
An us which is as multifaceted as a diamond
Recognizing both heaven and hell and the in-between in the
   life of the other
and the life of self
And beyond that
Deeper than that

Beyond all our imaginings
Christ
The Saviour
The one who calls us home.

Simple acts of practical service

Those who have experienced God's grace will discover the joy
of service. This is not the means of grace; it is the response
to grace, the reciprocation of Christ's love. Within any community there are many opportunities to serve, some more
glamorous than others. But there is no hierarchy of service.
Some of the most valuable acts of service you can do may go
unnoticed, like staying behind and doing the washing-up after
everyone has gone home. You may not even feel this is gospel
living, but in fact it is the very nature of it. After the ecstasy of
the transfiguration, there is always the toil, the drudgery, the
turning up, the dirty laundry. A Christian community must
constantly take care that labour and service is shared and that
no one feels oppressed and overwhelmed and that no person is
above a task or act of service. At the same time, we must not
underestimate or diminish the joy of serving others. It is our
pleasure to give and to offer. And if we are present even in the
smallest and most menial tasks, like moving chairs and making
sandwiches for others, will we not also be ready when Christ
returns as our guest? In the Nazareth Community, we want to
affirm the joy of 'loving and caring and sharing'. These are the
words of one of our International Group on the 74-mile walk
to Canterbury whenever he offered to carry a bag, or pump
up a bed, or encourage a tired pilgrim with his shared energy.
'Loving and caring and sharing' became the heartbeat of our
walk together. It is a prayer of Christ-like service.

In the *Nazareth Manifesto* a truth is expounded which is not
wishful thinking but the reality of our lives together. It is this
truth:

It is a miracle of grace that God meets our scarcity through the abundance we discover in those more apparently exposed to scarcity than ourselves. This is the lesson of Matthew 25.31–46. 'When did we see you naked?' is a question that echoes through our consciences. Jesus was naked on the day of crucifixion. He was hungry and thirsty on that day too. Hence his cry, 'I thirst.' (John 19.28) Jesus was also a stranger. Hence his words, 'He came to what was his own, and his own people did not accept him.' (John 1.11) He was sick – in Gethsemane his sweat became like drops of blood falling down on the ground. (Luke 22.44) And he was led away to prison after Judas' kiss. On each occasion his people failed to be with him. And so the irony of the six great acts of mercy is their simplicity. Give food, give a drink, welcome, clothe, care, visit. Not end famine, heal disease, solve the refugee crisis; just the simple encounter that requires face-to-face meeting, without a solution or a cure or even panacea to hand. Here is the promise: that if we can have the courage and humility to open up the encounter, we will meet Jesus. Whoever bemoans scarcity has been told where to find abundance.[1]

I

Service is recognizing the humanity of your neighbour

In our acts of service, we must never let the roles or the rules of operation overpower that simple truth. Do not let the sense of righteousness or the process you are adopting take away the humility and simplicity of this discovery. Our ministry is to create the opportunity, the sanctuary and the attentiveness to recognize in each of those who come, the image of God. Neither must we allow talking about service or networking about service to take over from the simple acts of providing it. Our minds can become so occupied by the network that we cease to be present to the face-to-face encounter. Similarly, we can become so preoccupied with whether we can provide solutions that we are no longer present to hear the person standing in front of us. Do not fear that we are not doing enough. The welcome of just one guest can be the welcome of Christ. One act of forgiveness, or peacemaking, or compassion, is one act of Christ.

Passing by on the other side

Who is my neighbour?
I am in this crowded room but the person I am talking to is
    not listening
It's like there are cataracts in their eyes
Their spirit is not here with me
They are looking past me to the next conversation
Our conversation does not converse, there is no connecting,
    more a sense of separating
'How are you?' I ask, lifting my eyebrows but not waiting
    for a reply as I push my way by
'Can I have a word?' my neighbour moves in like an iceberg
    – only a little visible but the unseen waiting to sink me
'Yes,' I think to myself. But I won't really hear it, haven't
    got the space for it. I can't save you or heal the wound in
    your eyes
I want to help, but I don't want to be involved
I want to pacify my guilt at arm's distance
I want to show the kindness of a stranger while
    surreptitiously planning my exit strategy
To leave the black bin liner of my old clothes at the refuge
    and go home
To show I care but still be home in time for supper
I want to give when it suits me.

Who is my neighbour?

We have locked out Christ in the labyrinths of austerity
We have locked out his freedom, his story and his beauty
We have not seen the rain falling on eyelashes
Or felt the gentle tug of a child's hand in the refugee camp
    asking for food
We have looked away
And blamed others
We are depleted by the poverty of our response.

Why is it that it is the broken who show me Christ?
Because it is through the cracks
That true life flows
When the shell and the façade are broken open
It is then that the treasure is shared
It is those who have shared the shadow of the valleys
Who have encouraged us up the mountains
Where together, for a few moments, we have stood in the sun
And longed for life to be like this forever
Their light is sometimes hooded, covered, hidden or
    cocooned in fear or shame
So you have to wait
You have to be present
You have to be face to face
You have to see the wound to know the sign of resurrection
And to know that beneath the pulled-down woollen hat
Is the halo of humanity
Against all the odds.

There is a human being in here

Hello,
there is a human being in here
Not an object
Not a type
Not an enemy

Not an irritation
Not a desire
Not something to be possessed or discarded
Not something that has come to steal your territory
Not a problem to be solved
But a human being in here
To be welcomed
And honoured
Recognized
Heard
Allowed space
To flourish
To grow
To give
To be with
In uniqueness
In fullness
The human being in here.

Service is just turning up

Service is not a public display that is over in an event
It is the daily turning up
It is the problem addressed that has no obvious solution
It is the washing-up after
It is the carrying back of heavy bags
It is the accumulation of unfinished need that lies heavy
It is in the kindness of the returned phone call or email
It is in the time taken
The being with when no one else was
The offering without recognition
The caring without expectation of thanks
Costing not less than everything.

I open my hands
To the God who transforms offering into gift
And service into blessing
I thank you Lord for the need you find in me
The place where compassion is born
And service becomes your grace offered
Your grace received.

Service is gift

The sleeping bag

I bought it at a camping shop last year
A three-season sleeping bag
It was warm and pleasing, the way good quality things are
One day, I was asked, as I often am,
by a man at the International Group
(for those facing destitution with no recourse to public funds)
for a sleeping bag
But I had none left, only this one which was mine
It felt wasteful to buy a sleeping bag for your holiday and
    then just give it away
But I thought of this man trying to sleep on the street
It kept nagging at me
He will use it far more than me
Or was it the realization that if I didn't give it away I would
    never be warm?
So I gave it to him, somewhat grudgingly.

He took it without realizing how much it had cost, that giving
Took it with no more thank you than if it had been a
    cheap one
Took as if it was his right to receive and my duty to give
Which it is
This year I have another sleeping bag

It's not like the last, and all night in my tent on holiday I lie
    awake feeling cold
Wishing I had the warmer one
When I told him before I left that I would need that sleeping
    bag, he laughed
'It's too dirty now,' he said, 'from sleeping on the streets.'
'Yes, but it's warm,' I said
'Yes it's warm,' he said, 'and waterproof in the rain – the
    best sleeping bag.'
I felt good when he said that
I had given him the best. My best
I will buy another, and give that away too.

The widow's mite

He was on the steps of our church and trembling with the
    cold
He told me that it had rained heavily in the night and his
    clothes had been soaked while sleeping
He was wrapped in a sky-blue crocheted baby's blanket and
    shaking so much I was worried he had hypothermia
I brought him into the church where it is warm and went to
    get him a cup of tea and a sleeping bag from the supply I
    had now bought
There are many like him on the streets
He was wearing just a thin cotton jacket
'You need a jumper,' I said
Another homeless young man rummaged in his small bag
'Here take this,' he said, pulling out a warm long-sleeve
    sweatshirt and leaving his own bag nearly empty
The trembling man pulled on the sweatshirt with the help of
    the one who had given it
And he drank his sweet tea
I could not forget the generosity of that young man's gift
More than half of all that was in his now nearly empty bag
And all day long I too felt warmed by the gift of that
    sweatshirt.

The blind who see

Abraham is blind
And he is kind
He is also homeless
Over the last few weeks I have noticed the way he has
    gathered round him a small community of other
    homeless people
They are looking after him with great gentleness, patience
    and respect
And he is looking after them,
bringing out their kindness
Multiplying it
Galvanizing goodness
It is a life-giving way
Both for Abraham
And for those who care.

I celebrated the Eucharist on the Third Sunday of Easter
I shared the peace of Christ with the congregation
Down the aisle towards the back of the church and there in
    the last pew
Abraham grabbing my hand – 'Father, I can see you,' he
    was saying, 'I can see you.'
Abraham had had the cataract removed from one eye
And again on the Fifth Sunday of Easter, 'Father, I can see
    you with two eyes.'
That is the Easter joy – the joy of seeing Abraham and
    Abraham seeing me
The Lord is risen indeed.

It's my pleasure

We begin to recognize the joy of giving for we give what is
alive in us. We begin to accept the joy of receiving as we recognize the life of the other.

Before I became an Anglican priest, I was teacher of English and Drama, and for four years I was a teacher in Yogyakarta in Indonesia at a Jesuit Teacher Training College. One of my students was a man called Agung. He was poor and I remember him telling me that his mother had sold her wedding ring in order to pay his admission fees to the university. In my first term of teaching his mother died and Agung had no financial support to continue, so I offered him a place to live at the house in the village just outside Yogya where I was living. We soon became very good friends. He had – how shall I put it? – a poetic, philosophical attitude to life. I was only being paid local wages as I was working for Voluntary Service Overseas, but we survived. And our house in the village became a wonderful place for gatherings, hospitality, creative ideas and discussion. I remember Agung built a brick bed from discarded bricks and planks of old timber with a thin mattress on top. When I set off anywhere he would call out: 'Jangan lupa, satu nasi dibukus buat Agung.' He meant, 'Don't forget to bring me a parcel of food back' – there was delicious street food – Indonesian curries with rice and sambal wrapped up in a banana leaf, the stem tucked back and pushed through the leaf so that the parcel was secure.

I didn't forget him. But after several years of this it was sometimes hard, especially at the end of the month, when money was short. 'Don't worry,' Agung would call out from his brick bed where he lay studying – 'Allah will provide.' 'The problem is,' I remember one day shouting back, 'it's not Allah who is providing – it's me.' To be honest it was not the providing that bothered me. In fact, I loved helping him – he was bright and creative and I could not have asked for a more loyal or better friend – no, it was not the giving, it was the lack of thank you. Why did he never say thank you? And he never did. Even though I paid everything.

And one day it just got to me: 'You know Agung, in all these years I've paid everything and you have never ever said thank you.'

Agung was quiet for a moment and then he said: 'I would love to be able to give to you as you do to me. Perhaps it should be the one who gives, who also says thank you too.'

'That's rich!' I said. 'You mean not only do I have to pay for everything, but I also have to thank you for receiving it!'

'Yes,' he said. 'In your English language what did you teach us? You said, when you give someone something and they accept it, you reply to them "It's my pleasure". Why do you say that? Are those just meaningless words? It is your pleasure to give. I have no money to give at the moment, I wish I did – but it is my pleasure to be your friend and brother in this country where you have come to live.'

Thirty years later Agung and his wife Lily Junawati came to stay with me here in London. It was like old times, though the roles have now changed. Agung wanted to pay for everything. When he left I found an envelope on the table. In the envelope was US \$1,000. The card read: 'Mas Richard, [which means my dear brother] – please accept this gift to help others like you helped me ... It's my pleasure.' I held the envelope, my eyes misting up remembering back to those days in Yogya where we became who we are. It was indeed my pleasure to be able to give, if only I had done more. I have tried to learn ever since. My dear friend Agung and many others were my teachers.

I have never forgotten these truths. Agung is now building a house in Yogyakarta. When I visited him he showed me the plans. It has a *pendopo* for gathering and telling stories outside and for eating 'nasi bunkus'. One of the rooms in the plan is marked Richard's room. I looked up at him: 'For you to come and stay with us – it will be our pleasure.'

Wealth

I saw a man driving a very expensive car today
A Rolls Royce it was
Down a narrow London street, past the bundled blankets
    and mess of the rough sleepers
And trapped by the reversing Tesco truck
I imagined how anxious the driver would be not to scratch
    its sleek polished sides
I wondered who sat in the interior beyond the shaded glass

I wondered how much of the real world they were missing
Its touch, its smell, its grime, its love
Behind the glass they were like an exhibit in the British
    Museum
Preserved in a controlled environment
Pickled
We all need the chance sometimes to travel in style and to
    taste luxury
But we also need the chance to get out and walk
I wonder how many lives could be transformed for the cost
    of that car.

I remember many years ago a rich member of my father's congregation coming to ask him if he thought it immoral when
there was so much poverty in the world if he spent £50,000
on a new car he wanted. My father was not one to judge. He
looked at the man with love and said that he thought it was
immoral. The man went away with sadness and bought the
car.

IV

Service is discovering compassion

Again and again, we will find our compassion is born out of
empathy. The realization of how easily we ourselves could be
there. Where they are. And actually the way we are there too,
for the 'they' is 'us.' Compassion is about the 'me' becoming
'us'. Living in a city we are often unaware of the stories that
people carry inside them. The reflections that follow may seem
extreme. Yet these layers of hidden life belong to everyone we
meet, if only we learn to listen with the ear of our hearts. Many
of those I work with are refugees or destitute. I have come to
realize they are not other – they are all of us who search for a
home. Be kind to those you meet, for we all carry within us the
wounds of our own wars.

Baggage

He walks past me
Hood up
His coat stiff with the grime of living on the streets
Black noble face
He pulls a heavy suitcase
The wheels have long buckled and shredded
So now the sound of metal as the edge of the suitcase is
    dragged along the pavement
All he has is here
And yet it's like a huge dragged burden
A huge load to pull with no future
Pilgrim but with no progress
And I bleed inwardly for him
Wounded by the scraping of those broken wheels
Longing to release this trapped man
From the humiliation our nation has inflicted upon him
Like a ball and chain
And I long for his freedom and mine
For we all have baggage we drag
And long for the kingdom.

Bus shelter

He has been asleep sitting up in the same bus shelter
For the last three years
Thick coat and hood covering his face
Head bent over resting in his folded hands
Propped up against the side of the bus shelter
His seat one of those narrow slats
As far as I know he is there every night, come rain, come
    wind, come cold
One day I woke him up and asked if I could help
He didn't answer, just put his head down in his hands again
We often talk of the poverty overseas
But none that I have seen

Looks more lonely than this
This is one among many whom the Home Office say 'has no
   recourse' to help.

Crossing the divide

He found it hard to manage his anger
He was on his own, not used to kindness
He had learnt to defend his space and few possessions
He was from Vietnam, but years ago everything had gone
   wrong
And hurt by everyone and the wrong he could not right
He waited for years in limbo for a way forward that could
   never come
Threatened, he would flare up – and resort to a violence
   that had seen him banned from everywhere
But over the years he came to our refugee group I saw a
   fragile trust grow
Caught off guard I saw his gentler-self open up
He showed me his young daughter the court had forbidden
   him to contact
On the cracked screen of his mobile phone and the woman
   he could not stop loving although he had not met her for
   eight years
He wanted nothing from us, demanded nothing, apart from
   his own space and a socket to plug in his mobile phone,
   with its cracked face and pictures of the family he could
   never meet
But over the years, kindness works its medicine
In the mornings he began to help me open up the heavy gates
He smiled a little and again I saw the gentle, fearful life
   within.

Then one day it all went wrong
And the years of building trust and mending were dashed
Some flash of anger

Some confrontation with a volunteer and he was outside
    again with all the stubbornness and hurt that had kept
    him on the streets so long
Refusing to come back, until that last day
When he came to say goodbye
He had agreed to be deported
There were tears in his eyes
I gave him a London sweatshirt, and he said he would hang
    it on his wall
I realized that here in this country he had had no walls
Except the ones he had built within himself for his own
    defence
On that day when I saw his tears, the wall came down in
    him and for me
And I knew that these years of building trust had not been
    futile.

Empathy with

When you meet people face to face
And see their humanity
It becomes hard not to carry them with you
Holding within you their cry
And longing for their joy
To be with people means that you know that there is no fix
    or easy solution
only this open wound
It is to know too that everyone has their own back story,
    which is never entirely as they seem
And can be told in many different ways
To be with someone means to be with them as they are, not
    as you would like them to be
It is to acknowledge the deeper and undisclosed narrative
    that you, and possibly even they, will never fully know or
    fully understand

It is to accept the mystery of a life and our ways of telling
   ourselves who we are and why we are here, and that has
   many layers
Prayer is not the diagnosis or the medication
It is the love of God for the person as they are
God above, God beside, God beneath
God with us in storm and in calm
For better for worse
In sickness and in health
It is this love that loves the person undefined by sickness or
   by wrong
It is this love that heals the soul not just now but for all
   eternity.

Andrew Carter

Refugee

I know this longing to belong
The energy, the courage, the dream or recklessness that will
　risk all
And cross seas and continents in search of hope or
　opportunity or love or peace or home
And I sense too the jagged alienation of arrival
The system which treats with suspicion
which deliberately relocates, imprisons, deprives and
　excludes
I see an island nation cut off from the compassion that is its
　life blood
and the justice and gift of sanctuary which a nation could
　truly celebrate
No one really wants to talk about our own hidden
　Lampedusa
Those hidden locked away places of exclusion
Our removal centres
Our Kafkaesque immigration processes
The endless waiting
Perhaps the years of failing to reply is incompetence,
　perhaps it is worse.

We have taken away their humanity and ours
Because we are led to believe they threaten our prosperity
Do we not also bear the shame?
They have crossed the ocean for freedom
And the hope that kept them going has been turned to the
　grey damp cold of rejection
They are trapped between the fear of the past and the
　despair of the future
They have gambled all, and it is only the memory of all that
　is lost that keeps them searching
How can we change this 'hostile environment'[2]
and discover again our humanity in discovering theirs?

The stranger

How precarious this path walking along the narrow ledge
Between seeking hope and the cliff fall
He walks past, hood up
So balanced
So alone
The perfect line
Looking ahead
His face in shadow
His destination unknown
A journey that still has no resting place
The magnetic mystery of another life
That fills with sadness
I am tempted to run after and call him home
But this is not his home
Instead I watch him pass until he is gone
This graceful transient life
That is not mine
And yet is
A destination I do not know
Only a loneliness I understand
Is it not he that calls me home?

The sky belongs to everyone

An Iranian who was homeless and seeking asylum here in London said, 'I often think I have nothing, nothing here. I have lost my home and my family, and my country and people think I chose this. I do not belong. And yet when I look at the sky, I remember that the sky belongs to everyone. It cannot be taken away. When I was locked up, I used to look out of the window and remember that. This prison was theirs, but the sky belonged to me too. They could not take it away. Who would not give everything for that sky?'

Andrew Carter

Service is staying with

He says he wants to but can't pray
I see the block of fear in his eyes like a prison wall
Unable to do the very thing that he has often told me
Opens him and brings healing
Breaks the trauma of the past
But now he knows he is locking himself into the hurt
Like an anorexia of the spirit which he cannot explain
Like self-harm
Shutting all the doors
And breathing in the exhaust fumes of his nightmares
Carrying within him the sins of the world.

It is only the gentleness of God which can break through
Not a battering
But as tender and soft as dew soaking into a sponge
A rhythm he remembers
As simple and as natural as breathing in and out
An instinctive pattern of prayer in the darkness

A discipline that can hold you fast in the waves
And even sometimes transform the blackness into the womb
   of velvet
And I pray a new beginning.

$$\boxed{\text{VI}}$$

Service is living the Beatitudes

'By the hungry I will feed you, by the poor I'll make you rich.'[3]
   One year at St Martin's we hosted the Templeton Prize
Ceremony. On the face of things, it was a prestigious formal
event. The guests were all sent the most beautiful invitations
and we were directed to our assigned seats. The front of the
church had a raised stage area that looked like a television
studio with modern high-spec chairs and the most amazing
autocue system that telescoped up into the air every time someone spoke. Around the church were flat screen TV monitors
for the ceremony, which was being filmed from various angles
and locations. Everyone had been invited to come in formal
attire, and our invitations were checked as we entered. The
introduction to the ceremony set the scene. We were told how
Sir John Templeton's vision had been to identify 'entrepreneurs
of the Spirit – those who devote their talents to expanding our
vision of the intangible and deeper realities of human purpose'.
We were told how spiritual progress – qualities of compassion
and care – had been scientifically proven to lead to higher qualities of life, success, motivation and wellbeing. The outstanding
person who had inspired 'spiritual progress' would receive a
prize of £1,100,000. It was a highly polished performance –
but it has to be said that until that point it felt a bit like we
were about to witness the release of a new Apple iPhone.
   Then the recipient was helped to the podium. Jean Vanier[4]
was elderly, tall and quite gangling. Despite the formal dress
of everyone present, he himself was wearing an ordinary
open-necked shirt and old anorak – he wrapped his tall frame
around the lectern and looked around the audience with a

smile that lit up the church. And without any notes or autocue or affectation, he told us that each one of us has to learn that every single person is important. This realization he said had come to him through the privilege of sharing his life with those with disability. While disability had in the past been seen as a thing of shame – to him and many others – it was so-called disabled people who had shown him the way to a relationship with God. 'You see,' he said, 'if you become the friend of the rejected – you are changed – you learn to live a life that is no longer a prison or a fortress, or a locked upper room but a belonging which opens us up – a belonging which is a becoming. This belonging opens up our own vulnerability – and it is here that God makes his dwelling. What we have to do in our world,' he said, 'is to rediscover that each person is precious. Those who rise up in anger have a story of humiliation that has never been heard. What people are yearning for,' he said, 'is to be seen as beautiful. What we have to do is to build relationships of trust and love from the bottom up.'

And then by way of example he asked a member of the L'Arche Community to read the passage from the Bible about the person who invited important guests to a wedding feast, but they all made excuses why they couldn't come. So the owner of the house said to his servants, 'go out into the roads and the lanes and bring in the poor, the crippled, the blind and the lame, so that my house shall be full.' We listened as the woman from L'Arche read. She was a person who would have been described as having an intellectual disability. But what was more obvious was that this was not disabling but enabling the story to be heard again in a way we had never heard it before. She read with care and attentiveness, pronouncing each word painstakingly, totally focused upon a parable which turned our Templeton gathering upside down. And then among the congregation members of the L'Arche Community began to hold up huge red hearts. We had not noticed them mixed among the formal suited guests but now they stood up, and the Holy Spirit seemed to be breaking loose and a song began.

I come like a beggar with a gift in my hand
I come like a beggar with a gift in my hand
By the hungry I will feed you
By the poor I'll make you rich
By the broken I will mend you
Tell me which one is which?[5]

It was a parable taking place in our midst – they started to fill
a table with bread and fruit and grapes, and then they began
to dance up the aisle without affectation or embarrassment but
with joy. Jean Vanier, held by his hands, and dancing in their
midst, surrounded by those of all types of ability and we in our
stiff formal attire felt our own inhibitions and disabilities dissolving and perhaps longed for the same spirit of brotherhood,
sisterhood which opened up a life of God's call – the possibility
of becoming more human. And so, too shy to dance, we did
that formal spontaneous thing – we clapped – clapped as loud
as we could because we had heard and seen a truth that had
come without invitation into our upper room and changed not
only the rules but if we were really honest, life itself.

VII

Service is visiting the prisoner and the
prisoner visiting you

We often imagine that others are other. It helps to demonize
because it distances us from the other and helps us separate
ourselves from the evils and transgressions that we fear. But
what if we really hear what Christ said: 'I was in prison and
you visited me'? What if we truly believe that somewhere, even
in the pain, horror and brokenness of wounded lives, Christ is
still present, waiting and longing to redeem?

In this section, let us imagine through others' eyes.

On the coast upon another shore
A family of fabulous creatures
Like pictures from an old story:
Whales stranded like refugees
Helpless victims of our tides
With a one-way ticket to oblivion ...[6]

A refugee in detention

You know when I came here I was poor
We had nothing but each other – I still see us now, in those
   first pictures
with our ill-fitting clothes in several layers to keep out the
   winter
filled with hope that we had arrived home
In the 'mother land'
We thought we would be living our dreams
We had not realized that this mother did not want us
Feared us
Told us we were bastards
Worse – told us nothing at all
But their eyes told us, and their newspapers, and their shut
   doors, and their all-night buses
And the cold taught us as it seeped into our bones and
   dulled the sunshine in our eyes and skin
We were nothing, worse than nothing, were dangerous
   nothing come to take their jobs and to tell them lies, or
   take their benefits, and steal their unaffordable housing,
   and sell them drugs or threaten their unfriendly children
   with knives
They did not realize we were beached whales
Swelling up on the wet streets, fed cold sandwiches and tea
   in polystyrene
In fact, it seemed, they took more care of the whales
A flotilla gathered around the one in the Thames
While on the bench by the Thames,
that they had deliberately designed so you couldn't sleep on it

76

No one saw me
I searched for my identity
They lost me in their labyrinths of immigrant unwelcome
Until they came to lock me up without trial
They thought I was stealing their country
They didn't realize there was no country to steal
I was the whale and I had nowhere left to swim.

Heathrow Removal Centre

There is an efficiency of sorts. A locker for your mobile
    phones and wallets
A logical process of checks: passport, proof of address,
    fingerprints taken
A door that slides open and shut
A holding area
A body search in a small side room
Another sliding door open and shut
More gates and barriers, locks and large bunches of keys
Like an old bus station with locked doors and no bus
Like a poor secondary school corridor with no school and
    no home-time
Like battery hens kept waiting for the egg that will never lay
This detention centre gives no explanation, but its message
    is pervasive
This is the place where your hopes and dreams of belonging
    end
There are rooms with computers and art and even a set of
    drums which someone is beating
as though his life depended on it
There is a courtyard and sky
But there is nothing that grows
No grass, no trees, no place for planting
No, this is a locked-in place
A purgatory with no hope of heaven
Some of them here have been locked up in this way for two
    years

No one has been charged
This is the place where people are prisoners for not
    belonging
I come away so ashamed of my nation.

Reflections of a man visited in prison

She looks at me with sad dead eyes that I know have cried
    so often
That now the tears have run out
I have longed all week for her visit, but now I long for her
    to be gone
'How's our boy?' I ask
I think of his birthday and see an empty room and a sad
    cake with seven candles and my son unable to blow them
    out because I am not there to watch him
'I'm sorry,' I say again
I can see that she thinks it's her they are punishing. I have
    it easy. I mean all I have to do is sit in a cell all day. She's
    got to get him to school, pick him up, pay the bills, earn
    the rent, face the neighbours, spend the sleepless nights
    alone worrying about the mounting debts and still find
    time to visit me
'I love you,' I say again
But sometimes love is not enough
And at night when she is gone, I hear her silent scream
And find myself praying she will come back again
And agonize that for the one I love most I have become one
    to despise
And I think of my son at his birthday party with no one to
    eat the cake
And the tears running down his face for both of us
And his playground like the yard outside my cell, littered
    with pain.

Reflections of his wife

I went to visit him today
I wanted to say so much and yet by the time I had got there,
    the bus, the walk, those depressing walls, that waiting
    room that stinks of dread, the checks, the body search,
    those bunches of keys – I was overwhelmed by exhaustion
And then his face, the face I loved and hated and wanted to
    hit and kiss, to blame and yet hold next to mine and never
    let go and yet leave behind forever
'I love you,' he said
But sometimes that is not enough. 'Your son loves you,'
    I want to say, 'and cries for you and asks when you're
    coming home and last week one of his friends in the
    playground told him that his mum had said that his dad
    was a criminal and he shouldn't play with him or ask him
    round, or come to his birthday party.' And I wanted to
    say:
'What good is your love if this is what it's led to?' But
    instead I didn't say a word
I wish I'd told him I loved him too, because I saw the
    wound in his eyes and yet I didn't have the power to heal
    it or bind it. And now I am home again and can't get him
    out of my mind but don't know if I have the strength to
    go back again or face our son when he asks me how dad
    is and when he's coming home
It's not just his life this is wasting – it's all of ours.

Reflections of a prisoner who longs to be free

I used to be
I used to be a chef
Now I work in these prison kitchens
Just keeping my head down doing my time
This time I am going straight
That's what I said last time
Until I saw my family did not want to know me

And I knew the friend who let me sleep on his sofa feared me
And after three weeks on the streets I thought fuck it
A legal high must be better than this
And for a few seconds it was
Until I hit the ground shaking
And I realized I was back where I started but this time lower
    than shit
So here I am visiting the sins of my past
I am going straight this time
Until the next time
You see you think they are going to let you go
But once you've been in here, they never do.

I was a prisoner and you visited me

They did not tell me that they would take God away
When they took everything else, those I loved, my home, my
    family, my reputation, my past
'Not God too, surely not God?'
But they left my guilt and it ate me
Night and day, it gobbled me up
Like a video on an endless loop it haunted and taunted me
'Look, even your God has abandoned you'
Forgiveness does not exist
Seven or seventy times seven – unforgiven
You think you will be free when they let you out?
You will never be free
God despises you
And then I saw him, naked like me
Stripped of all, he never said a word
'Remember me when they let you go,' I whispered
'Today you will be with me,' he said, 'in paradise'
A strange paradise this I thought as they led me back to
    my cell
But at that moment, for a moment it was.

For whatever you do for the least of my brothers and sisters

I have a dream of a place of forgiveness
Where wrongs are righted
And the issues that led me here are sorted
And we talk face to face
And I know how to face my anger
And I have a place to live
And can read a book
And apply for the job I want
And have the words to talk to the girl or man I like
You see they never taught me how to love
I know you find this hard to understand but you have to
    learn these things
If prison could be a place of learning, and healing and growing
Perhaps there soon would be no prisons
Only places of hope
Places of music and dancing
Places where God is not shut out
But actually with you for ever
Like God promised.

VIII

Service is hearing the cry

How can you say God loves me?

It had begun with her falling in love against the advice of her parents. This act of disobedience, she believed, had had catastrophic consequences, so that now as she looked back it appeared like the cause of years of suffering. I do not want to describe what she told me in detail lest I give the evil more substance and permanence before we, as it were, walk by on the other side of the road. Suffice it to say it included unimaginable violence against her and her children carried out by her partner

– torture, beatings, humiliations, slicings with blades, rape
and then, when she escaped, destitution, loneliness, guilt and
then further entrapment through trafficking by another man
unbelievably even worse than the first, as though passed on
from one evil to another. And the fear within her that because
of her that same suffering she has known will be visited upon
the next generation. Sometimes it would even appear better
to be dead. 'It is my destiny to suffer,' she said. 'No, no,' I
tried to convince her, 'it is not,' and then summoning up the
only words that would come into my head: 'God loves you.' I
meant it, meant it with all my heart. After her story, I longed
to believe it. 'God loves you.' But now her pain had become
a scream, ripped from her guts – a guttural primordial cry of
anguish. I have heard that cry before and there is no mistaking
it, for it comes from the horror of having seen evil face to face.
'Is this God's love? Is this what you call God's love? How can
you say God loves me? Is this life of mine – is this God's love?
Is this God's love?'

God's love powerless, immobile, found wanting. God's love
nailed to a cross.

I am defenceless, silenced by her cry. After those words there
can be no pretending. All I know is that somehow God's love
is this woman's courage; her love, her scream, her longing for
resurrection, Christ's cry that it is finished – no more suffering,
no more humiliation or pain. 'God loves you.' We part. But
her memory does not part. It haunts me, pursues me and cries:
'How can you say God loves me?'

Service is praying with

I meet with a woman who is seeking asylum in this country;
she is carrying a small child. She has come to ask me for my
prayers as she still fears being sent back to the violence. She tells
me those fears. I ask if I can pray with her. Perhaps she does
not understand but God does for she kneels down, cradling the

child and starts praying herself. She prays in her own language; it sounds like Aramaic, the language of Jesus – a prayer like a chant, a song of grief, soft repeated words, from the throat. I cannot understand her language, but I can understand the prayer, hear it deeply – she repeats the name of Jesus again and again. And there are tears on her face as she pours out her need of God.

I do not know this woman and I do not know if her prayer will be answered, but I can see her love for God and her love for her son. It is like light – illuminating her, shining out of her. I see a path with a heart. And I feel humbled – as though her prayer is for all of us and I am in the presence of someone very close to God, she holds on to her young son – like Mary holding Christ.

What can I say to her? I cannot promise that her asylum court case will be successful. What can I say? I can say nothing. I can only let her pray for me and the world: 'My soul magnifies the Lord, and my spirit rejoices in Christ my Saviour.'

'Amen, Amen.'

Service is costly

He wears a black woollen cap pulled down over his hair. I once saw him take it off and glimpsed the plaits beneath; but perhaps he feels his hair is too matted or knotted by the rain. He doesn't speak much. It is his actions which speak. And slowly over the weeks he has lifted up his eyes and his face has lit up into a smile and his kindness has filled the place. He came as a guest to our International Group – a place where we offer hospitality to those without recourse to public funds and end up discovering the hospitality they offer to us, so that we are no longer sure who is the guest and who is the host. It began with the washing-up – simply, quietly taking control of dirty dishes, washing and draining at speed, laughing when I tried to help. The sink becoming the place of hospitality and meeting – washing away the mess and grease, plunging into clean water. Then he began on the pots, the serving trays, the surfaces, the serving counters – cleaning at speed, so it gleamed, clearing away, putting back – his smile and laugh radiating outwards. He galvanized us. So that Sunday after Sunday the quietest became the one we all depended on most, the one whose presence inspired us all. Carrying huge bags of rice back from Chinatown, he carries two bags on ahead of me and before I am half-way back, has returned empty-handed to help me carry mine. Walking seventy-four miles to Canterbury on our annual pilgrimage and when we, the slowest group of pilgrims, have staggered into the church halls in the evening, which he reached three hours before, we discover he has sorted our luggage and found our sleeping bags and place to sleep. Nothing servile – but brave, self-sufficient, strong. This man has crossed Africa, spent time working to raise money for his passage in Libya, crossed the Mediterranean in a boat that almost sank, crossed Europe, spent months in the Calais Jungle. Got to the UK, God knows how. He has a kindness and an awareness of the needs of others that staggers. And yet he is so self-contained, demanding nothing – just this instinctive giving of self. Without complaint, without request, without moan, without profit, without motive: he generously gives and we are made richer by his presence. He is the beloved disciple.

Service is belonging

A tourist once entered our church and asked me loudly: 'Who are all these mummies in your church?' I didn't know what he meant at first. Then he pointed to all the hooded or blanketed sleeping people who sit in the boxed pews around the edges of our church. 'This lot. These mummies.' I was outraged. 'These people are my community,' I wanted to say, 'their snoring is part of our prayers.' Every morning you open up, there they are, waiting to come into the church and I never cease to be amazed at their graciousness and good spirits after a night on the streets, always offering to help push the heavy metal gates open. During the renewal and renovation, one of them said to me: 'I hope this is not going to be like a pub makeover. I mean this is our church. We spend more time in it than you do.' They do. They are a constant reminder that this is why we are here. That the church is not just some club for its private members or, even worse, a tourist shrine – it is the home of all. These people are the church, just as we are. A church grounded in the reality of people's lives. I remember the vision of Dick Sheppard all those years ago – the priest who was the Good Samaritan, and at times of depression and despair in his life the one who needed a Samaritan too. Returning from the trauma of the trenches, he described his vision, a vision that has animated St Martin-in-the-Fields and that by God's grace will go on animating it in its service for decades, please God even centuries to come.

This is what he said:

I stood on the West steps and saw what this church would be to the life of the people. They passed me, into its warm inside, hundreds and hundreds of all sorts of people, going up to the temple of their Lord, with all their difficulties, trials and sorrows. I saw it full of people, dropping in at all hours of the day and night. It was never dark, it was lighted all night and all day, and often tired bits of humanity swept in. And I said to them as they passed: 'Where are you going?' And they said only one thing, 'This is our home. This is where we are going to learn of the love of Jesus Christ. This is the altar of our Lord where all our peace lies. This is St Martin's.' It was all reverent and full of love and they never pushed me behind a pillar because I was poor. And day by day they told me the dear Lord's Supper was there on his altar waiting to be given. They spoke to me two words only, one was the word 'home' and the other was 'love'.[7]

XII

Service is realizing that we are all part of the body of Christ

Is this vision of home and love realizable, or is this just senti-mental? What I wanted to do was shout at that tourist. I wanted to tell him the names of those around the edges and their gifts and their qualities and to suggest that many of them were per-haps closer to God than he was. Not mummies, no, chrysalises – those waiting to break through all that has shrouded them in poverty. 'Unbind him, let him go free!' Jesus says to Lazarus.

But could I claim this? Where was the hope of resurrection? How many of us in the worshipping congregation knew their names? We are the church of the homeless and yet we knew very little about many of the homeless. And perhaps like many churches we often did not do anything because we were not quite sure what to do. We thought, like people often think, that we ought to do something for them, yet we might not be able to solve their problems, so we did nothing. Many of those sleeping in our pews were those with no recourse to public funds, and it would be true that if we tried to help them there would be no easy solutions to the difficulties. But was that an excuse to ignore their existence? Does the fact that someone has difficulties and you can't solve them prevent us from making relationships? I asked for volunteers among the congregation to discover if there was anyone willing to help provide hospi-tality for these people with no recourse to public funds. Forty people responded and in 2013 we founded the International Group to provide welcome for refugees and migrants who are facing destitution. It would not be an exaggeration to say that through this ministry we have discovered our neighbour and our neighbour is no longer a person simply on the edge but us, as we eat together, share together and offer one another the gifts of our hospitality. Who is the guest and who is the host? It is now difficult to tell.

We come from over thirty-five different countries. We speak

many languages. We have experienced many different cultures. We come from different faiths, and also faithlessness. We each come with our own wounds, carrying the scars of our lives in our bodies and scorched in our memories. We carry our own hopes, our own achievements and insurmountable needs. We are different colours, ages, sexes, genders, sexualities. We don't have all the answers. We know our failings. Some of us have money to generously share, some of us don't, but all of us have something to give. The greatest poverty is to believe you cannot help another, and it is a real truth that those who believe they have least in fact often have the grace to give the most. We all have the opportunity to be the Good Samaritan. We come from many different places to this place where our journeys meet. Who are we? The truth is that we are all the body of Christ.

XIII

Service is being there at the cross

I wanted to make a Passion Play in which the gospel would come alive. Each week we gather in this church – those at the centre and those on the wings. But for this play it is those on the edges Christ calls to be his disciples. There is M, who sits at the back, who cared for an old man in his home for fifteen years through dementia, and when he died, his relatives, who had seldom visited, asked M to leave the house and so he became homeless. There is big Len, who sleeps in the streets at night, but is writing a book in the public library by day and is one of the wisest people I know. There is J, who is an actor, and who has written his own musical but in the last four months seems to have aged twenty years on the streets, so that his face is now weary and his joints rusted by the cold, so that each day his walking becomes more difficult. There is Anom with his loving heart, disowned by his mother because he is gay; he has travelled from Indonesia, to USA to London in search of himself, and found himself and his partner John and the love and respect of our community. If only his mother could have recognized and celebrated the fullness of his humanity rather than holding on to the false gods of condemnation, reputation and fear of what the neighbours would think. How proud she could have been of him. She missed a gift of God for many years, but finally when she was sick and needy she rediscovered his steadfast goodness. There is Edwin, the reflective chess champion – searching for the meaning of life. There is the one with the black woollen hat pulled down. And there is Sam, who plays Jesus, and who comes from Afghanistan and at this church discovered the love of God. 'I don't want a God who creates half people. I want a God who creates us whole and wants everyone to be equal,' he told me when he first came to St Martin's. It's not been easy for him in the UK – arriving as a minor, learning a new culture on his own, beaten so badly in an unprovoked attack that he was almost blinded in one eye, learning how to love in a culture that seems at times impossibly confusing, free and yet controlled, compassionate yet hypocritical. The journey to the UK was an incredibly tough one. Perhaps the journey here in the UK is even tougher. After playing Jesus, he tells me: 'This is the best thing I have ever done.'

Christ's Passion has not ended. Our Jesus is not whipped but waterboarded. He is mocked by his captors who strip him and dress him in an orange boiler suit and take selfies of his humiliation or clothe him in the gold insulating paper of the homeless refugee. There he stands in tinfoil shimmering in the light. Our Pilate asks with a New York accent 'What is truth?' The young innocent Jesus screams from the cross 'My God, my God, why have you forsaken me?' or is it, 'How can you say that God loves me?' The news, as it always is, has been horrifying. A young Kurdish Iranian asylum seeker kicked unconscious by a mob in Croydon. Amo Singh, a shopkeeper, brutally assaulted and left for dead outside his shop in Stroud – after trying to prevent a gang attack against a Polish boy. And on a scale too terrifying to even grasp – horrifying images of the Syrian town of Khan Sheikhoun, with vivid news footage of dozens of people, many of them children, writhing, choking or foaming at the mouth and dead from breathing in poison after warplanes dropped bombs in the early morning hours of Tuesday. Meanwhile the UK paves the way for new trade deals with Saudi Arabia whose war against Yemen has already claimed more than 10,000 civilian lives resourced by a lucrative £3 billion arms deal with Britain. It is as though we, like the crowds in Jerusalem, have lost our moral compass.

Good Friday continues – the innocent are still being put to death in our world. Yet is it not on this Golgotha that the gospel becomes something which is not an appendage to life but where our lives themselves are at stake? 'Father forgive them, they do not know what they are doing.' Is it not here that the resurrection gift of peace becomes all that we long for? Melissa Cochran, interviewed about the death of her husband Kurt in the terrorist attack on Westminster Bridge, spoke about bearing no ill will to his killer: 'All I know is that he did not have the beautiful heart my husband had and I am sorry for him.' There she sits with tears falling, renouncing the hatred that would prevent healing.

> They come with such diversity, from so many cultures. At
>   the centre it is those who seek asylum who come without
>   artifice, mask or pretence, they centre us
> And this Jesus holds us, draws us closer to him
> And the tears are ours for the violence done to others
> His cry from the cross shakes us, changes us
> Makes us know that things will never be the same
> A terrible beauty breaking through all that harms and scars
> Opening up the vision of love greater than death
> Redemption of the flesh
> The hope of shared humanity.

Our homeless disciples in our Passion Play came towards the crucified Christ in bewilderment, their arms reaching out towards his body. Then the one who has a black woollen hat pulled down over his head, this man who doesn't speak much but speaks through his actions, takes Jesus down from the cross, cradles him in his arms so gently, places his body on the stone altar of our church with such compassion and respect.

Has he done this before? Has he carried Christ? Yes, every week, we have seen him. Perhaps he learnt to carry Christ through the struggle and the pain. This is the beloved disciple who leaned at Christ's side and upon whom God leans. Who is my neighbour? Is not this the one? The excluded one who has become our witness. And cannot we become this witness too? 'The body of our Lord Jesus Christ which was broken for you, preserve your body and soul into everlasting life.'[8]

Service is resurrection

I love opening these heavy iron gates to our church
With their padlocks and silted hinges that need shoulder
    strength to move
I love this opening up of the church not because keys make
    me the master of this house
But because there is a prayer of welcoming
Of letting iron gates and huge wooden doors become the
    letting in
The invitation for the outside to come in and the inside out
    into our streets
Of allowing this holy place to become the refuge of all.

Those who enter see refracted light
Pouring through the east window
And candles burning
A stone altar revealing the contours of time
Alive now
The place where sacrifice becomes freedom
Where iron bars bend in the east window to let the miracle
    of eternity in
This is what the Church should be
The opening up of Christ's tomb
The stone rolled away
The place filled with an ocean of light

The message of the angels
The ones who sang at his birth
But who were lost in the darkness of Calvary
Now sing their song again
Do not be afraid
He is risen!
The gospel filling our hearts
Leading us out of the church to the world beyond.

Resurrection is running towards those you love

How do you meet the risen Christ? What does he wear? How does he look? How has he changed and how does he change us?

In 2003, seven members of the community I was serving as a Brother and chaplain – The Melanesian Brotherhood – were taken hostage, tortured and murdered during a period of ethnic division in the Solomon Islands. It is an event my memory returns to every day. I wrote a book about them, *In Search of the Lost*.[9] In 2004, we were preparing the last scene for a production of the *Passion of our Lord*. Only Christ's own Passion could somehow give shape or make any sense of the horror of this tragedy. We would perform this Passion Play to thousands in the Solomon Islands both on Guadalcanal and Malaita, and in other countries. But like those disciples in the upper room after the crucifixion, it was as though the action had died too. We could act death, but then what? We had wanted a final scene of resurrection but did not know how we could ever express that, especially when our hearts felt mangled and broken. Those playing the disciples of Christ went down to the beach. We talked about how the disciples must have felt after Christ's death. We knew from our own recent lives and experiences something of the grief and loss they had experienced, and their feelings of guilt and the trauma of the brutality. And then we saw someone in the distance coming towards us, coming out of the morning light. Imagine he is one of the Brothers who had died. Imagine it is Francis! What would we do?

'Run!' Run as the two disciples had run towards the empty tomb. I would run fast for fear the one we loved would be lost again, run to catch the vision. And so we ran through the sea, ran with the spray flying, ran with all of ourselves to touch the one we loved and thought we had lost for ever, ran to reach him and know that salvation was real ... and in the waves he opened his arms. 'Courage, do not be afraid!' This would be our action of resurrection.

And what would we do together? We would eat breakfast.

Service is becoming part of the orchestra of heaven

Gavin Bryars wrote asking to take part in the annual commemoration for those who have died homeless. He said he was a composer and musician and wanted to perform a piece he had written, 'Never failed me yet'. The words were these. 'Jesus' blood never failed me yet, never failed me yet, Jesus' blood never failed me yet, there's one thing I know, for he loves me so ...' I was not at all convinced. I already had two choirs singing, Streetwise Opera and The Choir with No Name, both made up of members who have known homelessness themselves. This was a commemoration to give dignity and respect to those who had died in the streets not the place for performance. I was also unsure about the words. Many of those on our streets do feel failed, and the idea of Jesus' blood not failing them was an image of redemption that just seemed hard to grasp. Nevertheless, I invited him to come and meet with me to discuss his idea.

Gavin Bryars was a kind and thoughtful man and I liked him immediately. He spoke of hearing a tape of a homeless man singing in the street. Those words he had sent: 'Jesus' blood never failed me yet, never failed me yet, Jesus' blood never failed me yet ...' He was a composer. He had put the tape on a loop so that it repeated over and over again. Left it playing in the studio where he was Professor of Music at Manchester University and gone away. When he came back, he had found a whole group of students standing in the door mesmerized by the song of the old man singing. He passed me a CD and I turned it on.

The old man begins singing very softly. It slowly gains volume as it repeats over and over again. Slowly, almost imperceptibly at first, Gavin Bryars has brought in instruments, which seem to hold and enhance and deepen and broaden the song as though it were reaching out to include now not only the old man but all of us. It is a haunting sound. It is the sound of resilience and hope against all the odds, a sound that seems to get into your very bones. Of course I said yes, he must play the song at the memorial. He would use a recording of the old man's voice and then bring an ensemble to join in slowly. I suggested that maybe the two choirs could also join in the singing as it built, and Gavin readily agreed.

He arrived on the day with his other musicians. The two choirs were already practising. Unlike many other musicians I have encountered, he was thrilled to hear them sing and seemed in no rush and to have no anxiety to practise his own piece, which was going to be the centrepiece of the service. Finally, in the limited rehearsal time remaining, and very modestly, he practised. And the song silenced us and filled us all with the dignity and hope of the singer. The conductor for Choir with No Name brought us in at the required time, helping the two choirs and all of us to master the simple words and make them our own so that all of us became part of the song and the old man's song was our song too.

At that service 166 names were read out, all of whom had died in London in the last year. Above the altar was a huge picture of two holding hands, drawn by Don Pollard, an artist who has known homelessness himself and who each year has created an artwork for this service. One of the hands is a child's hand gently holding on to the fingers of the other older person. Which hand is supporting the other? It is hard to tell. Both hands need each other. Which hand are we? Are we not at times both of them?

Then the recorded sound of the homeless man begins to sing: 'Never failed me yet, never failed me yet, Jesus' blood never failed me yet, there's one thing I know, for he loves me so, Jesus' blood never failed me yet ...' Slowly members of the packed congregation move towards the altar and the picture of the two hands. On the altar they take a card, each card naming one person who has died in the last year and asking them to remember this name in their prayers. As the song is taken up by piano, and violin, and viola, and cello, and guitar, and then voices, it is as if the company of heaven have also joined in including 166 homeless people now honoured and given a dignity that perhaps, so tragically, many never found in life. The whole church is now singing, 'Never failed me yet'; God's faithfulness palpable in each one of us who have become part of this greater orchestra. It is a sound that moves beyond words, beyond the tune itself and seems to speak to your soul, your profoundest hope. What will survive of us is this. It is as though the song actually becomes that healing, that redemption, that love. What will survive us is this.

'Never failed me yet, never failed me yet, Jesus' blood has never failed me yet, there's one thing I know, for he loves me so, Jesus' blood has never failed me yet.'

Notes

1 Samuel Wells, *A Nazareth Manifesto*, Wiley Blackwell, 2015, pp. 28–9.

2 'The aim is to create here in Britain a really hostile environment for illegal migration.' Theresa May, former Home Secretary, introducing the Hostile Environment Policy in 2012.

3 Sydney Carter, I Come Like a Beggar, 1963.

4 Jean Vanier 1928–2019, Catholic philosopher, theologian and humanitarian, who founded l'Arche.

5 Carter.

6 Anonymous, *Koestler Voices: New Poetry from Prisons*, Koestler Trust, 2017, p. 26.

7 Quoted in Pat McCormick's introduction to R. J. Northcott, *Dick Sheppard and St Martin's*, Longman's Green and Co., 1937, p. ix.

8 Sections X–XIII have been adapted from a chapter by Richard Carter, which first appeared in *Who is my Neighbour: The Personal and Global Challenge*, edited by Richard Carter and Sam Wells, SPCK, 2018, pp. 265–71. It is included here with permission from SPCK.

9 Richard Carter, *In Search of the Lost: The Death and Life of Seven Peacemakers of the Melanesian Brotherhood*, Canterbury Press, 2006.

3

With Scripture

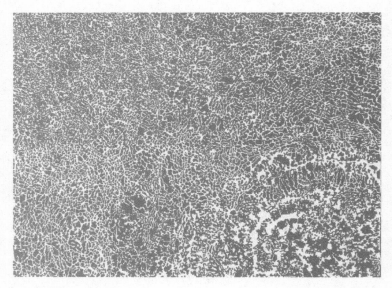

Andrew Carter

I

Scripture is learning obedience

Now every year his parents went to Jerusalem for the festival of the Passover. And when he was twelve years old, they went up as usual for the festival. When the festival was ended and they started to return, the boy Jesus stayed behind in Jerusalem, but his parents did not know it. Assuming that he was in the group of travellers, they went a day's journey. Then they started to look for him among their relatives and friends.

When they did not find him, they returned to Jerusalem to search for him. After three days they found him in the temple, sitting among the teachers, listening to them and asking them questions. And all who heard him were amazed at his understanding and his answers. When his parents saw him they were astonished; and his mother said to him, 'Child, why have you treated us like this? Look, your father and I have been searching for you in great anxiety.' He said to them, 'Why were you searching for me? Did you not know that I must be in my Father's house?' But they did not understand what he said to them. Then he went down with them and came to Nazareth, and was obedient to them. His mother treasured all these things in her heart. And Jesus increased in wisdom and in years, and in divine and human favour. (Luke 2.41–52)

In this passage, Jesus is found listening and asking in the temple. Part of our own rule of life will be to enter into Scripture in the same way – listening, asking, wondering about its meaning for our lives.

One moment Jesus is a baby and suddenly here he is aged twelve, and we know nothing really about what has happened to him in the meantime, other than that it has involved a long journey. The story of Jesus aged twelve, when his parents search for him everywhere and finally find him in the temple, is only found in Luke's Gospel. It is one of those moments of parenthood when you realize that the child that you thought was your child has a life that is other than your life and that you cannot contain or control.

On the surface of things, it's difficult not to be on Mary and Joseph's side. If Jesus is meant to be sinless, he comes pretty close to blowing it here and yet he seems so unaware of the worry and distress he is causing. Indeed, when frantic with worry his parents finally find him in the temple and confront him. 'Why have you treated us like this?' He seems to show no sense of remorse but responds, 'Why were you searching for me, did you not know that I must be in my father's house?' As if they are to blame rather than himself.

But perhaps what this story is showing is a different truth. The truth that even in the lives of those we love it is God who is at the very centre. If Mary and Joseph are able to recognize it, finding Jesus in the temple is the sign not of disobedience but a greater obedience – the meaning of obedience is to hear and to trust – to learn, to listen to the word of God. In fact, Jesus is doing just that – he is sitting among the teachers, listening to them and asking them questions. He is discovering the Word of God, which is all that he is, and which will guide him at every moment of his life. That same Word of God is also our way, our truth, our life. It is what holds us and anchors us in the one who will never depart from us. Like Jesus, we need to listen, to question, to discover for ourselves and to return to the Scriptures again and again. We seek an openness to the word of God, a spaciousness in us so that we allow the Scriptures to dwell in us and ourselves to dwell in Scripture. The Word made flesh. An obedience to God's Spirit within us.

I always feel a bit of trepidation when someone asks me for a Bible in this church. People who are homeless, people who are going through a hard time or grief, or those in need of consolation often ask for a Bible. I feel trepidation because I know what a difficult book it is to navigate. Reading the Bible is like life itself; it's going to take all of your life. It's a long journey – it's the journey to discover the fullness of the life of Jesus Christ and will only end in heaven. You will return to the same stories again and again always with new questions as you bring your life to the Scripture and the Scriptures to life. This holy listening, this attentiveness to the Word made flesh is essential to our rule of life.

Part of our way of life in the Nazareth Community is 'to dwell in the Scriptures richly'. Dwell with them, just as Jesus dwelt with them at Nazareth. You will find such challenge and riches in the contemplative reading of Scripture each day; dwelling with God's word; allowing it to permeate your concerns, your darkness, your desires, your past, your becoming. It is never easy, but this deeper listening to God's word at the centre of our lives is the way by which we learn to clothe ourselves with Christ and grow in body and in spirit. I cannot express better what this obedience to God ultimately means than to quote St Paul's letter to the Colossians and encourage you, as he does, to let the word of God dwell in you richly:

> As God's chosen ones, holy and beloved, clothe yourselves with compassion, kindness, humility, meekness, and patience. Bear with one another and, if anyone has a complaint against another, forgive each other; just as the Lord has forgiven you, so you also must forgive. Above all, clothe yourselves with love, which binds everything together in perfect harmony. And let the peace of Christ rule in your hearts, to which indeed you were called in the one body. And be thankful. Let the word of Christ dwell in you richly; teach and admonish one another in all wisdom; and with gratitude in your hearts sing psalms, hymns, and spiritual songs to God. And whatever you do, in word or deed, do everything in the name of the Lord Jesus, giving thanks to God the Father through him. (Colossians 3.12–17)

II

Scripture is *Lectio Divina* – divine reading which seeks communion with God

The prayerful exploration of the Scriptures is essential to the way of Nazareth. Our discipline must help us to 'exegete' the Scriptures: to discover the word of God for us and for our community. This means to unwind, to open out, to follow the thread, seeking the heart of the meaning of those words for our lives. Indeed, the unwinding often takes place within our bodies – our minds, our memories, our hearts, our lives. There are important tools that can help us in this process: discovering the context of the writing and writer; examining the sources from which the writing is drawn; understanding the passage of Scripture in relation to the whole, and the theological, cultural and practical issues it was written to address. All this is very important to our learning. But we also need to learn to enter into the Scriptures ourselves, both as individuals and as community.

While there is a need and hunger for Scripture, there is also often a fear of it: the sense that we can get lost in it or waylaid by passages of Scripture that appear disturbing or simply incomprehensible. *Lectio Divina* is a daily practice which will help us to enter into the Scriptures both as individuals and as a group. *Lectio Divina* means 'divine reading'. It is prayerful reading of sacred texts. It involves taking a sacred text and reading it with the conviction that God is addressing you through this text. What a revelatory thing it is to read the Scriptures prayerfully and discover again and again how the Scriptures need to be completed in the story of our own lives.

The method

The text is seen as a gift to be received
The passage of Scripture is read slowly
It is given time and space
It is allowed to filter into our own life and context
It is repeated, each reading taking us deeper.

The text questions us and opens possibility
It is a means of discovering God
It is a means of discovering our hidden selves.

The movement

In the twelfth century, the Carthusian monk, Guigo, described the four movements of *Lectio Divina* as:

1 Reading: selecting the sacred text and listening to it speak to you.
2 Meditating: a deep entry into the meaning of the text.
3 Praying: the reader's response to God in the light of this reading.
4 Contemplating: resting or living in the presence of God.

Guigo uses the image of eating to illustrate these different stages of digesting a text:

1 Reading selects the food and puts it into the mouth.
2 Meditation chews it and breaks it open.
3 Prayer extracts its flavour.
4 Contemplation is the sweetness itself which gladdens and refreshes.[1]

The image of eating is a helpful one. It shows the movement of the word of God entering into our lives. Reading can become communion. *Lectio Divina* moves beyond information and knowledge and becomes presence and transformation.

As we read the Scriptures, we search for the words or phrase that seem to be speaking to us directly. They may be words that lift our hearts or conversely trouble us or in some way arrest or hold our attention. Gerard Hughes used to say that you should look for the words that hit you in the guts. These are words that you should meditate upon.

Listening groups

Our method each week is to gather together after the Eucharist. We share a simple supper and then divide into listening groups. Each group consists of about eight to twelve people. Within the group we keep to a simple pattern to allow space for everyone and to guard against the group becoming dominated by only some of those present. In this practice we are not seeking to show mastery or cleverness or even our intelligence. We are allowing God to open up his word through the raw material of our lives. What is more, we are being given the unique opportunity to hear that process in the lives of others. As a group this is the practice we follow:

The method within a group

1 Three people in the group volunteer to read.

2 The text is read a first time with everyone invited to listen in the knowledge that this text is being addressed to each one of us.

3 There is silence allowing for space and for what we have heard to settle.

4 The text is read a second time, but this time each person is asked to discern a word or a phrase that seems to be speaking directly to them, to be addressing them or challenging them, or disturbing or exciting them. I wonder, which is the word or phrase that God is speaking to you through tonight?

5 Going round the circle, the members of the group then share with one another the word, sentence or lines they have chosen. But at this stage they do not comment on what they have chosen.

6 The text is read a third time.

7 Then going round the circle each person reflects upon the word or phrase or part they have chosen. They are asked to address how the Scripture is speaking to their own life from a first-person point of view rather than preaching or explaining to others in the group. It is an opening up, rather than a dispensing of knowledge.

8 If a member of the group does not wish to speak, they pass on simply with a gesture to the next person in the circle.

9 Listen to each person. Again and again, you will find Christ speaking in and through the lives of others, often in the person you were least expecting.

10 We allow the person space to speak without commentary or argument, interruption or interjection. We are non-judgemental and affirming of what each person offers. The facilitator or group leader may offer words of support or encouragement or thanks for a sharing but interfering or directing the sharing as little as possible. At times when someone shares something which may be painful or traumatic the facilitator may offer more support.

11 There must be trust for this process to work well, and this trust will grow as the group meets. It depends on keeping a structure that provides a sense of safety and acknowledgement that each person's contribution is valued and respected. Within the field of our lives, the Scriptures are the seed which can bear a hundredfold.

As we meet each week, we realize that the Scriptures become so much richer. It is as though we are weaving a tapestry together to which each in the group brings a different colour or image or thread. In this listening group, we see the text through different lives – one person may bring the grief she is experiencing for the loss of a loved one, another his experience of homelessness, another her experience and advocacy for those with disability, another his longing for asylum and belonging, another the insights and excitement of a recent conversion, another the academic study of theology or Greek, another the wisdom and truthfulness that has come from living with their own mental health difficulties, another their creative response as an artist. No one voice holds the monopoly on truth. God can speak through us all, and by listening to one another we guide each other back into the gospel – into the encounter with the Word made flesh. We discover this Word both as individuals but also as a community. No one voice should become dominant save Christ's voice – the voice and the actions of the one who leads us forward and permeates our lives. The work of the group leader is to bring the group back to the voice of Christ like the compass of a ship in which we are all the crew.

The contemplative reading of Scripture allows the Word to do its work

We do not come to debate or to argue, or to prove the wisdom of our insight or our superior knowledge

This is the Word of the Lord
We come to listen
Not to preach,
not to tell others what to do
Rather to allow God's word to do its work
Like the sea, tumbling and smoothing a small pebble
Or think perhaps of the way yeast does its work, fermenting
   life, raising all the dough
And, yes, like a seed, a mustard seed,
planted in the very heartbeat of your life
And splitting open as it takes shoot
The smallest seed, the greatest tree
The simplest words of Christ
Planted
Breaking open in our lives
Becoming the greatest truth.

We scatter the word
We let it fall
We wait in hope
We visit it again, reading a second time and a third
And we discern the word that is speaking to us, challenging,
   kicking us in the guts, or exciting us, or troubling us, we
   know not why
Holding
Calling
Promising
Demanding something more of us
God's Word has begun its work.

Now, after reading again, we begin to realize that we are
   not explaining the Word
Rather the Word is explaining us, speaking out of our very
   souls, telling our own story
As we tell His
And as we listen, we realize that each person who shares is
   also speaking Scripture
Telling Christ's story through their own flesh and blood
The wonder of God in the lives of others.

Returning again and again to the Scriptures

You will never know them
But they will begin to know you
They will hold your heart
And wrestle with you like Jacob wrestling with an angel
They will be like being lowered into the Pool of Siloam after
   a lifetime of waiting for the help and healing which it
   seemed would never come
They are like having your eyes opened by the kiss of Christ
Or your body touched, and cleansed when you thought that
   you, like the leper, would always be the outcast
This gospel will become written not on tablets of stone but
   upon your heart
It will bring you the knowledge of God's forgiveness when
   no one else could
Or simply allow you to touch the hem of Christ's robe so
   that his courage can flow through you even when you are
   unable to look him in the eye
This Word will transfigure you on the mountain but also
   lead you into the very valleys and darkness you fear
It will show you the betrayal you refuse to acknowledge
But run to welcome you when you return naked from the
   pig trough
It can become a spring of living water within you
Or anoint you with fragrant oil
And clothe you with the linen of resurrection.

God's word written in us

God's word is not just printed words in a book
It is the balm for the wound that longs for healing
It is the mercy that comes even in the pitch darkness of
   the night
It is the Word in the spiral of grief that disentangles you
It is the Word that reaches the lonely part of you and
   brings you in

It is the Hand of God held out in love against all the odds
It is the steadfast hope that whispers do not give up or
turn back
It is the light of the world and the lamp for your own feet
It is the cry that begins as Adam and Eve realize the
destructive power of their own disobedience
It is the cry that is heard throughout the Scriptures but will
only find its redemption in the name of Jesus
We will not know the meaning of the Scriptures until we
see Jesus.

$$\boxed{\text{IV}}$$

The contemplative reading of Scripture allows us to enter into the Scriptures ourselves

Meeting the risen Christ

I meet with a group of people at the Connection at St Martin's, which provides support for homeless and vulnerable people in London. This group is a weekly time we call 'Spiritual Space'. We read together the resurrection account slowly: Mary, outside the tomb believing the risen Christ to be the gardener. I ask them to imagine being a disciple coming early in the morning to the tomb of Jesus after they had just witnessed the agony of his death. And there coming towards them out of the light is Jesus Christ himself. 'What would you ask him?' I say to them, 'and what will he reply?' I am not sure if this contemplation will work. Perhaps it will seem like make-believe, a fantasy far removed from the tough reality of their lives where nothing is changed by magic. But quite the contrary. They have many questions to ask. 'What will their future be like? Why does bad stuff happen even when you are good? Why did God allow you to die?'

One person in the group's answers I cannot forget.

He is quiet in the group. So quiet in fact that I wondered if he registered my question or even knows what I was asking him to imagine. But he says this:

'Jesus held out his hands to me and I could see they were still bleeding. They were wounded hands.'

'What did you ask him?' I ask.

'I asked him if I could bandage his hands. I wanted to bind up his hands to stop the blood.'

'What did Jesus reply?'

'He thanked me but said he needed to hold up his hands like this in order to bless me. Bless me with his open wounded hands. He said that the blood was a sign of his love for me. He was showing me now. With these wounded hands he was blessing me.'

In the Nazareth Community we read the gospel using the gift of our imaginations to discover how the gospel is speaking to each one of us. And most important of all, we will listen to how God speaks through others.

Carol often asks very practical questions and I ask her:

'What would you ask the risen Christ if you had come to the tomb and saw him in the garden?'

And she replied, 'I'd ask him – "Jesus, how are you doing?"'

'And so,' I ask her, 'what was Jesus' reply?'

And she answers, 'He said: "So far so good."'

I listen and find wisdom and authenticity both in the question and in the answer. 'How are you doing?' Not that kind of rushed 'how are you doing?' as you brush past someone on the way into work without even bothering to stop to listen to the answer. But really: 'How are you doing?' I mean, after all, Jesus has just been through a betrayal, crucifixion and death, and now he has risen and come out of the tomb. There is a huge story here that needs to be both told and listened to. I would suggest we all carry such stories. Perhaps not as dramatic as Christ's death and resurrection, but also stories of countless small deaths, or struggles, or wounds, or fears, and also stories of glimpses of resurrection. 'How are you doing?' is a good question to start with.

In Carol's imagination, Jesus' answer is also revelatory: 'So far so good.' I've kept on thinking about that answer. It's hopeful but not overly optimistic. I mean, Jesus has been through the really terrible bit. He's out of the tomb of death. He's reached the plateau on the other side. You'd think he'd be ecstatic, but 'so far so good' also recognizes the story doesn't end here. True, he has risen from the dead, but he's still got a lot of work to do – for example, convince people, first of all, that he has risen indeed, and transform a group of frightened disciples locked in an upper room into apostles who are going to be brave enough to witness to his resurrection to the ends of the earth. He's got a Church to start. Who would wish that upon anybody? He's got a community to build, and he hasn't won over any of his enemies yet. His resurrection gift to his disciples is going to be the gift of peace. An incredible gift. But peace on earth is not an easy mission action plan. Two thousand years later and it's still a long way off, so this is a long-term plan! 'So far so good' is realistic: it acknowledges how far we have come but also the challenge of the future we cannot face alone. We are going to need each other.

The Spirit of the Lord is upon me

With the group at the Connection we read the following passage:

The Spirit of the Lord is upon me,
because he has anointed me
to bring good news to the poor.
He has sent me to proclaim release to the captives
and recovery of sight to the blind,
to let the oppressed go free,
to proclaim the year of the Lord's favour.

'I wonder what you would do if you had the power to change anything you wanted to change?' I asked, 'What would be your good news to the poor?' I am not sure what I expected those in the group to answer. All of them knew homelessness and the struggle of poverty and the powerlessness of life on the streets. Perhaps they would want the usual impossible dreams of winning the lottery or a house in Mayfair or Park Lane or celebrity success. But their answers were very different.

'I would like a place I could leave my suitcases and bags instead of having to drag them round everywhere like a constant sign of my homelessness. That would be my good news.'

'I would like a toilet in London that was open twenty-four hours that was clean and you could go to free without feeling like a thief or an intruder. For a modern rich city like London I think a free clean toilet everyone can use is not such a big thing. That would be my good news.'

'I would like to get my roller blades mended because before when I skated – I felt I was free – like a bird flying in patterns fast and live – like music.'

'I would like to make music. To play really well. Music makes people feel better about themselves.'

'And I would like a place I could recharge my mobile without feeling I was stealing electricity and to be able to top up enough to send texts.'

'Well I would like people to turn off their mobile phones so that the pings and the rings and the talking too loud and the light of their screens and the music in the headset stops. And people actually talk to you. That would be good news for me.'

'I would like the kindness I have discovered among people living on the streets to continue off the streets.'

'I would like to help people without them being frightened of me. Like help someone with a heavy bag up the stairs at the station without them looking at me as if I am going to steal it. I would like to help others and do something good with my life.'

'I would like to have my biometric photo ID back from the Home Office so I can work again after these many years of waiting. I really want to work.'

'I would like all those who have done stuff wrong to be given another chance, so you were not seen as rubbish for life, but could build a new life you could be proud of.'

'I would like an end to knife crime on our streets. For no kid to go out the back door with a knife in his pocket. I would like London to be a place where all felt safe without weapons and where there was opportunity for young people to make friends, and do creative stuff, like music, or sport and youth clubs and hanging out without fear.'

Amen.

I am struck how all these changes are real, practical, possible. The kingdom is brought a little closer not in fantasies or in casinos but in simple acts of change, beginning here and now, from the bottom up.

The storm on the lake

One of the Nazareth Community who has given me great insights into Scripture is Gemma. She always speaks and writes with disarming honesty. Gemma explained to me that when she was young she shared bunk beds with her sister. She was always on the bottom bunk and her sister was on the top bunk. Each night they used to share stories with one another. One night in the middle of one of her sister's stories she climbed up to the top bunk and realized her sister was fast asleep. But the story she heard continued. 'It was like an unsolved mystery. How could my sister have told me stories when she was fast asleep? And then six months ago, after all this time I worked it out ... it was my voices telling me the story. This is how my voices were born.' Gemma is a voice hearer and it's not easy because sometimes the voices can be quite delusional and scary or disturbing. And the thing about voices is that they seem real. This is why for Gemma her faith is so important. Somehow she needed to distinguish between the delusional voices she heard and the truth of God. Gemma's search to find the meaning and reality of God at the very centre of her being has not only helped Gemma, it has helped me and others too.

This is one of her reflections:

During one of my worst bouts of depression, all I could do was lie in bed and pray to a God that the depression kept me from fully believing in, 'Please God, take my life!' Clearly God didn't want to punish me. He didn't answer my prayer.

I believe there's a little piece of God in each one of us, in all of God's creation, called our soul. It's like a candle at the core of our being. Although in depression it feels like it, God cannot go out. What do I do when my depression keeps me from believing in God? At a loss for anything else to do, I began praying the Daily Prayers of the Church. To me these prayers seem steeped in thousands of years of belief in God. The belief of those who wrote the prayers little by little rubbed off on me. And part of the office is the Psalms. Prayers that seemed to be written by deeply fallible people – asking God to do their bidding, be their servant instead of us being God's servant. It seems like there is a psalm for every feeling and fear I experience.

The voices I hear are like the storm on the lake – crashing round and whirling up the world from which we need shelter. But there is no shelter from these voices. No running, no hiding. Can God calm the storm of these voices as Jesus calmed the storm? If he can then why doesn't he? Is he sleeping while we suffer? Is it because he believes we have no faith as Jesus accuses the disciples? But there is another story of Jesus having power over the elements. This is when Jesus walks on water and calms the wind. Jesus is not only God on earth, he is fully human. When Jesus walks on the water, he does not get rid of the water, he does not cast the wind behind him instead of against him. He lets them both be – but he rides the waves. Just before he rode the waves, he went up the mountainside to pray. He focused on God.

When we focus on God, the storm of the voices can be all around us, but we can be the calm at the centre of the storm. We can ride the waves as Jesus did. God is the calm at the centre of the storm as the voices rage all around us. Focusing on Jesus, we do not drown but become the calm ourselves at the very centre of the storm. We walk on the water with Jesus.[2]

Gemma is now Jamie. He always prays for me and helps me ride the waves too.

The rich daughter

You lack one thing; go, sell what you own, and give the money to the poor, and you will have treasures in heaven; then come and follow me. (Mark 10.17)

During our *Lectio Divina* she told the story of how as a teenager she had been jealous of her sister. How in the car with her mother she had listed the things her sister had got for her birthday like an iPhone, which she didn't get for her own birthday.

She told us that her mother, who was driving, had stopped the car and turned to her and said:

'That was so ugly. Listen to yourself.'

She said she had never realized before that something within her could be ugly. She thought ugly was a word that described your outward appearance. Not her inner heart. She had always worried about what she looked like on the outside but never the inside. She realized at that moment she did not want to be ugly within.

When her mother died, she remembered that word ugly and knew that all her life she would go on seeking her mother's beauty within.

Ugliness within was a grasping twisted thing
But beauty, real beauty of the heart untangled her
Turned her inside out
Opened her heart to love
Made someone beautiful both inside and out
It was her mother's gift that never died.

Reading Scripture is becoming the Scriptures

As the Scripture slowly permeated our hearts
We were opened up
Like the cracks or fault-lines leading back deep into our past
Were these still open hurts?
or were these wounds signs of our redemption?
For was it not in these pierced and wounded places that the
    seed of God's mercy was planted
And in this churned, pitted and broken land – ploughed up
    in memory –
the seed began to break open
And from within the tender shoot began to grow
One of us told the story of two deaths, the first his younger
    sister where he had wagered with God for her life and
    seemed to lose –
and one imagined a lifetime of grieving
And the other his mother –
not wagered for but abiding with,
present through the loss and darkness and beyond –
a sense of radiant light
A transfiguration of both
In which two deaths in eternity now met
And were gently embraced as he spoke of them
And were holding each other and him too
And the healing and the unity was not in heaven only
But also on earth
Both then and now
And the fruit of all the grief
Eternal life.

Participation in the Scriptures

We are not simply observers. We are not content simply to describe religion or examine it from the outside in. We come from a position of belief, and we try to understand more clearly what we believe and to establish what that belief means for us. We are not describing water, we are swimming in it.

We are not private individuals, simply putting forward our own views, opinions or investigations. We belong to a community, worshipping and believing with it. We learn Christ from one another and from being part of a community we call church. This is a pilgrimage together. Remember Moses and the forty years of pilgrimage in the wilderness and the search for greater understanding and relationship with the God who had called them out of slavery into a promised land. Remember too the disciples who followed Jesus and had to participate – they were called to follow – they witnessed, asked questions, saw, heard, touched, ate, drank, prayed together. They followed long before they understood. Similarly, we are not observers or onlookers giving objective opinions. We are not simply private individuals trying to satisfy our own needs or prove the intelligence of our insights. We are involved in Scripture and committed to grappling with it. The baptism has taken place, now we are seeking to discover the nature of that relationship and that is not always easy.

Reflection

While we are participating, we are also called to take a step back from the immediate experience of faith and reflect. Like the disciples, caught in the storm on the lake, we may have followed but now Christ demands more. Like those first disciples we must seek to answer the question: 'Who do you say that I am?'

We are called to reflect deeply about our faith and understand its meaning within the context of our lives (John 13.7). Jesus says to Peter 'You do not know what I am doing but later you will understand.'

VI

Scripture is finding a language

There is a great importance in language to share our experiences, to exegete or draw out, and to witness. Our aim is to express our understanding of God. We use language to talk about God, but the more we grow in our faith, the more we begin to discover that we are using a human means of trying to express a faith which is beyond human words. And while words may help us, we also become aware that they can also confine and limit us. Like any symbol, metaphor or poetry, their purpose is to point beyond themselves – to be part of our becoming rather than to imprison us in literalism. These words and narratives are parables forever being discovered. Think of how the following terms could both help or limit our understanding:

> 'Sitting at the right-hand side of the father'
> 'Lamb of God who takes away the sins of the world'
> 'Heaven' and 'Hell'
> 'Dividing the sheep and the goats'

St Anselm described theology as *'fides quaerens intellectum'* (faith seeking understanding). It is faith asking and raising questions in order to understand. We do not seek to be handed a book full of ready-made answers. In seeking God, we become explorers, those who embark upon a pilgrimage and journey of discovery. It will be the most exciting journey of our life and it will last the whole of our life. We do not study Scripture to persuade people who believe that they have some ready-made answers to explain their lives but rather to discover God already in the world, and to see the signs of his immanence and transcendence in everyday experiences and encounters.

Scripture also takes us beyond words. We are not being offered formulas for redemption. We are being brought into the light like the man who was born blind, whose eyes are opened by Jesus, seeing a new heaven and a new earth. We are not seeking explanations or rules to adhere to, we are seeking God. If we want to understand Scripture, we can only understand it by being transformed by our encounter with Christ in it. We are not being asked to accept a set of intellectual tenets but entering into something much greater – into communion with the Word made flesh. Nothing is so nourishing as pure faith. The words are the signposts, the call to 'behold the lamb of God', but they themselves are not the beholding. That beholding must take place in us:

> When Jesus turned and saw them following, he said to them, 'What are you looking for?'
> They said to him, 'Rabbi' (which translated means Teacher), 'where are you staying?'
> He said to them: 'Come and see.'
> So they came and saw where he was staying and they remained with him ... (John 1.38–39)

VII

Scripture is forgiveness

Once when I was teaching theology in the Pacific Islands, there was a student in my class called James Otumasia who had converted to Christianity. He was a man from the Kwaio tribe in Malaita who were known as fierce warriors and in the past head-hunters. In the class the other students would tease him about this heritage. Until one day he lost it with them all. 'You call yourself Christians but the Kwaio people have far more morality than all of you. Our people know how to respect one another and live together as a community – you do not.'

Later after he had calmed down, I spoke with James. I told him how glad I was that he had spoken out. And then I asked him the question that was in my mind.

'So why did you decide to become a Christian?'

A single word: 'Forgiveness,' he answered. 'There is no

forgiveness among my people. The Christian gospel is forgiveness. I need that forgiveness from Christ and so do my people.'
This is faith seeking understanding to live. This is the gospel.

VIII

Scripture is setting free

'Talitha Cum' which means: 'My child, get up.'
(Mark 5.21–end)

We begin with the story of Jairus, a leader of the synagogue coming and falling at the feet of Jesus and begging him to lay hands on his daughter who is dying. But then another situation interrupts this action. A woman who has been haemorrhaging blood for twelve years touches his cloak and Jesus' attention is directed towards her, and during this time the situation with Jairus' daughter gets worse. We notice what these miracles have in common. Both miracles are examples of outsiders intruding, as it were, on the action of the gospel: they disturb. These are awkward stories; they break with convention and they challenge us to see things in a new way. Both stories are about women and both show Jesus healing through touch and confronting the taboos of his time. These miracles are not just a holy transcendent magical event, confined to a particular place and period of time, but are miracles which touch our own lives too and seek to break through our own prejudices. They are miracles which invite us to see the risen Christ working these miracles in the context of our own lives.[3]

I try to imagine the situation of this woman who touches Jesus' robes. She's too afraid to approach him directly. She has been haemorrhaging blood for twelve years. What is suggested here, the commentaries agree, is a menstrual disorder. Menstruation would have made a woman unclean; in this case unclean for twelve years. In Leviticus there are many rules governing menstruation – the woman remained unclean for the whole period however long it lasted, during which time she was excluded not only from public worship but also from all forms of social interaction, and it was believed that anyone who she touched would be contaminated. This may sound extreme, but it is still a widely held belief even today in other cultures. In Melanesia, for example, a woman traditionally had to live apart from the village during her menstrual cycle. And even within our own society something of the taboo has continued. I remember as a child my mother referring to menstruation as 'the curse' – a description which originally linked menstruation to the curse placed upon Eve in the Garden of Eden in Genesis 3.16 and carries the connotation of suffering brought about by sin. This may sound rightly ridiculous to a modern mindset, but this denigration of women and their bodies was and is still too common. By touching Jesus, this woman with the haemorrhage reaches out against the odds. She defies the taboos of her time. And in that radical act of defiant faith, she will find healing in Christ.

But imagine how she feels as she is confronted before the whole crowd by Christ's words 'Who touched my clothes?' Not only her assumed uncleanness is exposed but the shame that she has somehow contaminated the very one to whom she has come for help. It is perhaps our greatest fear that we, our shame, our own sinfulness and failings, will be exposed in public and ridiculed and that we will be a source of shame to those we love most. This woman is not just reaching out 2000 years ago to touch Christ, she is reaching out for all of us oppressed by shame, prejudice and fear.

And yet now, contrary to all conditioning and expectation, contrary to all human prejudice and the insidious history of female oppression, Jesus is not speaking words of condemnation at all, he is speaking words of blessing and life. In fact, this woman who has fallen down in front of him because of the feelings of unworthiness projected on to her is now being called 'Daughter' by Jesus, and she is lifted up: 'Your faith has made you well – go in peace!' Peace, after years of feeling you are the outcast. Peace. You are the bearer of God's peace. You are acceptable to God. She has become, before that same judgemental crowd, the sign and witness of his risen life – the bearer of his peace.

And now we move back to the story that was interrupted – the story of Jairus' daughter, a young girl, who everyone thinks is dead. Jesus again uses touch – he takes her by the hand. Jesus is overturning another taboo, here the taboo of death: touching the corpse, again that which was considered unclean. He is speaking words of resurrection and life to her. 'Talitha Cum' – which means: 'little girl, get up.' And the girl gets up. He is raising up this child as later he himself will be raised up by the love of God. And there seems to be, in these two miracles, an overwhelming message for our times. Have we still not realized what it means to be made in the image of God? Are we not still treating people like objects, defining them by prejudice – rather than the Thou of his creation, longing to be raised up by word and touch?

James from our congregation phoned me. 'Father Richard,' he said, 'I promised you that you would be the first to know I have been granted asylum and the right to remain in the UK!' James was overjoyed. 'Can I tell the congregation?' I asked him. 'Yes, I want you to tell them all.' James is a gay man of great gentleness, integrity and courage. Born in Uganda, he knows what it means to be condemned and bullied, and physically beaten up because of his sexuality. He was arrested with two friends because of his sexuality. He never saw his friends again. He himself escaped death, but he knows the fear and the violence of homophobia – the police brutality and mobs that homosexuals in other parts of the world still face as a daily reality and which often the Church through their own condemnation of homosexuality are seen to condone. 'Tell the congregation I am no longer frightened to be gay. I am out and proud.' This year he celebrated Pride in London for the first time, walking with other members of St Martin-in-the-Fields with pride – celebrating that finally he has found a group, a church, a home and a nation where he can live, safe from violence and discrimination, and live that basic human right that no one should be persecuted because of the gender of the person they love. James danced the whole route and was still dancing the next day in church. James carries with him a rosary which he prays with great dedication. 'Why do you use a rosary?' I ask. 'I always want to remember God has done great things for me,' he replies. 'He has lifted up the lowly.'

Scripture is the story of coming home
(Luke 15. 11–end)

Coming home

He told of his grandfather
who said prayers and then they ate,
and after they said more prayers
His whole body lit up as he told us this warmth of the past,
his face became young again and the corners of his mouth
    raised in a smile
filled with innocence
But then he told us of the 'dark side'
A filthy alleyway in London
and the heroin and crack,
and the fighting for money and the next fix
His lip quivered, as though his face was about to crack open
like the shell of a fragile egg
'I realized this was no fun,' he said
'It was destroying me.'
'I had to get out, it was the memory of my grandfather's
    prayer,
somehow I had to return or I would be in this darkness
    forever.
It will take all my strength, it will take years to get back to
    where I was.'
We were listening to the Lost Son coming to his senses
And I am sure everyone in the room as they listened, like
    me, were longing for him,
willing him to return,

praying that this newborn man, emerging wet and
vulnerable from his shell
would make it back
and be clothed again
and dwell in his grandfather's love forever.

The prodigal daughter

There are some stories we would all love to end differently
and which perhaps seem too painful to tell. We all carry other
people's lives in our hearts and sometimes there is no happy
ending, only something jagged and open like a wound that
we long to heal. I have seen the pain and grief that Emma's
death has caused. And when someone dies so tragically, there
is always the endless feeling of 'if only ...' This is the nature of
love: it goes on hoping, and praying, and longing and feeling
the pain long after everyone else has gone home. The following reflection is based on Luke 15 and comes from the words
I spoke at Emma's funeral. They are included here with the
permission of Emma's mother who believes this story should
not be forgotten.

In the story of the prodigal son, the son who demands his
share of the inheritance, takes it and goes into a far-away
country. For Emma that far-away country began in 2004
when her father died at the age of 62. From all I have heard, it
would be fair to say that Emma never got over that loss. Emma
wrote beautifully and sensitively, and in her writing she later
described the time she heard of his death:

I was thirteen and I heard the phone ring and he left a
message. He had a new book of violin music for me and he
wanted to drop it round before he went to the dentist. By this
time in his life he had been made redundant from a job he
loved amongst the old dusty books of music in the library of
the Royal College of Organists in Holborn. When we were
children, we would close the rolling shelves together, into
which my sister and I would climb. That smell of old books

and the sound of Mozart playing while he hummed along – inscribing on manuscript paper, using an old-fashioned pen and bottle of ink, the separate parts of his quartet for strings for the Sunday service at the church in Petersham, where he was organist. It is here, not far from the river, under a tree, next to his mother and father, that my Dad was laid to rest.

How evocatively Emma describes the meaning of home, its sound its smell, its intimacy, its music and the grief of loss. Emma, after the death of her father, went into a far-away country. In the story of the prodigal son, we read that he squandered all he had on dissolute living. It is like trying to buy back happiness and home but in a way that leads to greater loss and emptiness. For Emma, this was high risk. She searched to answer her pain and loneliness in ever stronger cocktails of drink and drugs that were eventually to lead to her death.

All of us who knew Emma had seen the loving, compassionate Emma. This was a person who understood both the heaven and the hell of other people's lives because she had been there herself. She lived extremes. She was intelligent and insightful and was sensitive both to the beauty of life but also to others' deepest needs. On the pilgrimage to Canterbury each year, she would cook and help with such care for others as if she wanted to right the wrongs of the world. At our refugee group for those who are destitute in London, once again I saw her compassion and deep empathy and a wisdom that came from her own experience of homelessness and suffering. I saw too her longing for friendship and love and to somehow unwind her own memories and start again – to make something good from a life that had so much to offer but often seemed so wasted.

Those who knew her and loved her, like her mother, also saw her terrifying self-harm, her eating disorder, her addictions, her longing for love and the painful and frequently abusive relationships that ate away her heart and left her longing to escape into artificial highs to ease the pain. They saw her restless troubled spirit that longed to come and rest but couldn't: the cutting of contact, the long period of homelessness, the prison where she seemed so frightened, the demons

that seemed to pursue her and drive her so far away. And all
the time her mother watching and waiting and hoping that one
day things would change, and her sister trying to protect her
mother from further hurt.

Like the lost son there were times when Emma came to her
senses and returned home. But drug addiction is a frightening trap. It makes you a prisoner of yourself, it ravages your
mind, it fills you with fear, it forces you to beg from those
who use you. It takes you to the top of mountains so that for
a moment you think you are in heaven and it promises that
all this will be yours, but then it throws you off, down into
the deepest terrifying sump of darkness, to be attacked by
demons, paranoia, self-loathing and worst the insatiable desire
for more. In August last year from prison where her mother
visited her regularly Emma wrote:

> Who is this person inside?
> The quietness and kindness that turns against my own
>   built strength
> It doesn't help me to fight to be free
> I can stand on my own
> Yet I get so lonely in my zone
> It breaks down my spirit
> So I can feel myself get hit
> Changing my ways is so hard
> Diverting from my habitual path
> Requires strength and belief in myself and my reach
> Love, life, loss
> Are all part of my journey.
>
> From the past
> Look forward
> And hope for new strength, not fear
> The new beginning
> Is near.

It is the lost daughter longing to return, to break free, and love
again.

Her mother told me of a memory of opening the door of her

house and finding Emma outside, with no shoes, in vest and leggings, covered in dirt, nothing warm, like a bird thrown by the wind against her own window with broken wings. It is the lost daughter longing to return to her father and mother and sister but unable to find the way through. The cry for a love that will never fail.

Her last words to her mother were these: 'I love you so much' and the hug she longed to take away her loneliness. Emma was only twenty-nine years old when she died from a heroin overdose.

Sometimes trauma cannot be resolved. It can only be trans-figured by God. It is now finally we pray that Emma has gone home to the one who loves her unconditionally. She is the prodigal trying to ask for forgiveness as the loving Father runs to meet her: 'I have sinned against heaven and before you. I am no longer fit to be called your daughter, let me eat with the destitute.' But the Father sees her from a long way off. He sees not a sinner but his own daughter: he sees that her wounds are his wounds. The Father holds her in his arms and gently kiss-ing her he lifts her up: 'Quickly, bring my robe, my best one, put it on her, put a ring of my promise of love on her finger and shoes on her feet, wash away the dirt and tears from her face, for this daughter of mine was dead and is alive again, was lost and now is found – so let us celebrate.'

God has made us for himself and our hearts are restless until we rest in him. I am more aware than ever that God does not leave us even though time and time again we may turn away and believe that we have been abandoned. In that far-away country, he is still watching and waiting, even among the pigs he is there calling us home, visiting us in prison, never giving up on us, longing to hold us, to wash us and heal us. Our prayer is that Emma now rests in peace. And allows those who love her to know this healing too. This is the gospel – that the wounds of the world become the signs of salvation. Her ashes are buried peacefully next to her earthly father and grand-parents in the beautiful graveyard at Petersham, not far from the river, under the same tree, very near the church where the organ still plays.

Sometimes the healing that the world cannot give is found only in heaven where our Father waits for us with open arms and where the music never ends. As we go home from this grave it is as though we too have seen the darkness but have also been brought in from the storm by the grace of God. All of us are hushed by what has taken place. For we know that somehow, we have been touched by a love beyond our understanding that heals both here but also beyond the grave.

The Bible study does not end

When Barbara Brown Taylor preached at St Martin-in-the-Fields, she told this story. I want to include it here because it is a story of the gospel that continues to live with me and speak to our times:

> When the young white man with the odd haircut showed up at their Bible study, they did what the Bible told them to do: they welcomed the stranger so warmly that he sat with them for close to an hour before he remembered why he was there. Then he took out his gun and started shooting.
>
> All the right people stepped up to the microphone in the days that followed. Once again many spoke of gun control. The governor called for the death penalty. But it was the Christians people were waiting for. What would they say to the man who had violated their small heaven and taken their loved ones by force?
>
> At his court hearing two days later, he stood handcuffed before them, under court order to listen.
>
> 'You took something very precious away from me,' said a daughter of her mother. 'I will never be able to hold her again. But I forgive you. And have mercy on your soul.'
>
> 'It was as if the Bible study had never ended ...' one reporter said, listening to people ask mercy for someone who had shown them no mercy, to forgive him before he had

asked. Some sounded like they were still practising. Their hearts weren't in it yet, but they knew what was at stake. Violence had already taken the young man in front of them by force. It had taken nine people they loved as well, but it had not taken them yet. They still had power to resist that deadly force of hatred by doing what Jesus had taught them: turn the cheek, pray for the persecutor, love the enemy, welcome the stranger. In everything do to others as you would have them do to you.

It sounds like advice for angels, not humans – so unrealistic, so undefended, it's a wonder we repeat it at all. Yet there it is: the Christian teaching on how to respond to violence and prejudice when it comes. Sometimes it actually works to disarm the violence in others, which is why we know the names of Gandhi, Tutu and King. Its main purpose is to disarm the violence in us.

A few days after the church murders, a reporter interviewed someone who worked in a restaurant where the shooter often ate. When he asked her why she thought he did it, she didn't mention guns, or racism, or flags. She said, 'He always looked like he needed love.'

I wonder who taught him to hate instead? I wonder who is teaching a child to hate people like him right now?

I wonder who is teaching a community to love?

Note

1 See Christopher Jamison, *Finding Sanctuary*, Weidenfeld and Nicolson, 2007, pp. 60–6.

2 See Gemma Poncia, *Reflections of a Voice Hearer*, 3rd edition, Amazon Fulfillment, 2013.

3 See Jeffrey John, *The Meaning in the Miracles*, Canterbury Press, 2001, p. 98ff.

4

With Sacrament

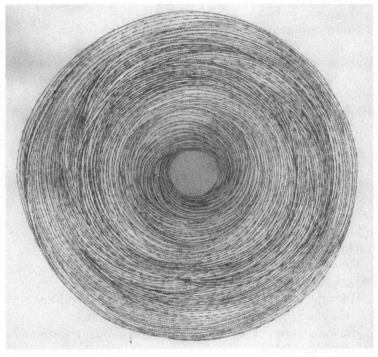

Vicky Howard

We are called to live in communion with one another and communion with God. How can we make this communion central to our lives? How can we become communion? The outward visible sign of Christ's reconciling grace? How can we come to this sacrament and make it live again?

It is the simplest of actions
Gathering
Confessing and Preparing
Listening to God's word
Reflecting on the meaning of that word in our lives
Taking
Blessing
Breaking
Sharing
Going out into the world as the bearers of that love.

This sacrament is and will be central to our community. It is the heart of our life of prayer around which all other life revolves. Christ makes himself present and we make ourselves present to Christ.

Sacrament is communion

Everything is Eucharist
The light breaking through our east window
The altar laid out in preparation
Those who gather – Eucharist
The more elderly members of our congregation with their
    ski poles, or frail balance, or aches and strains
and long stories of service and devotion in their creases and
    hallowed faces
The faithful returning to their familiar pews like carrier
    pigeons bringing news
The waifs, the strays, the tourists, the sightseers wandering
    in off our London streets
The stewards welcoming with pride
The together, the alone
All abilities and disabilities
The confident and the lost
All genders, all sexualities, all colours, all cultures,

the crumpled, the lonely, the different, the difficult, the needy
Those who carry heavy burdens
Those whose faces are filled with light and those whose eyes
    speak their pain
The beacons, the hatted, the colour coordinated, the
    shabby, the hooded, the sleeping,
the fragrant, and the smell of the struggle of nights on the
    street
The popular, the official, the joyful, the lonely
The hurting and the healers
The generous givers and the consumers of God's
    inexhaustible grace
Those whose needs spill out and those whose grief or pain is
    locked within
The noisy, the laughing, the contained, the devout, the silent
    witness, the buttoned up.

The red of the choir with wide mouths and beautiful voices
The children with a spring in their step and a glance at their
    parents as they carry their burnished candles sliced open
    with a cross of light
The Gospel read in our midst
God's story opened, scattered, shed and shared
A prayer weaving community – gratitude, hope, longing
    healing and heaven
A peace shared in touch of hand and glance of eye and
    mumbled words, but meant
A gathering
Christ remembered. Christ here now. Christ shared
An altar to which we have been called to come
Bread
Wine
Body
Blood
A presence that silences and stills
A funeral
A cry
A wedding

A feast
A new kingdom
Earth and heaven
Love offered for you and for the world
Come.

Again and again
At different times and places
But constantly
This ultimate gift for you and for a broken world
Even if they were to cast you out of the city
And leave you to die
This can never be taken away
This is God's unconditional love for you
This is the Word made flesh in you now and for eternity
This is communion.

In the Eucharist, Jesus is immobilized. He is reduced to a little piece of bread. The world needs him so much and yet he doesn't speak. We need him so much and yet he doesn't move. The Eucharist is the silence of God and the weakness of God. To reduce God to bread while the world is so noisy, so agitated, so confused. It is as though the world and the Eucharist were walking in opposite directions. And they seem to get further and further from each other. One has to be courageous not to be carried away in the world's march. One needs faith and willpower to go cross current towards the Eucharist. To stop and be silent and to worship. And one needs really strong faith to understand the impotence and defeat which the Eucharist represents and which is today what the impotence and defeat of Calvary was yesterday. Yet this powerless Jesus, nailed down and annihilated, is the God of the Impossible, Alpha and Omega, beginning and end.[1]

Vicky Howard

II

Sacrament is presence

Spend time in front of the altar

The candle is burning in the corner
Where the sacrament has been reserved
There is a presence here – in the shadows of this chapel
With its cold drafts and smell of derelict hymn books
The sense that here is a place where old men and women
    have prayed before
I would feel bereft praying here alone
Were it not for the candle burning and the knowledge of
    your abiding
I want your abiding to abide in me
Not to leave me to face the gloom and shadows alone
I who have known the empty house
Now know the goodness of this space infused with your light
Like a porcelain pot glowing golden
With the warmth of lit treasure shining from the inside out.

Return to my table

To this place of forgiveness
Where I will tenderly wash your feet
And offer you a place to be with me
Again and again
At different times and in different places
Constantly
I will show my love for you
I will give you my body
And my blood
For the forgiveness of your sins
A sign beyond words
A love beyond signs

Jesus remember me when you come into your kingdom
And Jesus replies to you
'Today you will be with me in paradise.'

Broken bread

The most perfect act is one of simple presence
As simple as a piece of shared bread
Do you want to save the world?
Jesus saves it with a piece of broken bread
We are so busy looking for more complex solutions and
    methods of control
That we miss the being with
What should you do?
That is not a question
Who am I?
That is the question
You are the bearer of Christ
You are bread for the world.

Exposition (Barrowfield Estate in Glasgow, 1986)

I asked a taxi driver to drop me off. He said to me, 'You
    don't need a taxi, you need a tank.'
This was a place where nothing would grow,
and the blocks of flats looked like a war zone, and the
    only place to park a car was the police compound or it
    wouldn't be there in the morning, or not much of it
The stairwells smelt of piss, cannabis and chips
and the windows were boarded up
There in an upper window, a candle flickered, lighting an
    icon of Mary
And there in this upper room the Eucharist was exposed
to the poverty of this place.

I arrived in this no man's land adrift and lost
Feeling I could not fall any further
I was suffering from a depression I had been fighting for
  months
But here was the place of healing
Like a man on a trapeze who has lost his hold instead of
  hitting hard ground
I found myself suspended in a safety net
It was here in this derelict estate that I found Christ
I remember it as a place of safety, peace and restoration,
glowing warm with the light
The Franciscans who rented this house were broken into
  three times in the first year
That was before those on the estate recognized they were
  the real thing
A stable in their midst
Where those who came and knocked at the door witnessed
  the incarnation among them
Even now nearly forty years later, I can return to that
  exposition and that altar
Return indeed throughout my life
and in my own derelict places of fear and dread,
there behind the broken glass of the break-in
I can see a candle burning
A luminous darkness
And a manger of hope
Here in the place of my desolation
The discovery of a treasure beyond, and beyond all price
The seed planted in the land where nothing else will grow
Entirely vulnerable, entirely inadequate, yet entirely present,
the very thing that would become the tree in which many
  could find shelter,
the Eucharist on the altar
Nothing
Yet everything.

Sacrament is incarnation

God bearers

He came to the midnight Mass on Christmas Eve
I saw him from the clergy vestry window
He was a single man with dark olive skin and a beard
He had a thick jacket pulled up around his ears and
  shadowed eyes
But it was the large shapeless pack on his back that raised
  my suspicions
We have all seen the photos of the perpetrators of terror in
  our newspapers
Those seemingly innocent young faces with soft features
  that have packed explosives together with nails and other
  brutal shrapnel
Where was this lone man from – I had no way of knowing
Perhaps the Middle East – Syria or Afghanistan or Iraq or
  Libya –
or perhaps North African – Algeria or Morocco
or perhaps even Bangladesh or Northern Pakistan
We are told repeatedly to be alert. But was I being foolish or
  needlessly stereotyping?
Something about the way he was carrying the pack on his
  back was unusual
I am attentive to these signs. Who in this day and age in a
  crowded central London building is not? You look out
  for people who for whatever reason don't seem to fit
He was not one of many homeless visitors – his clothes were
  too chosen, they were not ones he had slept with on the
  streets. And yet alone. No one with him, no group
And why that oddly shaped backpack?
I came to take a closer look
Down the stairs and along the north aisle

As I came towards him our eyes met and he shifted the pack
    on his back as though it were something heavy which
    needed protecting – a precious cargo or worse
And as I came closer and he turned away
And then I saw them – two feet and tiny shoes and then the
    child's head which I had not seen before nestling on his
    father's neck
And I heard a cry and I realized this father had turned to
    comfort the child he was carrying so tenderly that father
    and child seemed one
And I felt joy and instant relief
He was carrying his son – this precious backpack was a
    life – not death
In the place of fear and suspicion – a baby
God's salvation
God's Eucharist
God's love for the world
Calling us into that same story
Of carrying love
Of being the God bearers
The peace of Christ carried on his father's back.

Jesus' hands

I heard him swearing at the back of the church
I warned the vergers
He was drunk, and really angry
And when the verger approached it poured out
A barrage of vile expletives induced by alcohol and the
    misery of living on the streets
I went to get ready for the Eucharist, the words still ringing
    in my ears
And then later at the altar as I said the words of invitation:
'Draw near with faith, receive the body of our Lord Jesus
    Christ which was broken for you
and his blood which was shed for you, eat and drink in
    remembrance that he died for you …'

There he was coming up the aisle
I wondered if I should stop and get help to get him out
    before he caused another scene
I watched him coming, tottering up the centre of the church
    on unsteady legs
I waited for him to let rip as I stood on the sanctuary step
He knelt at the altar rail crossed himself and held out his
    hands
Should I refuse him after the barrage of abuse, I wondered
But as he knelt there all I noticed was his hands
They were thin, tapering, weathered hands
I could see the sinews of his wrists
The lines on his palms and the creases of his open fingers
I have seen hands like this before,
many pictures of hands like this nailed to a cross
They were Christ's hands
I placed Christ's body in those hands
I remembered that when God looks at us, he sees only Jesus
He crossed himself again and walked slowly away.

Embodying Christ

Kopano is playing Jesus in our Passion Play
But I realize his life at this time is painful and he is stressed
    by the unknowns he faces
He is finding it hard to settle
I know he is bravely carrying in his own body the wounds
    others have done to him
He does not attend rehearsal and I am anxious
'I can't do a Passion Play without Jesus
You need to be here,' I tell him
'Trust me,' he says 'I want to do this. I will be there.'
He comes, and I see the part of Christ growing within him
He seems taller, stiller, as though Jesus has given him his
    voice
and an authority, a dignity from beyond
He has learnt all the words of Christ by heart

And he is speaking them increasingly from the heart as
   though they are his own
'That was beautiful,' I tell him after the rehearsal
'I want to be beautiful, so beautiful that they will want to
   eat my body'
I look at him, but there is no pretence
'Take eat, this is my body broken for you'
This is the offering, his humanity, all that he is
And later his cry from the cross silences a packed church
'My God, my God, why have you forsaken me?'
I realize this is no fiction. He knows it for real
Told me about the way they tortured him because of his
   love for a man he refused to betray
'Father, into your hands I commend my spirit'
This is the beauty that the sinful violence of our world still
   puts to death
This is the meaning of Christ's body broken for us
Like Kopano, we carry in our bodies the death of Jesus so
   that his life may be revealed in us
And when we embody Christ
Christ embodies us.

The Last Supper

Daniel told me about Brian who had for thirty years slept
   on the same bench
outside St Andrew's by the Wardrobe
Each week he visited him with the street rescue team
They tried to persuade him to visit the hostel
But he did not want to come in
Too claustrophobic
Too many other people
This was his home – this bench
His ceiling the sky
But over the years, he learnt to trust Daniel
Then one day completely unexpectedly he said he would
   come

He was frail
His clothes were soaking wet
Daniel helped him
'Don't leave me sir,' he said so politely
'Don't leave me, please.'
He was wearing several layers of socks
They had been on his feet so long they had disintegrated
Had to be gently peeled away from his skin
Daniel washed his feet
'That must have been very difficult,' I said
'No,' said Daniel 'I felt so privileged that he allowed me to
    do this for him ...
It felt the most holy thing I have ever done in my life.'
It was sacrament
It was not long after that Brian died
It was as though he wanted to prepare himself for burial
'Do this in remembrance of me ...'

Embodied memory

I wonder when we look back at the past, what are the things
that we remember? In our lives we often think that it is words
which are important. What we say, the arguments we use,
how we persuade or convince. But I wonder how many of our
memories are sense memories, memories carried in the whole
of our bodies?

When somebody dies, we often find that those sense memories become very vivid. Brian Mears was a stalwart of our
congregation. He passed away in a hospice in Penarth in Wales.
I was fortunate enough to be able to visit him there one week
before he died. When I remember this meeting, I can remember
every detail. Brian's composure, his matter-of-fact understated
manner. Brian sitting there on his bed, with his face slightly
flushed and swollen by the medication and I facing him on the
chair. We celebrated the Eucharist together – a tiny piece of
bread shared, and wine, no more than a thimble-full held in a
tiny chalice. Then the cross on his forehead in oil.

I pushed him in his wheelchair, we found a door leading into the back garden overlooking the sea – at the bottom of the garden, a gate. 'Shall we escape?' I asked. Brian chuckled. 'Yes,' he replied, 'I have had that same idea, let's escape.' I pushed his wheelchair along the hill, both of us looking out to the vast sea, aware of the vast unknown that Brian was so close to meeting with such courage. 'When you go back to St Martin's,' he said, 'I don't want people making a fuss. I am eighty-six years old. What more could I ask? Dying is part of life.' A simple meeting but the details of the encounter etched on my memory. 'I think we'd better go back now,' he said.

What do I remember about my own father? He was a priest too, but I don't remember his sermons apart from a line or two. I remember his beautiful handwriting, the letters he wrote to me, my name on the envelope, and in the same handwriting written on the first page of the Bible he gave me, which I still have. I remember watching him do up a parcel so meticulously. I remember watching him shave in the bathroom and the sound the razor made as it cut through his stubble. I remember him tucking me up in bed and lying down next to me and saying how lucky I was to be going to bed and me thinking then why don't you? He was ill for about five years – losing his mobility. I remember his beautiful handwriting becoming wobbly. I remember his slippers still neatly placed at the side of his bed. I remember him lying defenceless on a wet bed when his catheter came out and my mother was crying because she couldn't cope and I was defending him and he was lying there defending her. 'Don't talk to your mother like that!' When he died, I remember the touch of his coffin, it was covered in soft fabric. He'd wanted hessian as a sign of Franciscan simplicity, the undertaker had used purple episcopal velvet, which we'd found amusing. I remember putting the side of my face against it, so I could feel close. Two years after his death I was walking down the road and I saw a woman trying to help her husband out of the car. She was struggling so I stopped to help her – easing the frail man to his feet, careful that his head did not hit against the roof of the car, or that he did not lose his footing and trip on the kerb. The wife thanked me, but as I walked away I could feel my whole body shaking and tears were running down my face. My body had remembered the many times I had performed this same action for my own father. That is what a sacrament is – the outward visible action or sign which holds within it the mystery of love and grace.

These are embodied memories, remembered not as formulas, or dogmas, or dead traditions but remembered through each one of our senses and the community who in this memory discover their identity and the meaning of their lives.

A group of friends gather in an upper room that has been prepared and then Jesus taking off his outer garments comes towards his disciples with a bowl of water and a towel around him. 'What are you going to do Lord?' What does he want of us? This one has called us, led us, opened our eyes to the miracle of God's presence here and now. What is he going to do now? 'Wash my feet?' Here in this washing, in this offering of self for self, an example we will never forget.

As if this washing were not enough, the revelation goes further still. Not only will I wash you clean he says, I will also feed you with my own body, my own blood given for you, the covenant, of my love for you. I want my body to become your body. I want my blood to become your blood. The sign of your forgiveness and the forgiveness you too must share. The sign that nothing, nothing, can ever separate you from my love for you. Not even my death.

He is here, just as he was then, washing away the dirt, sharing the bread of life – transforming the place of abandonment into the very place of his unconditional love.

Sacrament is going out into the world
as a bearer of God

Having drunk at the still spring
Let's take our faith outside
Into the raw beauty of the streets
Into each human encounter
Into the torn life
The wound that longs for healing
The need that has no answer
The loneliness longing for embrace
The sin longing for forgiveness
The blindness that needs to see
The random search for pleasure
The insatiable hunger
The broken heart
The weeping soul
The grieving memory
The life brittle with age and neglect
The mind programmed by trauma it is forever rewinding
The young person humiliated
The person mentally unwell lost in a maze of fear and
    delusion
The child trapped within who has never been nurtured or
    fully loved
The victim and the victimizer in need of redemption
The forgotten prison
The violent estate
The man whose poverty makes you turn away
The migrant searching for your home
The river choked with plastic
The city that can no longer breathe
The parched land longing for grace
This is your world too
This is where love calls us

This is the city that must become your dwelling place
This is the forsaken one crying out on the cross
Your sanctuary
Your altar
Your hands reaching out
Your resurrection
Your Good News.

Sacrament is beholding both transcendence and immanence

Abiding with Christ

When I was studying for my Bachelor of Divinity, I spent a year in a Catholic seminary in Melbourne. It was a year of formation which I still look back to with gratitude. I had gone with radical romantic visions of Catholicism. *The Mission* and 'Gabriel's Oboe' leading me up the waterfall. I imagined white cells, a stripped back simplicity and beauty, the aesthetic of austerity rather than a poverty of spirit. I arrived at a seminary that looked more like a large motel built in the 1970s in red brick. The Oblates of Mary Immaculate welcomed me with great generousness and graciousness. I remember the rooms were painted blues and pinks with quilted clashing bedspreads and carpets. Outside my bedroom door when I arrived the novices were playing indoor cricket in the corridor. There was compulsory sport once a week and each day an hour of 'community time', which I think involved playing table tennis, though I may be imagining this. It was an intense year for in many ways I felt restricted, cut off and a bit lost. I longed at times to escape and would arrange getaways up the highway to Waverly Gardens Shopping Centre where I met a dear friend who understood both me and the Catholic Church. 'How can something so beautiful feel so painful?' I asked. It was how-ever a vitally important year, and I look back at this year as a pivotal moment in my calling. Stripped of the familiarities of an Anglicanism that had been bestowed upon me so generously by my parents, this was the year in which I faced myself and the radical demands of the gospel. It was like a stripping down even, of sensibility and my previous freedoms that seemed at the time to be costing not less than everything. And through all of this the thing that held me captive was the sacrament.

The chapel was modern, clean and painted yellow, nothing at all ambient or atmospheric. But in it the sacrament was reserved behind the altar and a candle burned and it drew me back like a magnet and to the Mass, which they celebrated each day with such simple reverence. The chapel was always open, and I remember walking down the corridor late at night while the seminary slept and quietly opening the chapel door and then kneeling there with the candle flickering. It held me. In fact, it held me there in this seminary. And each night I was drawn back into this silent chapel like a deep yearning. I simply knelt there. It felt like everything and yet nothing I could explain. The word that I would use is 'offering'. This sacrament Christ was offering me was everything but also asking me to offer everything in response. It was beckoning to a vastness beyond me, vaster than the vast unknown of Australia: a landscape of God that led not to the familiar but ever further into the wilderness where faith is born. It was a future I could not plan for and to which the only answer was 'yes'. That chapel was like heaven in such ordinary that the ordinary could never be ordinary again. This encounter with Christ in the sacrament has always stayed with me. It was an incredible gift to be given by the Oblates of Mary Immaculate – an eternal gift. Writing this book, I returned to the Oblates of Mary, this time a small retreat house behind a railway tunnel in the East End of London. 'The City Is My Monastery' I wrote, the trains seeming to rattle the tiny room in which I worked and slept. The same reserved sacrament calling me to prayer in a room that looked like a dentist's waiting room – transformed by Christ's presence.

Stay awake with me and pray

I was to spend many hours kneeling in front of the sacrament in a very different context. It was when I was chaplain to the Melanesian Brotherhood in the Solomon Islands. It was during that time I have mentioned when in 2003 seven of our Brothers had been taken hostage by a rebel group on the island of Guadalcanal during a period of ethnic conflict. Later we were to hear that they had been murdered, but for three months we did not know this. At the Melanesian Brotherhood Headquarters at Tabalia, on the other side of the island from where we believed they were being held, I arranged a vigil for them throughout the night during those three months of waiting. My hour was from 2.00 a.m. to 3.00 a.m. In my diary I described that hour. It is in the middle of the conflict, so when I speak about 'fear' it is the fear for our Brothers held hostage and the fear too that we may be attacked:

At 2.00 a.m. I wake up. It is dark, and I don't want to turn on any lights as if it will disturb all that I fear. I am going over to the Chapel, as I do every night. Daniel, my Brother, wakes. He wants to come too. Silently we slip out of the house through the hedge and across the deserted grass, past the Community graveyard, then down the footpath by the side of the square. Bare feet on wet grass and then sharp coral, I know this way even in the pitch black. I have followed this same way at least five times a day for more than ten years. And yet still, as I approach the chapel, there is an anticipation, each sense heightened, as though a meeting is about to take place which is more than anything else in my life. Fear, but it is not like the fear of darkness: holy fear, an awe of something greater and beyond anything. It cannot be seen or quantified but it is longed for. At times it seems like nothing, a yawning emptiness, and yet it is everything. It is our hope. It is everything we are waiting for. Often I will leave this chapel feeling I have just missed what I came for, or the futility of my faith is mocking me, and yet I will long to come again and be, be more deeply. It is all we have to defeat

the darkness. There is a candle burning at the front; Novice
Jack Alec and Novice Ishmael are there praying; solid, silent
and so still, as they always are, as they have been since the
beginning, for they share this hour of vigil when everyone
else is sleeping.

I feel your presence in the night
The fragrance of God and man
I breathe in the stillness
And in the middle of night
Both flesh and spirit live
Live deeply
Live to the brim
Reach across time and space
And touch eternity
And I long for all to be drawn and held together by this
    invisible God
Whose love burns in the darkness with the life of the Son
And whose blessing touches us as softly as the rustle of the
    night wind and rain in the trees
How strange that when we are most abandoned we are
    drawn into Gethsemane
'Stay awake with me.'
How miraculously you wait for us just beyond our fear.[2]

VI

Sacrament is transfiguration

I am in the Basilica of Santa Maria in Trastevere, Rome.
According to St Jerome, oil gushed forth from the ground in
Trastevere at the time of Jesus' birth, a clear sign he wrote of the
'grace of Christ that would come upon humanity'. In the third
century, a church was founded where the miracle supposedly
took place. As I look up into the dome in front of me, there
are the most incredible mosaics, in rich colours of gold, bronze
and warm burnt umbers. The mosaic depicts Christ enthroned

in splendour, his left hand holding the Scriptures, his right hand around his mother also enthroned at his side. They are flanked on either side by a line-up of saints in ecclesiastical vestments, including, on Christ's left, Pope Innocent II. The altar is raised up about six feet so that the priest stands with his feet just above our heads. Above the altar is an ornate stone canopy supported by four porphyry columns. How high the priest seems above us. How hard it must be to be so raised up. What a long way to fall. I am filled with sympathy. I am very aware of human frailty, but what about God's glory? And then I too become involved in the Mass.

Despite the magnificence of this place, in fact the Mass which is taking place is disarmingly simple, the same familiar action and words though in Italian are instantly recognizable as the words I know. And suddenly I realize I am no longer an observer and this Mass is not a presentation or something declaimed; it is real, clear, transparent, and I am held by the words and actions as I stand there, as though a door has been opened into a darkened room and I am standing there in the light that is flooding in. Perhaps one could say that this is a place created to create the illusion of the sacred. Yet the opposite is what I experience, as though the illusion is the life I so often live, but what I experience here is the truth of things opened up. 'This is my body, given for you ... This is my blood shed for you.'

Gone for that moment is my cynicism and my suspicion of ecclesiastical pomp, wealth and power. I am acutely aware of the homeless Jesus of the streets, like Caravaggio's depiction of the child held in a doorway by a mother with bare and street-stubbed feet (which I have also gazed at in Rome). But I am also aware of the Christ who lifts up our eyes to heaven. This is the meaning of sacrament – the outward visible sign of a mystery so beyond us. God below, God above. Our faith becomes not how we convert others to Jesus but how we get out of the way and create the space and the opportunity for God to shine through: for God to do God's work.

Transfiguration is like that. Jesus shows rather than tells. He never sits his disciples down and explains who he is, but he leads those who are ready to the place where they will know it for themselves. We spend a lot of time looking down at our feet, but there are moments in our lives when we look up and see a greater truth.

In Rome I meet a very old and dear friend of mine. Her husband, who was the same age as me, has recently died and Liz's grief and love for him is palpable. She does not need to wear black for you to know how deeply she is in mourning. On the one hand she tells me she finds the organized Church impossible – it seems aloof, alien, cold, detached – and yet the churches around Rome are, she says, also the places she seeks sanctuary, for these churches alone are places where she can light a candle and open her soul to the enormity of life and death and the loss of the man she loves, and how on earth she is going to bring up her son without him.

In the Basilica of San Bartolomeo, I too go in search of answers. It is a place I feel I belong because one of the altars is dedicated to the Seven Melanesian Brotherhood martyrs, who before their deaths were for so long my friends and Brothers. On the altar is the cross and chain that Brother Robin wore around his neck, the black and white sash and symbol of their community that Brother Francis wore and Brother Tony's walking stick. I remember Robin's strong handshake, leadership and faithfulness. I remember Tony's kindness one night waking up to keep a fire burning all night so that we would not be bitten by malaria-carrying mosquitoes. I remember Francis, both his gentleness and his great bravery, as without weapons he protected the innocent from violence, and I remember each day his last word to me – the word 'courage'. Coming here feels like coming home because these small touchable memories of their lives connect me. Connect me to the simple chapel on the other side of the world, to the lives of these men I knew and love – now remembered here among the modern saints and martyrs – meekness and majesty. Nothing could be so human as those simple signs of their life; nothing could be so transcendent. I kneel for a long time in front of this altar in prayer believing they will intercede for me now just as they did for me so much in life.

Carl Jung argued that conflict can never be resolved on the level at which it arises – at that level there is only winner and a loser, not a reconciliation. The conflict, the grief must be somehow got above, like seeing a storm from higher ground. A transfiguration. Next to this altar where I have been praying is a small kiosk where I pick up a postcard. It is a mosaic of the face of Christ. I search the church for the mosaic but cannot find it. 'Si, Si,' says the man selling the postcards when I point to the picture. He takes out a key and leads me up a stone staircase to an upper room and there hidden away is this big oval beautiful mosaic of Christ looking down, gentle and strong, the Scriptures in his outstretched hands. The transcendent Christ, as though waiting for me, present in this locked upper room above the pain and loss of the path through which we find him.

And what is the message that I must take back when I go down those stairs? Well, the Scriptures are open in Jesus' hand. In Latin they read 'I am the way the truth and the life.' It is like looking into the face of the mercy of God. 'Tell your friend, tell your community, tell your own heart,' this Christ seems to say, 'I am the way and the truth and the life and I have set you free, not to live in the labyrinths of regret for all that cannot be changed. Your love has a present and a future and an eternity. Do not lose heart. Only my love can engender love, costly love, stronger than death. Look up and see my face. "I have said these things to you, so that in me you may have peace. In the world you face trouble and persecution. But take *courage*; I have conquered the world."' (John 16.33)

I am going to go back down the stairs and tell my friend who is grieving, I know there will be darkness again and there will be doubt. But it is good for a moment to be here in this place of transfiguration. And for a moment to know that seeking God means first of all letting yourself be found by God.

VII

Sacrament is becoming part of the body of Christ

I visited Chennai in India. It is a bewildering cultural and spiritual experience into which one feels thrown like a stick into a river of life. I arrived at the Mercy Home run by the Missionary Sisters of St Francis de Sales to whom I had been given an introduction by Michael Moran who is a member of the Nazareth Community, who has been much influenced by the gentle wisdom and devotion of St Francis de Sales. The sisters had heard we were coming and as we entered we were surrounded by what can only be described as sacrament – the outward, visible sign of God's grace. At least fifteen sisters welcomed us, had prepared for us, waited on us at table and showed us round. I wrote to Michael who always waxes lyrical about St Francis de Sales and 'living Jesus':

> Dear Michael, your Sisters of St Francis de Sales are the finished product. They are incredible – they treated me, and my friend Widi and our driver arriving at their door as if Jesus had just arrived. What a ministry they have. They are, as you would say, 'blooming where they are planted'.

I have never had so many sisters looking after me when we were eating, they had cooked curry without chilli for me specially because they thought an Englishman could not take hot food, and chips because they had heard that an Englishman eats everything with chips. At first, I thought that this was hospitality just put on for an Englishman, but then I went with them to meet more than 200 other men and women and children they had taken in off the streets, and who were now being so well cared for. Those who had in most cases been abandoned – the elderly, the sick, those with great disfigurement to their bodies, limbs and faces, a woman whose whole hands had been burnt away in a fire. And again I saw such dignity and light and joy as we prayed together and they grasped my hands in welcome.

'Namaste,' I bow to you. The place was so clean and light-filled. 'How is it,' Widi said to me afterwards, 'that here in extreme poverty we can find such hope and welcome while in the rich care homes of the West the experience is often one of such loneliness and unhappiness?' In a small chapel the Holy Sacrament was on the altar. It was the only air-conditioned room in the convent. Many were gathered here, and we knelt with them in prayer. This sacrament felt like the generator of the mercy that filled the whole community.

I remembered Mother Teresa's story about a sister who at first found it hard to care for the dying. She had found maggots in the wounds of one of the old men who had been carried in from the street. And the smell and the sight had made her feel physically sick. Mother Teresa had told her to look at the way the priest had celebrated the Mass that day, holding the bread and wine with such reverence and devotion – 'Now,' she said, 'holding that in your mind go back and care for this man from the streets with the same reverence.' Later she met the sister again. 'How was it, Sister?' Mother Teresa asked. To which the sister replied, 'Mother, all afternoon I have been holding in my hands the body of Christ.'

When you meet Christ, you feel transformed by the encounter. Go and do the same. Along the road out of Chennai are thousands of Indian Christian pilgrims walking over 400km from Chennai to the shrine at Valankanni where an apparition of Mary is believed to have taken place. It's incredibly hot and dusty and the pilgrims look exhausted, literally streams of them swathed in soft orange cloth as a sign of their pilgrimage, now grimy with sweat and dust. Remembering our own pilgrimage to Canterbury, I want to be with them and feel a great sense of solidarity, but there is no time – this pilgrimage lasts for at least two weeks. But how can we share a part of this sign of faith and hope? We buy boxes of samosas and mango drinks and we stop at the side of the road to hand out these small gifts. We and the pilgrims are left glowing by the joy of this encounter.

Our gospel is not words in a book. It is flesh and blood encounter with Christ. Sacrament. In India, both in the Home of Mercy and at the side of the road in the encounter, we bow to each other – I bow to you. It is a sign of the recognition of the divine presence in the other. 'Namaste – I see you.' If we saw the presence of God in one another, how different our world would be. If only we realized that our bodies are living sacraments.

VIII

The sacrament of the Eucharist is the remembrance of a death but also the beginning of new life

I remember holding a small memorial service at St Martin-in-the-Fields for a Congolese mother and her family, who had just learnt that her daughter had been murdered in the Congo while she had been trying to win asylum so that her family could be united. I remember visiting the family soon after they had heard the news, and her mother and the family were huddled, knotted up on the floor of their bare room sobbing with grief. And after a long time, when she had calmed a little, the mother asked me the same question we have often heard: 'What is the point of praying to God if our prayers are not heard?' Yet here in this mother was both the question and the answer. And the prayer within me was that she, and indeed we who joined with her, would not give up that struggle for love for if we did that would indeed be the victory of violence and hatred.

At the memorial service for this small daughter from the Congo, the victim of human brutality and war, we gather around the altar, the young son leaning on this holy table, looking up to watch a piece of bread broken – a sign of human brokenness and death which will be a sign, a sacrament of life and hope – and a cup of wine, Christ's blood – the sign of our forgiveness. And the Congolese family, led by their eight-year-old son holding a flickering candle, lead us out of the church into the light and we feel our hearts burning within us. This family – like lambs among wolves. Outside in St James's Park the sun is shining, the Horse Guards march past, a band is playing, flags fly and the helium balloons we have given the children rise up into a clear blue sky. This is the good news – the beginning of healing, that the first shall be last and the last first; that this mother, the very poorest, or the smallest child can become the bearer of Christ to the world. This is the meaning of the Eucharist: Christ has died, Christ is risen, Christ will come again.

Sacrament is discovering a new truthfulness in which we all are included

Each week the Nazareth Community meet for an informal Eucharist.

A Eucharist can sometimes feel like a performance acted out on our behalf by the designated ministers. A church can be like a theatre with a proscenium arch – most of the action taking place on a stage from which the audience is spatially separated. The congregation become the witnesses, the listeners to the prayers prayed on their behalf. They are read to and preached to without interaction. In the sacrament, they are recipients. The only things that are participatory are the responses to prayers which are prescribed and the hymns with words and a tune that they (mostly) adhere to. For much of the service, the congregation are static – they do not move, other than to stand up or sit down, until they come up to receive Communion. Most of the physical action of the liturgy is done for them.

In the theatre, many directors have experimented with trying to remove the divide between the actor and the audience to create a greater sense of involvement. The aim is to create not so much a spectacle in front of us but an event actually happening to us, in our very midst, in which we all become the actors. As we developed our informal Eucharist, we talked about how we could change the shape of our liturgy so that all could participate more fully in the action of this sacrament, while at the same time not losing its reverence – if all who

THE CITY IS MY MONASTERY

gather are called to be part of the one body then they are the liturgy themselves.

We gathered a group together to experiment with different ways we might do this. We experimented with not using the altar at all but gathering around a small table sitting on the floor. We experimented with movement so that the offertory became a procession around the church in which everyone participated. We experimented with paperless liturgy where there was no prescribed response. We held a silent Eucharist where no words were used at all but all of us were invited to participate in the actions that make up the Eucharist. It was beautiful. From these experiments and thoughts, we have created an informal Eucharist which has been used every Wednesday. Our liturgy has been formed and shaped through repetition so that people can feel familiar and comfortable with that shape and yet we have tried to allow for this liturgy also to maintain a sense of spontaneity and immediacy, the sense that this is not just a repetition of past actions but Christ made present and in our midst now.

In all of this we have been careful not to lose the sacredness and beauty of the Eucharist, nor its simplicity or power. Not 'do it yourself', but a Eucharist in which each one of us is called to be intimately involved just as those first disciples were involved as they shared the Last Supper or met the risen Christ when he broke bread at Emmaus. We have discovered that the most important thing is to keep this Eucharist as simple and natural as possible. We are not aiming at a performance but at something transparent: God's life in our midst and flowing through each one of us. We call this informal Eucharist, 'Bread for the World'.

This is the pattern we have developed.

1 All who come are warmly welcomed when they arrive. They are not given a service booklet but a single sheet which includes the hymns or chants and couple of responses. They are invited, but not forced, to take seats as near the front as possible. In front of the pews are some benches and wooden kneelers bringing a greater closeness. There is

no procession, but all those taking part take up their places among the congregation around the altar. This includes a small choir without choir robes who sit together.

2 The choir or soloist begins with a song that introduces or helps create the ambience or spirit of our theme. During this piece of music, two members of the community come forward and simply prepare the altar for the Eucharist – preparing a place for Christ. They light the candles, spread out the corporal, the white linen cloth, and place the pottery chalice into which they pour wine and the pottery paten onto which they place fresh bread.

3 The celebrant welcomes those who have come, inviting them to participate in this Eucharist and later to join us for a simple supper. We want to establish a sense of the generosity and beauty of Christ's invitation which is extended to all.

4 There is a simple participatory confession.

5 A member of our community reads the Gospel.

6 The reflection is usually shared and over the weeks has involved a large variety of people from all walks of life including those from the Nazareth Community, choir, guests and invited speakers. It has taken various forms: sometimes an interview, sometimes different speakers, sometimes something more participatory like the use of drama or godly play. It is important to hear the voices and reflections of some of the youngest or newest members of the community. Also the voices of those seldom asked to speak, like homeless people or those who may sometimes feel on the edge of more formal gatherings. These need to be sensitively prepared, and it helps to have someone interviewing who is known and can hold and weave this together.

7 After the reflection, members of the community lead prayers that respond to the theme, and all of us join in a sung chant response to each of the prayers.

8 The celebrant now shares the peace and invites everyone to gather in a circle around the altar – a circle in which all are included. There is a gathering hymn, song or chant as we gather.

9 The Eucharistic prayer uses different voices. We have tried to make it direct and immediate, allowing for spontaneity so that it can draw on the theme we have shared. The words of consecration and the calling upon the Holy Spirit are said by the celebrant, but we have tried to make these words present tense: something that is happening here and now and which unites all those who have gathered.

10 Standing in a circle around the altar, we say the Lord's Prayer together.

11 The sacrament is shared around the circle, those who do not wish to receive keeping their heads bowed as the choir sings.

12 At the end of the service, once again all those who have come are invited to continue the Eucharist with a simple shared supper and the chance to share thoughts and reflections with one another in groups.

13 The meal which follows the Eucharist is as simple as possible – usually bread and soup. The focus for this is not the food itself, the preparation of which could easily begin to dominate. The food after the Eucharist aims to continue the Eucharist as we talk and meet.

14 After this, we divide into 'listening groups'. We have found that between eight and twelve people in each group works best. There are simple guidelines for these groups described in Chapter 3 (see page 101). The understanding that we are here to listen to one another, that each person is given space and we use Scripture as the means of encountering how God is at work in the lives of others.[3]

This is an example of the full liturgy:

Sacrament is at the centre of liturgy

Bread for the World

GATHERING

Three candles are lit on the altar

We light three lights for the Trinity of love:
God above us, God beside us, God beneath us:
God at our centre
God on the edge

Music begins

PRAYER OF INVOCATION

We prepare a place for you
Come to us in the difference of every life gathered
Come to us in song
Come to us in Word
Come to us in stillness
Come to us in bread and wine
Come to us in flesh and blood
Reach out across time
Be present in all time

Come Jesus, be our guest,
Stay with us for day is ending.
With friend, with stranger,
With young and old,
With the lost and found
Be among us tonight
Our guest our host
The one who says all – all are welcome here.

Song or chant

Word on the edge

Reflection

Silence

PRAYERS ARE OFFERED

A *prayer of thanksgiving*

A *prayer of concern*

A *prayer of hope*

PRAYERS FOR FORGIVENESS

Because the world is beautiful
But beauty is easily destroyed
We need you
Lord Jesus Christ, Son of God, have mercy on us.

Because we are weak and fail
Because we often know little but pretend much
We need you
Lord Jesus Christ, Son of God, have mercy on us.

Because we cannot live without love
And often walk in darkness
We need you
Lord Jesus Christ, Son of God, have mercy on us.

Because you come among us
and hear the stories of our lives
and in the place of judgement offer healing for our pain
we need you
Lord Jesus Christ, Son of God, have mercy on us.

Because we curse you, and abandon you
And turn away and walk past
And are afraid
And let you die
But you love us to the end
And win a victory over all hatred
We need you
Lord Jesus Christ, Son of God, have mercy on us.

Because we have your message to proclaim
Because we have your kingdom to build
Because there are so many in need of your love
Because we have your life to live
We need you
Lord Jesus Christ, Son of God, have mercy on us.

And Jesus said, 'Your sins are forgiven'
In the name of the Father who created you and waits to
    welcome you home,
in the name of the Son who searches for you,
in the name of the Spirit who brings the healing of forgiveness
and calls you to do the same,
you have been set free. Amen.

THE SHARING OF THE PEACE

The risen Christ came and stood among his disciples and said
'Peace be with you'
Then their hearts rejoiced when they saw the risen Lord.

God of eternal peace,
who offers the gift of peace
and whose children are the peacemakers;
pour your peace into our hearts,
that conflict and anger may cease.

The peace of Christ is shared for all
Let us offer each other a sign of that peace

Song or Chant
during which all are invited to gather in a circle around the
altar

Lord Jesus Christ,
you have invited us to come to this table.
We have come from many places and experiences;
we have come with all our differences;
we have come to the place where journeys meet.
You have reached out to all on the edge
and called us into the heart of God.
The Lord be with you
And also with you

Reader
On the night that Jesus was betrayed he told us to prepare
a place for him. And then he offered us a sign. A sign of
how he would give himself to us to give us new life. He had
always loved us, and now he showed us how perfect his love
was.

Priest
While his disciples were eating, he took a piece of bread in
his hands, like this,
and he blessed it:
Blessed are you Lord God of all creation;
through your goodness we have this bread to offer,
which earth has given and human hands have made
it will become for us the bread of life.

And then he said to them:
'This is my body broken for you.
Do this in remembrance of me.'

Silence

And then Jesus took a cup of wine like this, and gave you
thanks:

Blessed are you Lord God of all creation
through your goodness we have this wine to offer,
fruit of the vine and work of human hands,
it will become for us the cup of salvation.

And then he said to them:
'Drink this all of you
this is my blood of the new covenant which is shed for you
and for many for the forgiveness of sins.
Do this in remembrance of me.'

Silence

Reader
His disciples did not understand these words but later they
would see Christ's body broken, his life poured out – his
death for us so that we might share his risen life.
The life he gave then, he shares with us now.

Priest
Lord Jesus Christ,
as we do in this place what you did once and for all,
breathe your Spirit upon us
and upon this bread and wine
that they may be heaven's food,
renewing, transforming, sustaining and making us whole;
and that we may be your body on earth,
loving and caring for your creation,
where all are welcome
and the poorest are fed.

Bless the earth
heal the sick
let the oppressed go free
and fill each one of us with your love from on high.
Gather your people from the ends of the earth
to feast at your table with all your saints.

Reader
Gathered here around this table,
called to share this same bread and wine
as one family we are bold to pray:

Our Father in heaven,
hallowed be your name,
your kingdom come,
your will be done,
on earth as in heaven.
Give us today our daily bread.
Forgive us our sins
as we forgive those who sin against us.
Lead us not into temptation but deliver us from evil.
For the kingdom, the power, and the glory are yours
now and for ever.
Amen.

Priest
Look, Jesus Christ, the Bread of Heaven is broken for the
life of the world.
The gifts of God for the people of God

Jesus Bread of Life
Bread on the Edge
Bread for the world

All gathered at the altar are invited to receive Communion.
Those who wish to receive a blessing bow their heads.

Song or Chant

Lord Jesus Christ
We have recognized you in bread and wine
May our hearts burn within us on the road.

Remember each day that Jesus is in you
Lord Jesus Christ
You are the Word for us to speak
You are the Truth for us to tell;
You are the Light for us to light in the darkness,
You are the Bread of Life for us to share.

Reader
Now all of us must go out into the world
And live God's love there
Look for Jesus in the oppressed and burdened,
Look for Jesus in those who have lost hope,
Look for him among the poor in heart,
Among the merciful
Among the peacemakers
Among the persecuted for the sake of right
Look for Jesus on the edge.

Priest
Go simply, lightly, gently
Go with obedience
Go with love
And the blessing of God Almighty
Father Son and Holy Spirit be with you now and forever.
Amen.

Song of blessing[4]

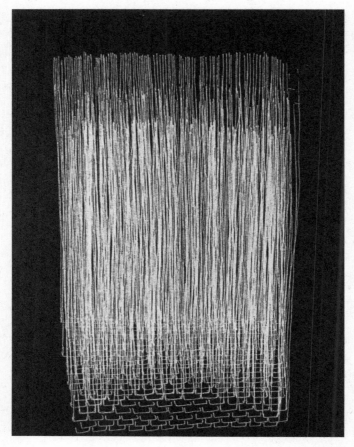

Vicky Howard

Notes

1 Carlo Carretto, *Letters from the Desert*, Darton, Longman & Todd, 1972, p. 130.

2 Richard Carter, *In Search of the Lost*, Canterbury Press, 2006, pp. 135–6.

3 Richard Carter, *Liturgy on the Edge*, edited by Samuel Wells, Canterbury Press, 2018, pp. 22–5.

4 Ibid., pp. 26–32.

5

With Sharing

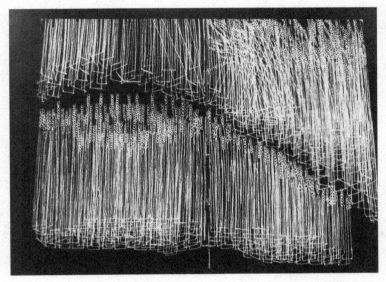

Vicky Howard

The Christian gospel needs to be lived. It needs to be shared.

We are a gathered community coming together to live our rule of life but often called to live that life independently and on our own. This will make the need for our own commitment greater because for the most part we will need to depend on self-guidance and establishing the pattern of religious life for ourselves.

What are the qualities of this life that we will share?

1 **A greater simplicity of life**

'You want to follow Christ, and not look back, remember that, as you walk in his footsteps, you will be irresistibly drawn to share, and to a great simplicity of life.'[1]

Let go of the things that keep you from seeing Christ face to face and seeing Christ in the face of your brother or sister. There are many things that burden us that we simply do not need. Only you will be able to discern the things you need to let go of. Gently strip away those things that have over-occupied your mind and heart and create a generous space for the encounter with God.

2 **A beginner's mind**

Remember that we are all beginners in this path of discipleship. The youngest or the oldest or the one you perhaps are tempted to overlook may be there to share the greatest wisdom. Be attentive to the voice and actions of each community member. We are all novices. There is no hierarchy in God's love. We are all the beloved. No one person is the expert. Each day we begin anew.

3 **Renouncing possessiveness**

Brothers and Sisters have traditionally in religious life taken a vow of poverty. Christ himself willingly embraced a life of poverty in the world. 'He was rich but for our sake became poor.' 'He had no place to lay his head.' The members of this community will need money to provide for their needs and those of others. Money is also a gift that some can offer with gratitude and others share with gratitude. The members of the community will seek to live both generously and responsibly. Each living within their means. Each guarding against the idolatries and false consumerism that can so easily dominate and deplete us. In living without possessiveness, we will aim to grow more aware of the needs of others. We will both feast and famine with the community: meaning that in times of plenty we shall be happy to celebrate and to share and at times of scarcity and struggle we will also be there to share that scarcity without complaint and surprisingly, often with joy. There is no point in wearing a hair shirt when you have accepted an invitation to a party. At the same time, when there is scarcity, humbly step back, let go of your own demands until all are fed. If your host offers you the fatted calf, without realizing you are on a diet – give thanks to your host and share without rejecting their hospitality. In our way of life, there needs to be a generosity which is more important than our own righteousness.

4 Obedience

At the heart of our rule of life there is an obedience, an obedience to God and to this community we have chosen to serve. This is not a crushing obedience but a path of respect that opens you up to a greater freedom to offer and to serve without selfishness or favour. Obedience to Christ is not life-denying. It is not there to mark your failures or increase your guilt. It is there to bring life. Remember Christ's words:

> Come to me, all you that are weary and are carrying heavy burdens, and I will give you rest. Take my yoke upon you, and learn from me; for I am gentle and humble in heart, and you will find rest for your souls. For my yoke is easy, and my burden is light.
> (Matthew 11.28–30)

This obedience requires a willingness to offer one's time and giftedness generously and not in search of individual reward, always realizing how much we receive reciprocally. Obedience is not about oppressing yourself with your failures. It is not a hardening of the 'oughteries'; it is about listening and discerning. It is about creating the very condition in which each member of the community may flourish. What at first may seem like loss is in fact the soil that allows more to flourish.

5 Poverty of control

One of the ways we have learnt to survive in an individualistic society is by creating private territories where we are in control. A community can sometimes become obsessed with its own procedures and rules. I remember arriving at an empty campsite and being told I could not book in because they had 'already put the computer to bed'. I remember my brother and I joking that the procedure for booking into this field seemed more complicated than the NASA Space Station. A community without helpful rules of operation can quickly become a burden to the few. Yet rules should always be there to support and sustain and help communal life to flourish. That may sound obvious, but too often and too easily rules acquire a life of their own, creating unnecessary hierarchies and processes of control and administration. I remember when we first started the International Group that all the volunteers wanted to wear the smart aprons we had bought and stand behind the counter serving food. On the one hand we could have said this was 'servant leadership', but on the other hand the striped apron became a sign of the organizers as opposed to those being organized. Our challenge then was to break down those divisions so that guests could also become volunteers and anyone who was helping would wear an apron. This may seem a small thing, but it is enormously important in creating community not to create a division between donors and recipients but to encourage the sense that we all can be both – the guest could become host and host would also see themselves as guest. We also noticed how easily new rules could creep in. For example: 'There will be no showers after 3.00 p.m.' so that we could wash the towels and get away quicker; or 'We do not wash coats.' Now there was sometimes reason for this if there was a lot of washing to do, but what about when it was clear that a person's coat was very dirty and there was enough room to wash it? There were, on the other hand, simple rules that were enhancing to the whole community. 'Leave the basins or the showers as you would like to find them'; or eating together at the tables provided rather than standing up or taking food into other rooms. A few months ago, when a large group of us went to stay with the Focolare Community[2], I asked Mary, who was in charge, if she wanted to tell everybody the rules of the house in which she was staying. She simply responded: I have no announcement of rules only that you make yourself at home and treat the place as you would your own. What a beautiful rule – to treat a place with the respect you would your own.

6 Openly Christian

One of the rules we made in the International Group was that we will always begin our meal with prayers. We will not be ashamed or try to hide the fact that we are a Christian community. At the same time, we are a community that respect people of all faiths and those of none and give them the space and the opportunity if they want to honour the traditions of their own faith. Muslims, for example, are provided with takeaway food during the fasting month of Ramadan. We are also careful in the food we prepare, using food that is halal so all can eat and avoiding pork or beef. We aim to be a Christian community, proud of our own faith and respectful of all. Is that not what we see in Jesus Christ? This is an example of the grace we pray, which I first heard prayed by Mallie Lightbourn who was herself one of the greatest examples of hospitality and inclusion I have ever met:

Lord God
In a world where many are hungry, we thank you for the food we share
In a world where many are lonely, we thank you for our fellowship.
In a world where so many live in fear and mistrust, we thank you for the example of unity and peace.
In a world where many do not know the love of God, we thank you for that love which is ours today and which we share.
In the Holy Name of our God we pray.
Amen.

7 **Creativity and participation**
Participation will always involve an element of risk. It takes time and effort to create trust and fullness of participation, but the results can yield a hundredfold. One of the greatest joys of community is to discover the talents of others and see them flourish in a way that no one was expecting. For example: to see someone growing in confidence so that they are not just able to tell their story but hold a congregation spellbound; to participate in a theology group led by a homeless asylum seeker whose theology is not just in his head but in the story of his life; to a see man of great dignity who has been homeless and sleeping outside our church for many years become a steward and helper of others with such natural graciousness and care that only someone who had been there themselves could know; to discover what a joyful thing it is to see someone arrive tired, angry and despairing and see them leave three hours later after a shower and hot food, with clean clothes and some hope restored, knowing they will be welcome here again. As we grow together as a community, one of the greatest gifts is that slowly we will learn the gifts that each person brings are shared by all and that together we can also bear one another's burdens.

8 **Table fellowship**
Throughout the Gospels, Jesus continually shares food and fellowship with those he meets. Eating together is at the centre of our Christian life. Food brings people together in common fellowship and sharing. The table becomes the sign of our unity and the hospitality we offer to one another. At this table there is no segregation. All are welcomed, saint and sinner alike. The only ones who are not welcomed are those who choose not to come. The guest, we are told, comes as Christ to our door and the welcome we provide is the sign that whatever we do for the least of our brothers and sisters we do it for Christ. But at the same time the host is also himself or herself a sign of Christ, welcoming all to the table.

9 **Unity**

For a community to become a community it also needs time together and patience, learning to live with the idiosyncrasies and frustrations of those very different from ourselves. There will be frictions to overcome, and irritations and conflicts to be faced, but that too is part of one's life together. We meet each other as we are, and the miracle of the gospel is that we learn to live together despite our differences, forever in need of reconciliation and forgiveness. Within our Nazareth Community, we seek to create opportunities each year to be together. Of all of these times away, a time of retreat is particularly important. Each spring there is a silent retreat that members of the community are invited to attend.

10 **Spiritual accompaniment**

We all need some guidance and discernment upon the way. So each of the community will have someone to accompany them. They will meet every two to three months to talk, pray, reflect and discern. With the person who is accompanying you, you are invited to make your way of life your own, deciding how you will live the different aspects of silence, service, Scripture, sacrament, sharing and Sabbath in a holistic and integrated way. Perhaps the secret of this journey is not to fear, but to open one's hands to this call to follow. It is important not to over-commit but to do simple things well. Less is often much more. As you find more time to pray, you will also discover that the compassion within you and your empathy for others is opened up. It will need discernment with the person who is accompanying you to discover the right path, which will combine both balance and trust. Your guide is not your director. They are there to listen, to encourage and to help you discern the path which has the heart of Christ.

I

Sharing the Church

Learning to share the Church

There was a cross on the wall of this Norman church
Made by the crusaders they said
And a smell you can only find in churches
Of damp, wooden pews, hymn books and hassocks on hooks
There was a curtain around the organ so that you couldn't
    see the organist's feet dancing
And there were old people who smiled at you
And gave you orange cordial in white plastic cups and
    custard creams,
after you had sung choruses at Sunday School:
What, never thirst again? No, never thirst again!
What, never thirst again? No, never thirst again!
And whoso drinketh, Jesus said,
Shall never, never thirst again!
This church was the place I imbibed my faith
Kind and welcoming, and homely in an otherworldly sort of
    way
Like an eccentric great aunt or grandmother,
who was there at your baptism,
and watched you grow up
Or a Bible with pictures that drew you into the story
For it had your name inside, written in your father's
    handwriting
It became as part of your life as cornflakes or toast,
but created a home within and formed the seasons of your
    life
Like coming home from school in winter
Or the smell of Christmas in the air
Or setting off for the seaside in the summer
Church was like your family
This church formed you in kindness,

in knowing it was right to help others
And in gentle tolerance
That knew in whispers that things went wrong
And things were not always what they seemed
But accepted those they whispered about with mercy.

I reached an age when I stopped going regularly
because it seemed at that time something you grew out of
or did for your parents
while there were more interesting things to do on Sunday
    morning
Like stay in bed
Yet it had already become part of me
My identity
As part of my life as breathing,
breathing in a narrative of redemption
which shaped my life
And at the centre this man Jesus
Whose gospel had inhabited me without realizing
Until I tried to leave it behind.

Our home was like the church extended
We didn't worry about money
We welcomed all people home for tea
My friends loved this open house forever able to expand to
    include them and others
The elderly Vi Lathbury who I rescued when she got stuck
    in the lavatory
The drug addicts who came to breakfast with shaking hands
Mr Sumption who sometimes slept during the day in our
    spare room, I knew not why
Anne who was dying from cancer and wandered along the
    corridor at night wild-eyed and increasingly emaciated
    and I discovered one day in the larder when I was looking
    for biscuits and she for her painkillers
In this church and home
I learnt that people and the way you treated them
were always more important than what you owned

And when things went wrong there was forgiveness
And a God with whom you could rest your head against the
    pew in front
Tired from your paper round
Or with thoughts full of dreams and longings and desires
This was a God who did not change with thought or feeling
    but loved you, the way you were
It was a church that did not seem to demand much
But in fact was everything
Asked everything
It formed me
It took my life
And held it with generosity
And when I left it behind thinking I could manage alone
It took me back
Led me out of the wilderness
It was there watching and waiting
Praying for me
Praying within me
If I knew then what I know now, I would never have gone
    away
If I had not gone away, I would not know what I know now
Which is that this church contains the treasure for which it
    would be worth giving your life.

Sharing the Comfortable Words

One of the parts of The Book of Common Prayer order of Holy
Communion I have always loved is the part which is known
as the Comfortable Words. They are just that, comfortable
words, comforting, redemptive – Christ the saviour to whom
we can return, however bad the journey, however much we
feel we've messed things up. We all need to be comforted.

These are the words:

Hear what comfortable words our Saviour Christ saith unto
    all that truly turn to him.

Come unto me all that travail and are heavy laden and I will
refresh you.
So God loved the world that he gave his only-begotten Son,
to the end that all that believe in him should not perish
but have everlasting life
Hear also what Saint Paul saith
This is a true saying and worthy of all men to be received
that Christ Jesus came into the world to save sinners
Hear also what Saint John saith
If any man sin, we have an advocate with the father, Jesus
Christ the righteous and he is the propitiation for our sins.[3]

These were words I learnt off by heart like many others. In
this Norman church where I was a server, I would kneel at the
altar, my father celebrating. I remember the service beginning
in silence and then the Lord's Prayer beginning almost like a
whisper. As though the priest was praying out of the silence –
his own prayer becoming our prayer too, interceding for us,
enveloping us. I remember as a child enjoying the sound of that
word, *propitiation* for our sins. I had no idea what the word
meant, but I liked it anyway.

What I loved about these words is the way they spoke of
Jesus. Not a theology I understood or could even begin to
explain but Jesus Christ who said we could come to him just
as we were and it was he not us that would make everything
alright, it was he who would refresh, who would save, who
would advocate and who would be the propitiation, he who
would prevent us from perishing and grant everlasting life.
This was the God who loved us not because we were good
but because God was good. Though I had no understanding
of how this theory of salvation worked, I came to believe that
nothing is beyond the redemptive power of God, and nothing
was outside the possibilities of his love.

Sharing the Church

Julian of Norwich, the fourteenth-century anchoress, who lived a life of seclusion and prayer, in her *Revelations of Divine Love*, written during the terrifying time of the Black Death, wrote this revelation of trust:

> And the Lord showed me a little thing, the size of a hazelnut, on the palm of my hand, round like a ball. I looked at it thoughtfully and wondered 'What is this?' And the answer came. 'It is all that is made.' I marvelled that it continued to exist and did not suddenly disintegrate; it was so small. And again my mind supplied the answer. 'It exists both now and forever, because God loves it.' In short everything owes its existence to the love of God. In this little thing I saw three truths. The first is that God made it, the second is that God loves it and the third is that God sustains it.[4]

This may sound a very simple insight, but it is a very profound one. One of the most important things in these times of uncertainty is to hold fast to those truths that we are made by God, loved by God and sustained by God. This revelation of divine love is part of our own flourishing but also the flourishing of others.

Sharing Nazareth

We have all heard people say that they don't need the
    Church to know God
Indeed the Church can often seem more like the wounder
    than the healer of the soul
But our faith is not a private thing
The Church must be the place where prayer speaks beyond
    self
Where we enter shared space
Where each single person together becomes the bearer of
    Christ multiplied

And the prayer of another deepens your own
And the beauty of another is for you to rejoice in
Though we ourselves think we have a hundred St Martin
   cloaks to share
It is the one with no cloak who shows us Christ
This church is not a space we own but rather holy ground
Where we leave our shoes at the door
For here we all have bare feet
And are all equally in need of Christ's tender washing
Walk softly into this mystery
Beyond our own song, however well we sing it,
we will hear the song we cannot sing alone.

Sharing Christ beyond the Church

In her autobiography, *A Rocking-Horse Catholic*, the twentieth-century English mystic Caryll Houselander describes how an ordinary underground train journey in London transformed into a vision that changed her life. I wonder if you have had any such epiphanies:

> I was in an underground train, a crowded train in which all sorts of people jostled together, sitting and strap-hanging – workers of every description going home at the end of the day. Quite suddenly I saw with my mind, but as vividly as a wonderful picture, Christ in them all. But I saw more than that; not only was Christ in every one of them, living in them, dying in them, rejoicing in them, sorrowing in them – but because He was in them, and because they were here, the whole world was here too, here in this underground train; not only the world as it was at that moment, not only all the people in all the countries of the world, but all those people who had lived in the past, and all those yet to come.
>
> I came out into the street and walked for a long time in the crowds. It was the same here, on every side, in every passer-by, everywhere – Christ ...

I saw too the reverence that everyone must have for a sinner; instead of condoning their sin, which is in reality their utmost sorrow, one must comfort Christ who is suffering in them. And this reverence must be paid even to those sinners whose souls seem to be dead, because it is Christ, who is the life of the soul, who is dead in them; they are His tombs, and Christ in the tomb is potentially the risen Christ ...[5]

Sharing the blessing

The trolley

She is a busker and homeless
When I asked her, she said there had been no blessing
'Nothing,' she said, 'Apart from the fact that I am still alive.'
'It's been a hard week, like those words in the song I sing
"through many dangers, toils and snares I have already
    come"
But I can't think of anything good this week.'
Yet later she grew animated
'There was a blessing,' she said, and she couldn't wait to
    tell us
'I had this trolley to wheel my bags, but it had become old
    and rusty,
awkward – more of a hindrance than a help I thought
I got rid of it, thought I could carry my bags, but hadn't
    realized how heavy they were
They weighed me down, drained me
Then I remembered a friend who worked in Lush
She told me to come to her if I was ever in need
I walked all the way there carrying these bags
I just turned up in Lush and there in Lush were these shopping
    bags with extending handles for people to shop with
That would be perfect I said
So my friend asked the manager if I could have one

"Take one, it's yours," the manager said
I couldn't believe it when she said that
I was waiting for a "no"
That was my blessing,' she said
'This is my blessing,' she said pointing to the basket on
　　wheels.

Two-wheeler

He told us the story of his five-year-old son who has a new
　　two-wheel bicycle
He had seemed too young – a long way from mastering it
He took his son to the park and suddenly his son was off
Snaking down the path
Wobbling but riding on two wheels
And it felt a joyful moment
We all felt it
A rite of passage
And we all remembered too
That first time on two wheels
It was the day before I went on holiday
In our house in Chessington – the concrete slope beside the
　　kitchen
The fear, the wobble, the excitement of reaching the bottom
　　without falling off,
the racing heart
All holiday I remember longing to return home, so I could
　　do it again
And everyone in the group could remember
That moment of personal achievement and joy
Balancing on two wheels for the first time.

Sharing the journey

Pilgrimage to Canterbury

Lord I want to walk with you
I want to walk along pavements
Across the Thames and down the river
Weaving through people of every nation
And every culture
To smell chicken and chips, see furniture stores, and
    Lewisham
And kids spilling out from school
To be stared at crossing roads and junctions with my name
    around my neck
to feel your ground, slowly freed from concrete under
    burning aching feet
and then suddenly hear the song of birds
to breathe outside air
to taste rain and be quenched by it
I want to feel wind that makes indoor skin burn with life.

And to ache not from sitting but from moving,
to know the shape of hills by walking them,
the rhythm of each step walking life into place
Seeing again –
shapes of leaves and shades of green,
softness of grass and sting of nettles
Hearing again – a world free of traffic and sirens,
the movement of wind and the snap of branches, and the
    grasses rustle
Snatches of conversation, the sound of the rain
I want to climb stiles and negotiate cows and cross boundaries.

And as I walk I want to be open to the lives and stories of
    others,

from every part of the world through whom we are all
   enriched
To see the generosity of the human heart to come out of
   hiding,
to witness again the to and fro of human goodness set free
Not valued for house or job, or wealth or status but for
   human kindness.

And I want to arrive – and hear the cheers of welcome – for
   the last shall be first
To taste food and the bustle and hospitality of church halls
Sandwiches
And plates of labelled home-made parish cakes
And hot bowls of water
And podiatrists and reflexologists tending feet
And shepherd's pie
And dark cups of well-brewed tea
To know that we have struggled but together;
to long for comfort and see it shared,
a welcome where, for once, all outside can come inside
and the inside can come out
And there is no difference between us because we are all
   pilgrims on the same journey.

'Loving and caring and sharing'

He is frustrated and hurt
And who can blame him
It's like a maze set up to torment
With no seeming way out
A system which employs people to tell him why they
   can't help
I see this young refugee who has travelled so far
In search of belonging
I see in his eyes the longing to help and to please,
the beauty of his humanity

His potential, the coiled energy, like the spring of a leopard
   kept in a cage
I see the pool of fear and despair which threatens to overwhelm
The storm clouds waiting
The anger and despair that can engulf
In his face like broken glass
I see his goodness, his generous heart, Christ within
The extra mile he will go again and again not only giving
   his coat but his shirt as well.

It's all about 'loving and caring and sharing' he says as we
   walk together
'Loving and caring and sharing'
A rhythm, a hope, a way forward
Loving and caring and sharing
The treasure beyond all price
This untapped life present now
I see him walking this balancing act like a man on a high wire
Below the drop, the terrifying fall back into the darkness
he has tried so generously, so sacrificially to escape
and yet so precariously, so agonizingly vulnerably – this
   path that is of God
Loving and caring and sharing
The fear and the heartbeat
The cross and the resurrection
We will not be judged by sin
We will be judged by our loving and caring and sharing.

Sharing baptism

Anne Duffin died just before her ninety-third birthday. She had
been an inspiration to many of us: intelligent, practical, rooted,
entirely dependable, she participated in the life of this church
for sixty years. 'What did you love about Anne?' I asked Alison
Hardwick, one of her closest friends at St Martin's and a quiet

saint in her own right. 'She was the most tremendous example to me of how to live with faith and grace. I could always turn to her,' Alison said. Yes, you could always turn to Anne, because you knew Anne was turned to Christ. In her meditation group, which she led come wind or rain, that's what we did each time we met. She turned to Christ, and she taught us to do the same. Physically we learnt to do that. To turn to Christ with our whole bodies and gaze upon him. To be filled by his presence. That's what she taught. Right through all the struggles I was going through, she taught me simply to turn to Christ. And that turning anchored me. I am still learning to do that. This is the central call of our baptism. Do you turn to Christ? Yes, I turn to Christ.

And when in baptism we turn to Christ, what happens then? Well, we are told that when Jesus himself came to be baptized the heavens are opened. The heavens are opened for us too. It's like entering into a new dimension of living, for yourself but also beyond yourself. It's hard to explain to a person who has not experienced this epiphany what it means. God's world has entered your world. God's love has broken down the barriers. There is a height and a depth and a breadth opening up.

And there is a sign, a sign of a dove and the Holy Spirit descending upon Jesus. And the realization that this is what our baptism is. That dove is descending on you. That the heaven beyond – the kingdom of God – is not just something out there; it is in us. The Holy Spirit has made its home in our mortal flesh. You may feel lost or frightened, but God's Holy Spirit is within you. You may feel alone, but God has made his home the very stable of your own life. You may feel torn and pulled in all directions. But be still here and now, you are standing in the beam of God's love. You are God's manger.

And then finally those incredible words – the voice from heaven that speaks: 'You are my Son, the Beloved; with you I am well pleased.' With baptism comes the promise that these words are not past tense, not words meant for Christ alone but that miraculously we have been included – here and now and for eternity. God is saying to each one of us: you are mine, you mean everything to me.

How often we have heard a different message from religion. The message that we are unacceptable, sinful, outsiders, shameful, condemned. But this is not the story of our baptism. The song of our baptism says I love you no matter what. I will never forget you. You are my beloved. You may feel dirty, but I will wash you. You may feel unworthy, but I will clothe you. You may be ashamed, but I will lift you up; you may be hungry and thirsty, but I will give you living water and the bread of life to eat. There may be a time in your life when you feel you believe you are totally abandoned and you would gladly eat the pig food, but you are still my beloved; you are still my daughter, my son. You are the dwelling place of my love and you will be with me in paradise.

It's a big event, baptism – the biggest – this turning to Christ, heaven opening, the Holy Spirit dwelling in us and the voice of God telling us that we are beloved, that we mean everything to God.

Sharing is encountering that which we do not own

I heard Rowan Williams speak at St Martin-in-the-Fields about 'encountering that which we do not own'. He speaks with a simplicity that makes you feel he is articulating a truth you have always known, but like all real wisdom, what seems at first simple has a huge resonance and depth of truth for the whole of life. When we really encounter someone fully, we are actually invited into an unknown – into territory that we do not control or possess. It is a relationship without ownership. It is the space before God where we do not claim to know all the answers, and where we cannot fix everyone's problems. And this discovery, though outside our control, is also exciting and liberating because it is the place of real meeting – of seeing and being seen, the discovery of the other and also discovery of the unknown self. Rowan spoke of a meeting between two Rwandans who had been on either side of the genocide – a Tutsi and a Hutu. He said how tense they all realized the encounter would be and how impossible to arrive at a superficial reconciliation that would deny the enormity of the suffering that had taken place. The only way to cross the divide was 'to create space that belongs to neither of them but makes space for both'. Encountering the other means encountering the one you do not own in the place you do not own. To create a space for the other that belongs to no one but makes space for all.

How difficult it is to encounter the other in a space we do not own. I remember when we were invited to visit the Ahmadiyya Muslim community in Morden for a shared lecture. They would speak about their faith. We would speak about ours. I remember I fielded a number of telephone calls, anxious about registering for this lecture:

'Why can't I use the St Martin's site to register?' they ask.

'Because the mosque uses a different registration website,' I try to explain. 'The details are all there in the flyer.'

'I don't understand it,' the person replies. 'They ask me if I have any dietary requirements – why do they want to know that?'

'Perhaps because they want to feed you?'

'Why?'

'Because that's part of their hospitality. That's the meaning of encounter – we are encountering that which we do not know.'

'Oh,' says the surprised caller 'Well, I'm not sure if I'll be hungry!'

Sometimes you can't win. That's the nature of sharing and encounter. No right way, no wrong way, just different.

Sharing space

As all of us know it is not easy to live together in community, loving one's neighbour as oneself. I remember when I was living as a monk in the community of the Melanesian Brotherhood, visitors often used to say to us, 'You Brothers are such an example to us. You seem to live together with such unity and peace.' And I used to think 'little do you know!' It is never easy and there are always difficulties, divisions, tensions, jealousies and rivalries when people live closely. True love of neighbour, of which Paul speaks, is costly love, love that costs Jesus his life. It is not a love that simply excuses all. Inclusive love does not mean that anything goes. All of us know how difficult Christ's love is to live out. Brother Roger of Taizé used to tell his monks that community was total – it costs nothing less than everything. One of the Brothers told me of how once he had tested Brother Roger as a joke, taking a piece of cheese from his plate while he ate. 'You have taken my cheese,' said Brother Roger. 'Ah yes, Brother Roger, but today you said that community was total.' 'Yes,' said Brother Roger, 'but community also respects the edge of my plate.' His words are important. Community respects the space and humanity of the other. The business of living and dying with love for God and neighbour involves giving both oneself and someone else the space and the room to find one's connection with God. That needs trust. Whoever we live and share with, be it in the family or the workplace, there will be conflicts of interest and tensions between us.

For several weeks the International Group have been holding a course here at St Martin's on relationship building. We were asked to draw a circle around ourselves to indicate the boundaries we draw when interacting with others and we reflected on these boundaries. One of those in the group gave the example of stewarding for St Martin's. She told the story of how earlier in the day she had seen someone who was obviously homeless on the steps of St Martin's. He had his bags everywhere. She described how she squatted down and talked to him, as friendly as possible, and then began to move his bags out of the way of the steps and the entrance to the church, she thought helpfully. But the man became extremely angry and upset and told her not to touch his things. As we reflected on this situation, we began to see how actually what was taking place was a conflict of territory. For the steward, the steps were St Martin's steps – they needed to be clear in order for people to come into the church. She thought she was helping the man. Subconsciously this was our territory and she was sensitively (she thought) helping him out of the way. But for the man, the steps were his territory – the place where he had slept the night and his bags were his private property – in this case more than that, his home – his sleeping bag etc. What becomes obvious is how upset we can become when we feel that our territory is being infringed on or threatened. Just think about it for a moment. How many of the tensions and conflicts in our world at the moment are about the anger and the violence that breaks out when territory is threatened, or invaded, or attacked? If we look at this on an individual level, we can notice how we ourselves may respond when we feel our territory is being taken away. The person at work who doesn't respect our authority or dedication or tries to take over or control us; the guest who does not show gratitude; the train which is far too full so that the person with a season ticket can't find a space; the person who takes advantage or pushes into the queue in front of us; the family member who never tidies the house or cleans your basin; the friend who enjoys your hospitality but never reciprocates; the person who threatens your job; the neighbours next door who are building an ugly extension far too close to the fence. 'Who do they think they are?' All these scenarios are examples of where our territory is threatened. The boundaries we fear that others may cross – like the English Channel.

Straight afterwards with my renewed understanding I went upstairs onto my landing where a kind member of St Martin's was depositing a huge box of second-hand clothes for refugees. 'You can't put it there, I'm afraid,' I heard myself say. 'But it's for the refugees,' she responded in amazement. 'It might be, but this is my landing and there are no refugees actually living on my landing, only your boxes,' I felt like telling her. But I didn't, I just thought, here I am defending my territory like everyone else.

Sharing is overcoming division

Beware of all jealousy or possessiveness within a community
It is an ugly thing
It turns openness and generosity into competition
It turns sacred space into private territory
And freedom into the desire to manipulate or control
Root out in yourself all that would stifle or spoil the life
    spirit of another
Explain gently and honestly the space that you need to the
    one who leads
We all need to realize how easy it is to allow the seed on the
    footpath to be carried away by our projections,
to become the intransigent rocky soil that withers the life of
    others
Or to choke another's growth with our thorns
It is in good soil which we all will grow
Rejoicing in the nourishment that we provide to one another
Together yielding a hundredfold
In community we are constantly called to open wide our
    hearts
To become together the parable of God's abundance.

Sharing love is recognizing the pain of love

There are times when separation leaks
And each time you remember
It leaks a little more
It tastes bitter this leaking
Like grief
And you fear it will poison your soul
And perhaps you think of a hundred ways of running after
Or holding on
Or making them feel the pain they have caused you
How can you catch again the wonder that just was?
That which you seemed to share so completely
That which you believed in

And thought was given forever
Until the gift was torn away
And what you thought was your inheritance became your
    desolation
Perhaps all you can do now is watch and wait
Wait with grace and open heart
Wait with the love that was
And is
And because it is real
Refuses to spoil within itself the one it loves
But prays for them to become
The full person God wants them to be
How can we pray
For the one who has left us behind
And accept without poison that they must find their own
    way
To the same God
Who like you is watching and waiting for their return.

VI

Sharing is discovering the community of the dispossessed

Up the road from the steps of St Martin's Lane Ian McKellen is playing King Lear with such raw and recognizably flawed humanity that it makes you weep. At the beginning of the play, full of his own self-importance and largesse and drunk by the power he has always enjoyed for so long, he conceives a plan of huge vanity, dividing up his kingdom publicly between his three daughters to show his munificent generosity. It is probably one of the worst retirement plans ever conceived. His first two opportunistic daughters, Goneril and Regan, launch into lavish expressions of filial affection. 'Sir, I love thee more than word can wield the matter, dearer than eyesight, space and liberty ...' etc. It is only Cordelia, the third daughter, who refuses to act out this charade: 'I cannot heave my heart into my mouth,' she says. For her, love is a gift, a sacrifice, not a commodity to be bargained with. When Cordelia fails to respond as he expects, Lear is distraught and furious, renouncing all his paternal care for her, and tells her that she will be a stranger to his heart forever. 'Therefore begone! Without our grace, our love, our benison.' We become acutely aware that this division of the kingdom is not really a gift at all. Lear has given in order to possess and in this he fails spectacularly and in fact never recovers. How many of us have been guilty – giving in order to possess, influence or control?

It's a family argument, but Shakespeare's genius is to show an intimate, family division magnified onto a national, cosmic, timeless canvas. A fault-line, a rift, opens up visibly in front of us; there is no going back. Shakespeare is showing that the movement of nations, the redrawing of empires, wars, the deaths of thousands of people are balanced on tiny decisions, moments of blindness and pride, moments of envy and possessiveness, where a flaw is revealed in a leader, and from that moment this enormous fault-line emerges, which goes on getting wider and deeper until there is no going back. If you think I am exaggerating just think about the politicians of our time – think of the Iraq war, think about Brexit, think of Tony Blair, think of Boris Johnson.

Jesus' own disciples were not free from such faults of pride. They too wanted to own their Messiah and their saviour. They don't like the idea of a future that will involve suffering and betrayal and even death. But Jesus, astonishingly, turns everything on its head and says this. 'Whoever wants to be the first, must be the last of all and servant of all.' It's the opposite of our power or pride games – it's not about possessing at all, it's about an encounter without ownership. It's the kingdom not of the possessed but of the dispossessed. And these disciples are going to learn how to live that kingdom, not through pride, but actually outside a city wall, where, like King Lear and in the company of the wounded and the broken, they will learn the meaning of love and truth. Beneath our own royal robes, as Lear says, we discover 'the same bare forked animal'. Unaccommodated, we are all subject to the storm. Storms are no respecters of rank or position. Our shared humanity, vulnerability and mortality make a mockery of the hierarchies of power but at the same time point towards the love and the truths that are immortal. The disciples learn to distrust the self and put their trust in God. And in so doing to find their true self.

VII

Sharing the dance

When my niece Molly was nine years old, she came home from school saying that there was a play at the local theatre called *A Midsummer Night's Dream*, and her headmistress had told them that they needed schoolchildren to play the parts of fairies. Molly had never shown a particular interest in performing, but she thought she would like to be a fairy and so she filled in the form and applied. Her father became far more alarmed than her when he discovered that 600 other children had applied for the parts of four fairies and that Molly would have to audition on the theatre stage in front of a panel of selectors. He emailed me to ask me how on earth she should prepare for this ordeal. 'Just let her be herself ...' I replied, 'if they choose her it will be because they want someone who is natural and kind. She always seems to be far more interested in what others are doing than trying to show off herself. Whatever you do, don't make her feel she has to perform. It doesn't seem her nature.' A few weeks later, Molly went for her audition; she followed on from recitations, children singing, dancing, performing tap and ballet routines. Her father was doubled up with anxiety when he saw the line-up, fearing his daughter would be publicly humiliated. Molly came on the stage and said that she was going to do a dance she had learned for a school assembly. They asked her what music she was going to use, and she said that it was in her head. And then she danced without music, just simply without embarrassment. Later in the afternoon, the theatre phoned to say that Molly had been chosen. 'Are you sure you've got the right name?' her mum asked on the phone, 'she was the one who did the silent dance.'

'Oh yes, quite sure she's the one, her dance was really unaffected and beautiful, she was so attentive to others, that's what we want.'

Picasso, in his old age, said, 'I have spent all my life learning to paint like a child.' Peter Brook, who has been one of the most innovative and acclaimed directors of contemporary theatre, writes that the performance of a child presents a tremendous challenge to an adult for often the adult will struggle through intellect to reach the point which the child has arrived at naturally. But the moment a child tries to perform he becomes unattractive. When a child is not acting, when he is just being, then what we see is full and complete. One is in contact with something very precious, 'the image of life flowing'. 'An actor,' says Peter Brook, 'has to forget making an impression, he has to forget showing, he has to forget fabricating, he has to forget making effects, he has to get away from the idea he is there as a show piece and in its place he has to open himself to the notion of being the servant of an image that will always be greater than himself ... What are we making?' Brook asks, 'We are making relationships. But we can't make relationships, we can only let relationships because that is the heart of what any story, any play, anything human, is about – relationships.'⁶ The word Brook comes back to time and time again is transparency. In a word, we are learning to unmask rather than mask. We are discovering how to be truer to a deeper humanity. That is what true sharing is about.

Sharing our spiritual journey with a guide

They say that spiritual guides are given as a gift to you when you most need them. If you discover a guide who can really listen, inspire, help you discern, challenge and hear your inner story with love and lightness – and find joy and hope even in the darkness – then it is indeed a huge blessing. Perhaps we do not always discover that person and the guides we meet are more like friendships, or even encounters or transitory meetings where we scarcely realize the significance until later in our lives. I wonder who has been a guide or a companion to your own faith journey? Remember, a companion is one who shares bread with you along the road. A spiritual companion may seem quite ordinary. But perhaps if we are attentive to the blessing, the breaking and the sharing – they are sharing Jesus. We used to call these guides Spiritual Directors, but perhaps this sounds too directive or paternalistic. Often this accompanying will be much more like a dialogue or even the movement of the Trinity in which you both share your life but are also very aware that God is part of the conversation sharing Christ's life with you.

I am very blessed in that for twenty years I had the same person to accompany me. His name was Fr Simon Holden, a monk from the Community of the Resurrection. I did not choose him; he was chosen for me when I was studying at the College of the Resurrection in Mirfield. He was wise, always challenging and surprising, often amusing, or irreverent, very human but always open. He opened my eyes to see in my life and struggles the workings and the calling of God in ways I had not always realized or believed possible. And as the years went by, I also realized that he was not only accompanying me but I was accompanying him, and indeed this speaking and listening, this listening and speaking, this reciprocity, was a huge mutual gift from God.

Several years ago, we discussed leading a retreat together in which we would share some of our conversations over the last twenty years. 'What would be our theme?' I asked. 'How about *The Meaning of Life*?' he suggested playfully. We settled on *The Path with a Heart: Conversations on the Meaning of Life*. He planned to join me to give this retreat with me to those at St Martin-in-the-Fields, but when it got nearer the time he was not well enough to travel down. So we planned to give the retreat the following year in the monastery at Mirfield. But then I heard from members of the community that Simon was not well and quite anxious and confused at times. They wondered whether he would be well enough to cope with it. But the retreat was fully booked – he was a popular man with a group of disciples. When I arrived at Mirfield to lead the retreat with him for All Saints and All Souls, I asked him if he was still up for it. 'What retreat?' he asked. 'I feel as though I have one foot here and one foot in eternity and sometimes I am not quite sure where I am.' Together however, gently, we decided to go ahead. There was no need for us to worry for as soon as Simon slowly shuffled into place in the chapel it was as though God was his muse and this was the gospel of his life which he was sharing.

We talked about longing

'What do you most long for?' I asked.

He paused and then twinkling with delight, for he loved his audience, he said,

'I long to disappear.'

I was surprised by his answer. 'I hope not immediately,' I replied.

He laughed. 'It's not about obliteration,' he answered, 'it's about the me becoming us … It's crossing the line of separation and becoming part of the heart of God. It's difficult to talk about in words,' he said, 'it's impossible to define. You surrender your freedom and yet you enter a greater freedom. You surrender your own heart and discover God's heart. You see there is only one life and it is God's life. Finding intimacy with God is like going home, to all that we are and all that we long for. It is a return to the "I AM". Intimacy is God – it is like crossing the line from separation to everything you have ever longed for.'

We talked about waiting

'Scripture is about waiting and the longing for God.' It begins with paradise and the fall. It ends with the vision of heaven and earth reunited. Through Scripture, there is a longing to return. Waiting for freedom in Egypt; waiting in the desert to discover the promised land; waiting in Babylon to return; waiting for the Messiah; Zechariah and Elizabeth waiting for a child; Simeon and Anna waiting to see salvation; Jesus waiting in Nazareth for his ministry to begin; John the Baptist waiting for the one who would baptize with the Holy Spirit and fire; Israel waiting for the bridegroom; the soil waiting for the seed; the man waiting for thirty-eight years for healing by the pool of Beth-zatha; waiting for forgiveness; those who waited by the foot of the cross: those who waited by the tomb; those who waited in a locked upper room.

'Jesus teaches us to live the now even when waiting,' said Simon:

'Think of a brilliant waiter at a restaurant, so attentive and alert that you do not even notice them until you need something and then they seem to know without being asked. Or a nurse in a hospital that you have been unaware of until in that moment of need in the ward at night when they are suddenly there by your side helping you through the pain or the fear.

'The fear is not knowing what is going to happen to you next. And in old age in particular, you often feel you have lost that knowledge. I live in the constant realization that at any moment I may drop down dead, but that makes now an exciting opportunity. Not living in the past, not living in the future, but living now. If I can only unite myself with Christ's presence now, then each simple action, each simple action I perform can become an expression of Christ's abiding.'

We talked about wonder

Simon told the story of the pupils of a school who had been asked by their teacher to find out the seven wonders of the world and when asked the following day one of the class had replied: 'To see, to touch, to hear, to smell, to taste, to move, to breathe.' They were right. What wonders these are.

'A person who knows the wonder of God lives within the mystery of God without ever being able to define or contain that mystery. The wonder of my life is that I am a person who receives now the attention of the creator of all that is – and so do we all.

'The Church needs to live that love of God. It needs to love. Often the Church gets in the way of God's love and when it gets in the way it gets it all wrong. I remember being in the centre of Leeds and suddenly realizing that God has a personal knowledge of each of these people I was seeing in the street. He created them, he remembers them all, and does not forget. It was an astonishing thought, and I was filled with wonder and gratitude.

'To rediscover wonder, we need to rediscover silence. Not fixing or thinking we can solve the world, or accumulate more in order to control or defend, or gain, but learning to listen again, to listen to ourselves. Most people don't listen to what God's love is saying. We need to allow God the space to sow in our hearts the seeds of life.'

'How did Fr Simon get on?' his fellow Brothers asked after the retreat. 'He shone,' I said. 'He always does when he has an audience,' they laughed. 'Ah yes,' I replied, 'but today the me became us.'

Sharing home

I want to go home to the one who is always waiting
In the stillness of my heart
Above the storm clouds
And deeper than the currents and the waves of the vast sea
It is the place where conditions, failures and shame cease
Where wounds are healed

And the wrongs of the past are dissolved into a greater mercy
And all will be redeemed by your love
That is the gospel
A love that unlocks all that we are and all that you long for
us to be
So that we may walk in the paths of peace forever.

Notes

1 Brother Roger of Taizé, *The Sources of Taizé*, GIA Publications Inc., 2000, p. 19.

2 Focolare is a movement of spiritual and social renewal, founded in Trent, Italy. They have an ecumenical centre for unity in Welwyn Garden City where our community has held quiet days and silent retreats.

3 The Book of Common Prayer, The Communion 1662.

4 Julian of Norwich, *Revelations of Divine Love*, Penguin Classics, 1966, Revelation 5 on p. 68.

5 Richard Rohr, *The Universal Christ*, SPCK, 2019, pp. 2–3.

6 Peter Brook, *The Shifting Point: 40 Years of Theatrical Exploration, 1946–87*, Bloomsbury, 1989, p. 198.

6

With Sabbath

Helen Ireland after Thomas Bewick

On the seventh day God rested from all that he had done.

Rest is given to us as the culmination of creation. It is not something to be ashamed of but to be cherished. This is not a commandment banning activity or joy – rather it is the recognition of all that we seek and have been given as gift. It is the stepping back in wonder and thanksgiving. It is the replenishing of the soul. The gift of rest, not as something earned but given. The whole of creation moves towards this time of Sabbath, and our lives have no meaning simply as cycles of survival without this arrival at the place of wonder and rest. This is not the day off, it is the day of ... We do not go back to work; we work to go back to the Sabbath. Holidays are holy days. They are days of rest, and rest is a beautiful thing. It is time for us to see that all God has created is 'very good'; I wonder how we live time hallowed by God and inhabit this time of blessing. I wonder how we can create days of wonder.

God blesses time. He consecrates it as holy. Creation is not complete until God rests on the seventh day and contemplates all creation. When we rest, we imitate God – we enter into the rhythm of God's time. In order to do that we need to disconnect from our compulsive busyness. Sabbath is like a recalibration. And if Sabbath is God's time, it does not end in the keeping of the Sabbath – the Sabbath enters into all our time. When we keep Sabbath, everything we do can be infused with that sense of God's presence. Each day there can be Sabbath spaces which reconnect our immortal souls with our reason for living. Each of our silent times can become windows of this Sabbath time infusing the day with God's time: opening up a new dimension of our lives.[1]

$$\boxed{\text{I}}$$

Sabbath is the gift of time

'You're always so busy,' he said, 'if people were to describe you, that's what they would say, "he's so busy". But is that a good thing to be so busy? I knew you would be there in the moment of crisis, at the hospital bedside, at the side of the dying. But what about now? What about present to the person in the ordinary, the long term, the moment where there is no drama just months of being unheard?' I know he is speaking truth to me. I want to be present, really present but I feel dried up. I feel there is none of me left, like my blood has been transfused and I am dried up. I feel the battery is flat and the bulb growing dim. I need to be recharged by God. I need the forced smile masking emptiness to become the smile of God again. You cannot fake this without becoming fake. You can't keep spinning all the plates. Sometimes perhaps you have to let some of them fall. You have to know peace within your own heart in order to be able to share peace. To try to heal despair with your own despair can deepen the wound and the longing. You have to be plenished yourself to replenish others. You too need God's time and like Mary, rather than Martha, to sit at the feet of Christ. Choose the better path. Open the shutters behind your eyes and be held: 'He will rejoice over you with gladness, he will renew you in his love; he will exult over you with singing.' (Zephaniah 3.17) He will bring you home. He will gather you. To be held by love. That is Sabbath time.

Silent Retreat

We came inside and it was spring
Leaving the fresh snow outside
Its soft white blanket marking our footsteps to the door
And silencing the din of our lives
As we discovered Focolare[1]
The hearth and place of warmth
A generosity of welcome that received us
And gave us their place as though it were our own
I pulled up the blinds to let the light in
An open and spacious place
With clean soft colours
Yellows, whites and olives
A simple circle of chairs
Daffodils in three pottery jugs
Opening signs of spring
And spring in our hearts too
As we let go of our defences and controls
And let God expand in us
At times as thrilling, chilling and as life-giving
As a gulp of winter air
As dazzling as snow covering the earth
Yet as warm as a fireside with windows and doors that open
    out and welcome in.

How can we learn from you and be this hearth too
This fire of God's Spirit that radiates warmth
How can we create a space to live with generous hospitality
   and attentiveness?
A pattern and way of life that creates both space and
   acceptance
Belonging and yet freedom
Expectation and yet mercy
Warmth without shutting out the mystery of this fall of snow
We found true hospitality here
That got out of the way but was still present with us
And allowed buds to open
While still rejoicing in the wonder of winter outside.

| II |

Sabbath is realizing the mystery and miracle of life

We are such stuff
As dreams are made on; and our little life
Is rounded with a sleep.[2]

A few years ago, I was in hospital. And actually, strange to
say, I found it a deeply contemplative experience. At first there
is that very human dilemma of wondering whether something
was seriously wrong with me or was I just making a fuss and
being a nuisance. Then when people start rushing around and
you start getting hooked up to drips and you think perhaps
this may be serious, it can actually be an experience of what it
means to be mortal. Days and nights become indistinguishable,
and it's all about human bodies in open-backed hospital night-
gowns lying on beds, medicines, and flesh and blood, lots of it
– blood tests, blood pressures, cannulas and drips, and grunts
and calls and snores, and food trollies and bed pans, and opening and closing curtains and teams of consultants, nurses and
students scooting between beds with laptops on wheels talking
above you and through you.

Sabbath is trusting in God. In hospital there is a lot of waiting. My first thought on being in hospital was 'what about
...?' What about all the things I should be doing? What about
all those plans and things in my diary which won't happen? I
remember saying to the consultant when he came on his ward
round on the first morning that I would have to be out of
hospital by Sunday because I was organizing the Crib Service
in Trafalgar Square. He replied with a smile, 'Well, I'm afraid
you are going to have to tell the Almighty you are not going to
be there!' At first, it's profoundly worrying because I have con-
ditioned myself to think that my life depends on fulfilling my
obligations, and that to be abandoning them seems profoundly
reckless or hard on those who are having to pick up my work.
Until I begin to realize that things carry on ... of course things
carry on. And sometimes you have to let your fondest held
projects go.

Sabbath gives you time to become aware of what's happening
around you. One of our strongest instincts is self-preservation,
in other words survival. If you are in pain, you obviously don't
want the pain to get worse. If you think you are in danger,
you don't want to be abandoned or forgotten. These survival instincts are basic and often fierce. On my first night, I
remember having very little awareness of anybody but myself.
However, what slowly breaks into your awareness on a ward
is also the needs of those in beds around you, and becoming
increasingly receptive to the bodily wellbeing of others. Like
dear Christian in the bed opposite me who was very much
sicker than I was. One night he asked the question, 'Is it day
or night? Am I still alive or am I dead ...?' And then, 'How do
I know that I'm alive?' Profound theological questions. What
I found most moving was the way the nurses cared for him –
they were so gently present to him during that journey into
the shadow lands of human mortality. I was aware too that
everyone in the ward was not being judged on wealth or status,
or importance, or even age – it was simply about those most in
need at a particular time of medical care. So, if a case was more
serious or more life-threatening, then that case took prece-
dence. If I had to wait longer for my scan because someone

else's need was greater, there was a justice in that, rather than a reason for complaint. And I watched roles changing around me – the patient becoming the carer – Michael in the bed opposite who had seemed so very frail after his operation now growing stronger and able to encourage others on the ward. 'You look so much better,' I told Michael. He did. Michael beamed and asked me, 'And how are you getting on?' On my first day I had resented the other people in the ward. Time, speed, attention to me had seemed the priority – what emerged after the first few days was a more generous patience and spaciousness. In our frenetic world we do not have the chance to live that graciousness as graciously as we would like.

Sabbath is about being present to now. I have read that using a mobile phone while driving can be far more dangerous than drunk driving. It is because the mobile phone takes away your presence. It leads to a different virtual reality. In a *Guardian* article that I read, the reporter described taking his young son for a walk with his mobile phone and realizing his interaction with his mobile phone was far more compulsive than his awareness of his young son with him – to the point where he looked up and realized his son had wandered off without him realizing it. In contrast, visiting hours in hospital are like a throwback to a bygone age. People actually take the trouble to visit one another in hospital and spend time with you, sitting on a plastic chair by your bed. No diversion, no agenda, no TV, no email, no meal, no escape. Just simple face-to-face presence. I was aware of how good people are. How sensitive and sympathetic they want to be. And how good it is just simply to have time to chat to people with no agenda other than the kindness of their visit. Isn't it strange that when you go home from hospital no one visits you anymore to talk because they think they may be disturbing you. In hospital I also got cards and letters. Real letters in the age of terse emails of 'Hi' followed by request or demand. How lovely to decipher handwriting again and the personality it communicates.

Sabbath time is about thankfulness. One of the people in my ward spent a lot of his time complaining about what was going on: the food, the regime, the frustration, the doctor's diagnosis or lack of one, the nurse's instructions, the lack of clear progress. These things may well have been both frustrating and true. But I was also aware of how unfair a culture of entitlement and complaint can be and of the blessing: food, care, expertise, medical skill, medicine, people all trying to make you better completely free of charge. And then at the end of a week you walk out like you have just received this massive gift, and no one gives you any bill or even expects you to say thank you. Isn't that like the experience of God's grace all around us?

Sabbath time is also about the time to pray. 'Lord Jesus Christ have mercy on me.' God's mercy – the gift of God, underpinning all that we are – all of our lives. It's sometimes only when we are a little stripped down, like this in your hospital night-gown, and tubes coming out of your arm, that God's presence is once again uncovered. I have tried so hard to be efficient and self-sufficient that I have not fully realized my need of God. There is a man I know who is homeless who never misses Morning Prayer in our church. 'Have you always been so faithful in your prayers?' I asked him. 'No,' he said, 'only when I am in trouble.'

'Where did you learn to pray?' He is silent for a moment. And then he tells me quietly: 'In prison that's when I realized I needed him most.'

'Well, I learnt to pray again in hospital.'

Sabbath is discovering sacred space

Holy Island: A prayer looking out to sea

In the still place
I see now
The cross on the island
The tide coming in
The pile of stones on the shore
The shape of the ripples on the water

The greys of the sky
The shape of the gull's flight
The silver of the breaking wave
The head of the seal breaking the surface of the sea.

The seals have swum in to look
I am still
I can see for miles
There is nothing between me and you
No defences
I enter into a transparent luminous world
The place where sky and sea meet
And dark clouds become infused with golden light
I need your life to enter mine

I who have known your shadow have also basked like these
    seals in your light
Let me be with you
Let me swim in this gently furrowed water
Mirroring unblemished your heaven
Let me know your peace
As the seals cruise away
And the light fades.

Easter break

I am here sitting on a rug outside
Feeling my bones uncrunch
and ease back into place
My body rehydrating
My lungs expanding
As I breathe in fresh air
Even my guts are unwinding
I have turned off my mobile phone
And this morning my mind feels like a pool of stillness
I have slept well and felt the sleep like a silent draught of
    healing

Unlock the aches of my life
I have stood under a shower that does not dribble but gushes
Hot water
And then as I turn the lever and brace the cold
I feel the burn of the icy water of Scotland and I am fully
 awake
Now kneeling on my stool
My field of vision expands and deepens
I see silver birch trees
Rocks and mossy grass
A stone wall
Beyond rising hills of mossy yellows and greens
And above that, high up, snow like icing sugar dusting
 brown majestic crags.

Sabbath is coming and seeing

Pilgrimage to Lampedusa

The Lampedusa Cross is the cross the Nazareth Community share.

When, at the beginning of John's Gospel, the two disciples ask Jesus where he is dwelling, he says, 'Come and see.' There is an openness to that invitation. 'Come and see' does not mean you've got to answer this problem or can solve this mystery, it simply says you've got to be open to it, attentive to all that is about to happen.

Early in the New Year I set off on a journey by myself to both come and see. It was a spiritual journey to a place which had inspired my imagination and my faith – a pilgrimage. For me this journey had begun when Jill Cook, one of the curators at the British Museum, brought a Lampedusa Cross to the Festival Day of the Friends of St Martin's. Jill told the story of how, on 3 October 2013, a boat trying to cross the Mediterranean sank off the coast of the small Italian island of Lampedusa, an island more than 200 miles from Sicily and 120 miles from North Africa. In that terrible tragedy, 359 migrants drowned. With the help of the coastguard and local fishermen, 155 survived and came ashore near Rabbit Beach – a beach considered one of the most beautiful beaches in the world. Many of those survivors were Christians from Ethiopia and Eritrea. How could anyone respond to a tragedy of such terrible consequences? Mr Tuccio, a member of the local church and a carpenter, collected some of the timbers from the wrecked shell of the boat and in his workshop made simple crosses, which he gave to the survivors. Later, when Pope Francis visited, he made the Pope a cross from the same timber. This Lampedusa Cross became a symbol for our times. Made from the wood of the wreckage, it told the story of the movement of migrant people to Europe in search of a home – the story of their displacement, exodus and search for a country that would accept them and of the many who have drowned crossing the Mediterranean in search of that hope. One of these Lampedusa Crosses became part of the British Museum collection.

When Jill Cook brought it to St Martin's, it silenced us. At the Eucharist we placed it on the altar and the symbol of that cross seemed to transfix each one of us. It palpably spoke of the tragedy of our times – but more than that. It had a presence that you felt in your very soul – it silenced words yet spoke to me of why I am ultimately a Christian. 'Nothing, nothing in all creation can ever separate you from the love of God which is yours in Christ Jesus.' This cross with the blues and reds and yellows of the boat seemed to say 'Come and see.'

I flew from Palermo in Sicily in a yellow and white old-fashioned retro propeller plane with only about fifteen passengers on board. I found myself looking through the window down at the vast expanse of rough sea – the white waves breaking – and I imagined being lost in that huge sea. Indeed, what I would do if this plane were to come down among those waves? In the last few years more than 250,000 people have made the journey to Lampedusa as a stepping stone to the West, and many lives have been lost.

The island is a rugged and barren place where little grows.

The islanders inspired the world by their response to the refugee crisis. But it's hard when the boats keep arriving, and hearts have hardened too. There is always the choice of not seeing and turning away. 'What about us?' many are now saying, 'what about our lack of a maternity unit, the damaging effect migrants are having on the tourist business that sustains us, what about our own lack of fresh water and opportunities for our young people?' Recently Lampedusa elected a new mayor on a platform of putting the needs of the islanders first and a much tougher response to refugees – with a locked immigration detention centre with no public access. I hired a bicycle and for three days I rode around the island. I saw few migrants as they are now locked up on arrival, but the spirit of their exodus is everywhere around you. On my balcony I looked out each day and saw the sun and the moon and the sky meeting the sea. I cycled to Rabbit Beach with its steep path down the cliff. In January I am alone. Summoning up courage, I take off my clothes and swim. Sensing the incredible mystery of our lives: we too are all no more than matchwood in the vastness of the sea. How mortal we all are. I am aware of the wonder of life and the courage that leads people to cross oceans and to dream of a better kingdom. I think of the fishermen's prayer I prayed in the South Pacific – 'Be good to me O Lord, for the sea is so vast and my boat is so small.'

I am aware of how much of the Bible is about people in exile longing for a home. Believing that *beyond* there is a promised land and yet in fact discovering God in this exodus and often painful struggles of the wilderness. I am aware of how we are actually all part of this exodus. However much we build our own boats and believe that we are invincible, ultimately we all have to push out to sea not knowing where we will arrive. In a small deserted chapel, I kneel. There is a statue of the Virgin Mary and the story of how through her intercessions a man was miraculously saved from the sea. 'Hail Mary full of grace,' I find myself praying, 'the Lord is with thee, blessed art thou among women and blessed is the fruit of thy womb, Jesus. Holy Mary Mother of God pray for us sinners now and at the hour of our death.' And for the first time this rosary makes complete sense to me. Here in the unknowing of our time – where we cannot be sure, where we have no certainty or ultimate control – where it is so easy for the human heart to harden and for us to reject the love of God that alone transforms our world. Here and now, I pray this prayer and see a mother holding on to the child she loves in her arms, praying for us all now and at the hour of our death. Mary holding the Christ-child, but the Christ-child in fact holding her. Christ alone embracing our hopes and fears, the times we overcome and the time we face our deaths. Only this love is great enough.

The next day, I visit Mr Tuccio in his carpenter's workshop. He can speak no English and I no Italian, but we do not need words. I have come to see. He embraces me. Timber from the wreckage of the boat is still piled in his workshop alongside the photo of him kissing the hand of Pope Francis. At my request, he has made small crosses for those who will join our Nazareth Community at St Martin's, and I thank him. 'Si, si,' he says, and taking a small piece of wood from the wreckage he skilfully cuts me a small Lampedusa Cross – which I am wearing today – 'Si, si, piccolo, piccolo,' he says as he hangs it round my neck.

And then, 'Portala con te come segno della resurrezione che nasce dal dolore.'

'Take it with you as a sign of the resurrection that is born in pain and struggle.'

I have indeed come and seen – the meaning of prayer, the sun's light, the breaking lengths of wave, water, cliff and sea – and the human search for salvation.

And I have come to see the courage and hope of the human heart that opens my heart up to the lonely wonder and mystery of life. A cross held in my hand, a cross whose wood has known pain and death and yet speaks of the heavens opened and the angels of God ascending and descending on the Son of Man.

Sabbath is forgiveness

I am on a pilgrimage, walking to Santiago de Compostela. I have been walking for nearly 30 days and have walked more than 500 miles. I have met and talked with many people. Everyone you meet has a reason for walking. And the walking often releases their reason so that they share it with you. An older gentleman tells me his wife had a hip replacement last year and they are doing the walk together. About five miles a day. In a refuge one night I meet Ciara and Matias. They are sharing the bunk above me and the next morning they tell me they are walking to Santiago for their honeymoon. They did not need to tell me. Their love is so evident. But my constant companion on the road is Patrick from America. At first, he refuses to attend all of the pilgrim Masses. He has had enough of the Catholic Church, he tells me. But slowly over the pilgrimage I notice he has begun to slip in, at first just at the back but later with me. I learn over many hours of walking that he has split up from his girlfriend and beneath he is hurting, and one day he tells me: 'I am walking because I heard that if you get to Santiago you receive instant forgiveness of all your sins.' So we walk on along roads through towns and cities, across the plains and through the hills and mountains. On and on we walk, sometimes gliding, sometimes plodding, sometimes each step forward an effort. But the further I walk, the lighter I feel – it's as though my body is rediscovering that for which it was created and each day I wake up joyful to be walking again.

The last week of our walking, two Catholic priests from Ireland join us. 'Can you believe this?' says Patrick, 'Me who wants nothing to do with the Catholic Church, find myself walking with three priests.' 'In order for your sins to be forgiven,' one of the Catholic priests lets slip, just as Santiago is in sight, 'you still have to go to confession.' 'Well, that's typical,' says Patrick, 'I've walked 500 miles and the Catholic Church has still managed to stitch me up because there is no way I am going to a priest for confession.' We arrive in Santiago. It's Sunday. My first day of rest after a month of walking. Tears are in my eyes as we look round during the Mass at the Cathedral and see the people who have walked with us. Today is the day of rest – the coming together of all our combined stories – and it is good. I visit the tomb of St James. The pilgrimage is complete but not quite. I say goodbye to Patrick and make my way to the station, only to realize that something is missing. I have left behind my Melanesian Brotherhood walking stick. I return to pick it up. But there's something else. When I go into the hostel, Patrick is still there. 'Patrick,' I say, 'over the last 500 miles you have told me all your whole story and you have given the fullest and most honest confession I have ever heard in my life and you have heard my story too. Look, I'm a priest too ... can I share with you that prayer of absolution?' 'Would you?' Patrick asks. 'Lord Jesus Christ, Son of the living God have mercy on us. Your sins are forgiven, in the name of the Father and of the Holy Spirit. Amen.' Patrick is beaming from ear to ear. And I am too.

Thus the heavens and the earth were finished and all their multitude. And on the seventh day God finished the work that he had done. So God blessed the seventh day and hallowed it, because on it God rested from all the work he had done in creation. (Genesis 2.2)

Sabbath is presence

Isn't that something?

I like when
the music happens like this:
Something in His eye grabs hold of a
tambourine in me,
and I turn and lift a violin in someone else,

and they turn, and this turning continues:
it has reached you now.
Isn't that
something?

(Rumi, thirteenth century)

'Will we have a glorious orchestra this time next year?'
I hope so: my thinking is that through God's grace the
orchestra has already begun.

Nazareth

They came into the church amidst shafts of sunlight
Stilled
If ever I needed a sign it was here
As springtime filled the cold grey corners of winter
And the doubt which lingers,
and which wonders if the daffodils will ever grow again
Is now blinded by your grace
Our east window refracting the rising sun in ripples
the centre becoming a white golden pool of molten light.

We gather, overawed –
first in prayer
And then later in chairs, in a circle and on the floor
Sensing a mystery greater than us,
greater even than the sum of our diversity
Eyes opened
Recognizing the signs of your presence
A peace we cannot explain
Did we not all feel our hearts burning within us on the road?

VII

Sabbath is tasting the gifts of God

On the door of the baker in Fiscardo, Kefalonia was a hand-written message both in Greek and English. 'Closed, fresh bread baked morning 7.00 a.m.'

I woke early and walked about half a mile from the place I was staying, along the edge of the sea, to the bakery. The bakery was open; you could smell it from 50 metres. I entered the bakery and behind the counter there was warm bread, crusty and risen, in wooden racks. Just as I entered, a boy arrived from the kitchen with another tray of hot olive bread. I pointed to one of these, and the woman took it in her hands as if it was something precious and beautiful, which it was, and wrapped it in white paper and handed it to me. It was still warm and the crust crunchy to touch. I began eating it on the way back to where I was staying, as I walked slowly along the beach, tearing off pieces with its salty black olives, and savouring the taste. It tasted as bread should taste – of the land, the sun and the sea. It was like tasting creation: the growing grain, the harvesting, the grinding, the olive groves on the hillside. And I felt that this is how life should be: real bread, simple and delicious, with time to touch it, smell it, taste the full flavour, and with no need to disguise or preserve the taste with a thousand additives. I know everyone sometimes gets feelings like this on holiday, and we all have to get back to the reality of supermarkets and the real world ... but wait a moment. This was the real world, this bread, real and simple ... you could not get any better. This was reality. As simple as bread. Real bread in which you tasted life. Later in the day, I sat on the beach and watched people playing in the sea. No computers, no TV, no mobiles, no amusement arcades, no confectionary, sauces and burger bars, just a beach and water and the sun and the shade of olive trees. And I watched people interacting so naturally it was like goodness come out of hiding. Whole families, grandparents, parents, children so at peace with themselves, with each other and the environment simply standing in the sea talking. And I swam, ate bread and ripe tomatoes, and these simple actions were like a prayer.

VIII

Sabbath time means living in the kingdom of God now

When I was living on Holy Island in Northumberland, I was visited by my friend whose two children sat in the car watching separate DVDs on their own screens with earphones. I asked would they like to explore the island and the sand dunes, and they said the island was 'boring'. In fact, everything for them seemed boring. So I said to the two children, 'I'll give you a challenge – for the next two days you are here you are not allowed to use the word boring. If you say the word boring, I will fine you £1 each time. But if you get through two days without using the word, I will give you £5 each.' They rose to a financial challenge and managed it. We walked across the shallow water like the ancient pilgrims to the island even though they complained the water was cold. We climbed the watchtowers on the way, looking out to the horizon where the sky joined the sea. They saw the swirl and then the heads of seals basking near the rocks and heard their honking cry. We walked round the whole island and climbed up to the castle. They ran across the vast windswept sands and watched the rivulets flow, and join up in pools as the tide came in. They wrote messages two metres high on banks of sand in the dunes and watched the sun go down into the sea. And their true characters emerged from the DVD and the boring: scrubbed and infused with sun and salty air so that they shone. In fact, at the end of the two days they had won their bet but wouldn't take it. Their mother said they said later that Holy Island was cool and 'live' and not at all boring. It was not 'loads of stuff', it was just simple, as simple as all goodness is. It's not that I am attacking the modern world, it's just that we have to rediscover those values which we have often buried under too much stuff we do, or have, or think we need. This is Sabbath time where we see once that everything God created 'is very good'.

Sabbath is hospitality

Afternoon tea

Up the steps and through the door
I enter the story of her life
Here it is gathered like a collage, a woven tapestry, a
    dancing hanging mobile
Every room different
Books and chimes and piles of magazines
Patterned teacups, pictures, hangings and icons on every
    coloured wall
Into the corridors and rooms of her goodness and gifts of
    her healing
Into the accumulated memories of her life
The gifts of the Spirit, the longing for light
And today the light is pouring in
filling the space with warm colours like the inside of a tent
    at sunset
Inviting you to look out and see the tops of the trees
Here in the midst of the city
A roof garden
A small oasis of peace
A place of hope and tranquillity
A Patmos cave of sacred memories
A monastery in the city
With hot scones
And large wide-brimmed refreshing cups of tea
As the chimes jangle on the doors
I participate in a poem of life

Where Christ, me, the Buddha, Rumi and the Sufi mystics
all find sanctuary.

Sabbath is thanksgiving

For life
For mother and father
For beloved brothers and sisters, nephews and nieces
For education and teachers who opened your mind
For a home that welcomed
For loyal friends
who continued the conversation each time you met as
    though you had never been apart
For beauty which astonished
For books you read and couldn't put down
For films and theatre and art that opened your eyes and
    stayed in your heart and gave you a new language –
    expanding your humanity
For music that moved you and took you on a journey
For the beauty of those you love and held your heart
and quickened and warmed you,
and in whom you tasted eternity
For travel and discovery
and the journeys that took you to new cultures which filled
    you
For the natural world alive with miracles
For this city
For the astonishing amphitheatre of life
in which you are but a small fragment of fashioned clay.

For Christ who has called you and saved you and gone
    ahead of you to show you the way
For his love which lives forever
For Sabbath time – the time to be thankful.

Helen Ireland after Thomas Bewick

Notes

1 See Mark Scarlata, *Sabbath Rest: The Beauty of God's Rhythm for a Digital World*, SCM Press, 2019.
2 Prospero in Shakespeare's *The Tempest*, Act IV, Scene 1.

7

Staying With

Helen Ireland after Thomas Bewick

Growing

Through this silence, sacrament, sacred study, compassionate service and sharing, you will grow. Through love, we grow. Silence will be the soil of this growth. You may not think you are growing; like the growth of a plant it takes time, and you won't be able to see the growth each day. You can't pull up a plant to check how its roots are doing – you just have to trust and keep the practice going. Yet you will find that over the months something is unlocking inside – that there is a shifting within. And the things you thought would always hurt you, or overwhelm you and which consequently you could never face – though they still hurt – have been brought into the light, so that the wound, no longer concealed has become your sign of grace received.

As you begin to grow, you will begin to see yourself for what you are. You will be humbled by this and grateful. For here lies a greater freedom. You will see your moods, and your deceptions, and the changing weather of your feelings, and the games you play – but you will not be deceived or the victim. And you will see your goodness without pride – like a butterfly emerging from the chrysalis.

You will see the life beyond self. The life beyond your preoccupations and beyond the anxieties that feed fear. A truth. A life radiant and beautiful. A life made by God. A life of blessing which invites you to become blessing too.

I

With steadfastness

Return

Return again and again
For how quickly we can become disorientated and
    separated from the source of our being
Nothing can separate us from the love of God
But we do not see that if we turn away
How quickly we demand our share of the inheritance and
    lose ourselves in a foreign land
We too must come to our senses
All we are searching for, we have already been given
God is not beyond us in the never-never land
God is here and now
Watching and waiting
His forgiveness comes before our repentance and our return.

Keep coming back to your practice

Not beyond
But here and now
Find the gap in the dialogue
Find the space in the crowdedness of your mind
Find the silence that your anxiety wants to invade
Find the Spirit within that you have ignored or suppressed
And enter again into that silence
Like a swimmer entering a pool
Whatever the weather, the pool is still there
Inviting you to discover in this immersion
The homecoming you long for
Keep on returning
Keep on seeking the God within.

Persistence

You may feel your life is running away like a river without
    banks
Within you this call:
Keep the discipline
Hold the stillness gently but steadfastly
Let go of all that tempts you to turn away and miss the
    miracle
Or squander the treasure without price
Discipline means to learn, to listen and become a disciple
This yoke is easy, its burden light
You may come with trepidation
When actually this is an unbinding
A setting free
A return to your truest self
The spontaneity and spaciousness of God at your very centre
You are dissipated by the random chase
The confusion of multiple choice
While all the time here and now
God is waiting.

Hoping

When you thought you had lost your path,
beneath all your fears,
I am there
When meaning is gone
I am that meaning
When truth seems hard to find,
I am that truth
When even love seems a bitter thing
I will take that bitter cup from you
and you will taste the wine of my forgiveness
Come back with me to the centre of the things
and be held, not torn.

Each day is an opportunity for hope
And hope will often arise from those deemed hopeless
Learn to hope in God even when hope seems impossible
    and beyond
Learn to hope in God's grace even when the rules of the
    world cry out that your values have no currency
Learn to hope in God's love
Hope as tender and ephemeral as a new shoot
But which can make the desert bloom and the song birds
    return.

Tides

Imagine you are a rowing boat
Floating in the estuary
Sky blue, wooden gunwale, clinker built
Nothing flashy, sturdy, built by hand
And this boat is anchored
Its bow fastened to a yellow buoy
Imagine that anchor is Christ
And as the tide comes in gently, the bow of the boat comes
    round to face the incoming tide and rise

And as the tide goes out, the rowing boat turns round to
face the receding water
Receptive to the flow
Today the estuary is still
The rowing boat too is still
There is not a ripple, just this gentle turning round to face
the tide
At other times this estuary will be rough, and the rowing
boat will ride those waves, be rocked, though still held by
the anchor and still turning to face the tide
You are that rowing boat
In calm and in storm still turning to face Christ
Rising and falling
Riding the tides.

Roots

There is a fear of being left behind
And so we run faster
And our souls run dry
We pass many along the way, but we cannot converse
Because we fear stopping
Lest we never catch up with expectation
And become part of the spillage
And so control and efficiency, managing and the transactional
take the place of human kindness
But what if you stop
And turn off the engine
And face the chaos
At first this stopping will feel dangerous as though you are
waiting to drown
Or are like driftwood with no direction
But how about we face the stopping
Face the stillness
Face the wreckage of purpose
And allow the roots to grow down again
Roots that have been torn away

Allowing them to find water and nourishment beneath
And the branches and leaves to reach slowly towards the sky
Allow the buds to form and those tight knots of growth to
    unclench
Uncurling in sunlight
Releasing in fragrance and colour
The hidden life, more wonderful than anything predicted or
    planned
This flourishing of God.

Staying with and letting go

Each day I am pared down
Stripped of something more
How can I let this tearing become my liberation?
This less become more,
this absence become my presence?
The letting go become the shedding of all that weighs me
    down
So that like David
I am not encumbered by the heavy armour of defence
But free and barefoot
I know what it is like to be tied to many things
But I have been touched by the beauty of your agility
Your life unbound
That beckons me
To walk softly on water
To calm the storm
To pick up my bed and walk
To run
And find within the tomb the cloth unbound
And the call to seek you
Because beyond this grave there is a Sea of Galilee
Teeming with life
And love.

Negative capability

This phrase was first used by the poet John Keats to characterize the human potential to pursue a vision of beauty even when it leads through intellectual confusion or uncertainty: 'when a man is capable of being in uncertainties, mysteries, doubts, without any irritable reaching after fact and reason'. In fact, the sense of unknowing becomes the catalyst or the very thing that focuses, intensifies and enhances the search for a greater truth. There is an importance in staying with the discomfort of the unknown, fear and the unresolved, because it is in that place that we reach the borders of what we are and discover what we could become. Thus this uncomfortable place, or place of trepidation where there are no quick fixes or easy answers, can become the place of transformation. It is often the very things we fear and our own lack of certainty that help us to break through all pride and discover the truth of living at ground zero. Perhaps it is here that we will learn what it means to live by faith and by love. It is in this hard place that the face of the unknown can reveal to us the face of the beloved.

Staying with the seasons

Winter

The place is so spacious I hardly recognize it
Stripped back
Without the leaves more gaps and openings
For the steely cold blues of the sky
Dark silvers on the surface of the lake
The trees stand black and naked against the light
Their twisting curves reaching up and out
their branches an intricate latticework through which
    winter light pours
Black silhouettes of buildings with their light-filled windows

Now the oranges of dawn
The sound of the wind
The cold seeping into the backs of my fingers as I write
The autumn leaves have been cleared
It's much more empty and spacious now
As though waiting for the year to begin
I can live with the whole year
I can find hope and promise even in this empty space.

Spring

Pale blue sky
Golden light
Bringing the park into focus and clarity
A blaze of white light streams through the branches of the
    trees
The other side of the lake lit up like a Merchant Ivory film
Fresh green grass
Willows weeping
But here in the foreground
The joy
A carpet of yellow daffodils announcing that life and beauty
    win
Irrepressible living yellows
Like hundreds of trumpets in a fanfare of spring
The first squirrels of the year like trapeze artists
Leaping between branches like runners in the air
Above the lake, a single gull slowly glides.

May

Sun through new leaves
Fresh white light
Long shadows
The smell of new grass
And birdsong, which is weaving a nest of tunes
I see the contours and shades of green

The shape and depth and openings
Through which the light comes and diffuses
And softens all
God's spotlights
Like a theatre of creation lit up
Leading me into the shape of this landscape.

I came with so many cares
And fears of letting others down
And being let down
Sinking
And yet here I sit, held in light
Softened by it
Called into the spaces,
through the trunks of the trees,
through shadows and light
Into the haze of morning
Finding here the space to also be lit up
And hold the warmth of that light within as I return.

Summer

Early morning
Eyes half-closed, filled with rays of light
And even in this early morning I feel the warmth of the sun
The sky is streaked with arcs of light
The grass looks greener
The leaves look thicker
The tops of the trees highlighted by the sun
Cast bold shadows across the park
The church bell chimes
Striped deckchairs lie in piles waiting for the crowds
It costs £8 for one day
What a wonderful thing it would be I think
To sit for a whole day in the park soaking up the light
I check my watch and rush back for another day
I hope the summer park comes with me.

Autumn

I have come back each week to the same place to see the
change
Today the branches are almost bare of leaves
And the ground is thick with crackling browns, yellows,
bronzes and golds
A squirrel comes so close
And sits back on its haunches
Front legs open as though to embrace me
The lake seems stiller and deeper than ever
Its surface reflecting the deep colours of autumn
I catch the cold in the air
The smell of the coming winter that excited me as a child
With memories of bonfires and fireworks and coal fires and
the nights closing in
These seasons are the miracle of God's natural world in our
very midst
I could have missed all this
I just had not noticed all that was happening
I was too locked in to come out and see the gold.

Through

Through the rain
Through the autumn, the winter, the spring, the summer
The shadows, the clouds, the sunlight,
beyond the weather, this being, this rising, this life.

III

Staying with truth

I love this blessing:

> Go forth into the world in peace;
> be of good courage;
> hold fast that which is good;
> render to no one evil for evil;
> strengthen the fainthearted;
> support the weak;
> help the afflicted;
> honour everyone;
> love and serve the Lord, rejoicing in the power of the
>   Holy Spirit.

It seems a good place to start. Hold fast to that which is good. How often even in small things we find that once we have embarked upon the path of untruth, deceit multiplies; not only have we lied, but we are forced to tell more lies to cover the initial lie. This is a slippery slope for the more we hide and lie to conceal the deception, the greater it grows until we become so tangled up in the deception that we no longer recognize what the truth is. We saw the consequences of when a nation lies to itself in Nazi Germany, and many other examples since. It does not necessarily begin with the desire to do evil. I think of the former courage of Aung San Suu Kyi in Myanmar, but now her refusal to acknowledge the persecution and ethnic cleansing of the Rohingya people. I think of the effects of climate change and what is happening to the world and our continuing refusal to acknowledge the consequences of our way of life. Truth has power, but so too does the denial of truth. The abandoning of truth has its own power and momentum and generates a tangled web of deception and often destruction. The wilful abandoning of the truth has another name. It is called evil.

Contrast this with the accused Jesus. If I am feeling over-whelmed, I visit a painting by Gerrit van Honthorst that usually hangs in the National Gallery: *Christ before the High Priest*.[1] Christ's hands are tied. In front of him the accuser's finger points in accusation. Yet the first thing one notices is the stillness of the Christ figure. It is as though his very body is refusing to respond to the venom of the attack. Rather, his posture seems almost languid. The white robe, which follows the relaxed pose of his body, is bathed in the light of the candle. The tension and piercing stare of his inquisitor is juxtaposed with an openness and a translucence in the figure of Christ. There is no defensiveness in Christ, rather it is as though we're being invited into his very heart. Look at Christ's eyes. He returns his accuser's stare with a beholding. 'Why askest thou me?' (John 18.19) Why not question yourself? The gentle Christ is the most powerful, tallest presence in the picture as though he is soaking up all the falsehood and defeating the lies. Holding fast to all that is good, even here giving back to no one evil for evil. In contrast, the High Priest is trapped by the chair and table and the law books in front of him. Though Jesus stands accused, it is as though the roles are reversed and his accuser seems the frightened, startled one, who is in fact the one on trial for though he claims the books of the law as his own, he does not belong to the Truth. Here the High Priest interrogates the Truth but is unable to realize he is looking into the face of truth and refusing to let that truth in. In the High Priest we see the skull beneath the flesh and are reminded of our mortality, but in Christ we see the Word made flesh and are reminded of our immortality.

I took a group of people who have known homelessness from the Connection to see this picture. We stood gazing at it in silence for a long time. 'What do you think?' I asked. 'That's the finger, the wagging finger that is always accusing me,' Don said. 'Wherever I go, whatever I hope for, I always see that finger condemning me.' He went up close to the picture to point out the finger for us and immediately one of the security wardens rushed over, wagging his own finger: 'Do not touch the pictures, sir!' 'That's the finger,' Don said, 'the finger that if you are homeless you get pointed at you again and again. Remember,' he said, 'that when you point your finger at someone else there are three fingers pointing back at you!'

But what about Jesus? There is no wagging finger there. His hands are tied. No accusation, rather an invitation to come in. It's as though he is saying the real kingdom, the real authority, the answer to all your fears is within me. The kingdom of heaven is here within my very heart and though you will put my body to death in the most painful way imaginable, you will never ever be able to defeat the love of my heart.

I once talked to my spiritual guide Fr Simon Holden about a difficulty I was facing in which I felt the pain of an injustice done to me. I have always remembered his response: 'We will come up against those forces that seem to deny all that we are and all that is true. The question is not "will I face those moments of trial?" but "will I be poisoned by them?"' Will I, when facing injustice, become the unjust? Will I return the hatred, return the exploitation, return the violence, return the lie or become infected by it so that I no longer know the truth? Or can I discover Christ within me? Can I transform the wagging finger through the sacred heart of Christ?

His stillness
His silence
His open heart
His wounds for love
The power of his gentleness
His open translucent compassion for the world
I am not seeing the death of Truth; in him we are seeing
    salvation.

I think of Moses coming down from the mountain after his encounter with God, his face so full of the light that he had to veil his face. I heard an Orthodox priest speaking of the way our faces were mirrors. Mirrors of the love of God. I wonder if I can mirror the Jesus I see in this picture. Holding fast to that which is good. Giving back to no one evil for evil.

Staying faithful

'For we walk by faith,' says St Paul in his second letter to the Corinthians. But how easy is it to do that, to walk by faith? Is it even desirable? In the age of risk assessment and the increasing need for constant vigilance and accountability, can we really afford to walk by faith? Walking by faith may seem like walking blind – putting trust in an unknown and unquantifiable, even non-existent God. Is it walking without due diligence? Or is it the opposite? Could walking by faith actually mean walking with your eyes, your heart and your deepest human intuition wide open?

Two Melanesian Brothers came to stay with me. They are not used to the big city. They live in a group of islands in the South Pacific that, though threatened by global warming and rising sea levels, actually has one of the lowest carbon footprints in the world. Drop Melanesians in the middle of London and not surprisingly they look astonished by the mad scrum of people and traffic and noise and the speed of this rush – a rush so busy that in the morning it's almost impossible to get across Church Path without being swept away by the incoming tide of commuters or even cross the road on a green pedestrian light without being mown down by cyclists accelerating towards you like a cavalry charge in Lycra. No thick velvet night or the sound of crickets and panpipes, rather 24-hour neon, the scream of a busker's trumpet. As Brother Michael sits staring out of the window on to the endless pandemonium of Trafalgar Square, I explain to him jokingly, 'We call this civilization.' But Brother Michael's constant refrain to me throughout the week has been, 'Do not worry.' He means it. 'Do not worry.' You see he doesn't worry – because he is living by faith.

I asked these two Brothers to lead the evening Eucharist at St Martin's 'Bread for the World'. English is not their first language or even their second. Brother Michael has never been out of Solomon Islands before and has never had to speak in English in public. And yet now they are both leading the reflection. What's more, a lot of people have come into the church to listen to them. 'Don't worry,' says Brother Michael.

But I am. I am worried for him. How will they cope? Will he say anything? Sometimes if Solomon Islanders don't know what to say, they sensibly just keep silent – but how will that go down in front of our congregation? I think of a Western back-up option. I know, I will use PowerPoint: set up a screen in church, show photographs of where he's come from, keep people occupied. But later I drop that plan. It seems like a cop out. No, let these Solomon Islanders be who they are. For better, for worse. 'Don't worry,' says Brother Michael again, smiling. 'Live by faith.'

So, standing in front of the congregation, I ask him, 'How do you live by faith?' In answer, he tells a story. A story which happened a few years ago when he and a group of five Brothers and priests were crossing the sea in an open canoe to visit the Christian community on the remote island of Vanikoro. One hour out to sea, their boat was hit by a large wave and simply sank. There he was, he and six others in the midst of the rough and shark-infested sea. 'Are you a good swimmer?' I asked him. 'No,' he replied, 'I am a bush man. I have never swam.' This is true, in the Solomon Islands the 'saltwater people' living by the coast are the fishermen – the swimmers. But the 'bush people' who live up in the hills are the farmers and gardeners, bartering their sweet potatoes and bananas for fish. So here was Brother Michael, a bush man in a rough sea unable to swim. 'What did you do?' I asked.

'I prayed,' he said

'But what more?'

'When my head went under water, I saw how the others with me were moving their feet and paddling their arms and I copied them.'

'How many hours did you do this for?' I asked

'I did this for twenty-one hours.' By this stage our congregation at Bread for the World are transfixed. You could have heard a pin drop.

'You mean you swam like this for twenty-one hours?' I repeated.

'Yes,' he said. 'If I panicked, I knew I would drown, so every one hour the six of us came together and we prayed together, through a whole day and a whole night in the sea. We kept praying. When very thirsty the rain came so we opened our mouths and drank.'

'What about the sharks?' I asked.

'I don't know,' he said, 'we didn't see any. Perhaps our prayers made them sleep.'

'What was your prayer?'

'Well the priest prayed a long prayer, but mine was a short one – help!'

After twenty-one hours they made it to shore. Every one of them survived. By the end of this story everyone in the church was listening to Brother Michael as though he were the Dalai Lama imparting a life truth. 'What would you like to say about faith to this congregation?' I ask. There was a long silence. I thought that Michael was not going to say anything and then he said 'Smile.'

'Smile?'

'Yes, smile. You must smile because God is smiling at you. We are God's smile. And don't worry. Live by faith.'

'But,' I said, 'how in the face of all the difficulties we face is that possible?'

Brother Michael replied, 'Love – the answer to all your questions is love. If you want to have faith you must first love – love God and love your neighbour as yourself.'

On the way out of the service, one of the congregation said to me, 'That was the best service I have ever been to.'

'Why?' I asked, 'what was wrong with all the other ones?' Surely she'd heard these things before.

'Yes, but this was like the real thing,' she said. 'It was like God was really present.' There is no mistaking the real thing.

Living by faith. I wonder if we can live by faith not just in the Solomon Islands but here in the centre of London. Not as fantasy or escape but live by faith with our eyes wide open.

It is clinging which is our death

We are wary of trusting, cynical of putting our trust in anything beyond human power or control. We are often so bent over, looking down at where our feet may slip or fall, that we are unable to look up and trust in the presence of God. Our faith has lost its confidence and we as Christians can lose that simple dignity and beauty of looking up and recognizing the grace of the One who has come to set us free. In his book *The Snow Leopard*, Peter Matthiessen, who is a Buddhist writer, describes a scene which often comes back to me. He and a group of Sherpas are walking along a narrow ledge in the Himalayas in search of the snow leopard. There is a cliff face rising on one side and a thousand-foot sheer drop on the other. He says that the path is wide enough to walk along and that if it were not for the sheer drop he would walk along it easily. He describes the Sherpas walking with their heads held up, poised and balanced despite the heavy backpacks they are carrying. They seem to glide along the path without waver or wobble. In contrast, he describes himself – bent over his feet, fearing each footstep, clinging to the weeds sprouting from the cliff face which come away in his hands. He writes: 'it is our clinging which is our death.' How true of our own lives. The more we cling, the more fearful, the less balance.

Holding fast by letting go

The less longing, the more presence
The less we bang on the door, the more it opens for us
The less we demand, the more we see the beauty of the gift
The less we expect, the more the joy of the surprise
The more selfless, the more self
Clamorous need shuts us off from the needed
'It is our clinging which is our death.'
The less we cling, the more we embrace
The less we fear, the more we love
All joy reminds us

It is not a possession but leads us onwards
Our love is a taste of things to come
Go lightly
Go simply
Feel the beauty of balance
A breathing out
A breathing in
A shared breath
A letting go so that we may be held forever.

IV

Staying with suffering

One thing that Jesus does not shy away from is the fact that in the world there is suffering – real suffering. In fact, he tells his disciples that he himself will suffer, and if they want to follow him they will have to take up the cross and suffer too.

The disciples are understandably confused. None of them want to suffer. It's not why they followed Jesus in the first place. Today, this is perhaps truer than ever. There is a sense in the Western world that suffering is something that happens out there to someone else but should not happen to me. The suffering and loneliness of old age is often hidden away in care homes where relatives may seldom visit. With an illness, the focus is usually on the treatment plan rather than the reality of the life of the person themselves. The suffering of mental illness has been for so long hidden away and is only now beginning to be talked about. When someone dies, we employ strangers to take the body away, clean it, dress it, embalm it and apply make-up, so that when the relatives come they will not be shocked to see mortality. How different from other cultures. And look at the addictions of the modern world – be it drugs, or alcohol, or gambling or sexual addictions, shopping addictions, cosmetic surgery, health products on the market, or the insatiable busyness of our lifestyles, the endless messaging and selfies on social media – are these not in some ways bids to escape suffering?

Look at me, I'm doing well! I'm having a good time! In fact, there is so much aversion to suffering that when we do suffer we feel that something must have gone seriously wrong. There must be some way of eliminating this – a drug to take, a person to blame, a court case to win, a perpetrator to punish.

I have a very powerful memory of my great aunt shortly before she died. She was lying in hospital looking lost, vulnerable and frightened, and so alarmingly thin. I knew she was dying. All my life, she'd had people running around after her. She'd had money and homes in both Canada and London – she had taken me out to restaurants and theatres and cinemas and, for me when I was young, being with her had felt exciting and luxurious and wonderful, but now here she was in hospital crying out: 'Tell the doctors to do something. I can't stay here,' she was saying, 'tell them to do something.' And I was acutely aware that there was nothing more they could do. My beloved aunt was dying, and there was no way of escaping that suffering. I could only be with her as things were. And I recognized that in so many ways she seemed so unprepared for death. The problem is that we think we have time. We have only now.

A couple of days ago, a dear friend phoned me and told me that she had been diagnosed with cancer of the bowel. A few weeks previously, I had been trying to reassure her that the pains she was feeling in her stomach were probably not something serious. I had tried to tell her not to worry about the biopsy that she was having and that I would pray for her. 'By the way,' she added, 'they have also found I have seven cancerous nodules in my lung.' She told me so matter-of-factly, as though she didn't want to worry me and went on to ask in her usual compassionate and caring way about how I was and about what I'd been doing and the projects we were organizing to help refugees. When I came off the phone, I was shaken – shaken most of all by her goodness in the full face of her own suffering. We both knew those signs were not good. But neither did that suffering define her, she was the friend I loved, the wonderful human being I know her to be, not the diagnosis. I saw her kindness, her courage, her humanity – her soul force – I saw her immortality. Suffering can be about running away from the reality of life, but suffering is also when you stop running and face the truth of life – this is where I stand, how then shall I live?

When Zen Master Shunryu Suzuki Roshi was dying of cancer, he told his students: 'If when I die, if I suffer, that is all right you know, no confusion ... this is just suffering Buddha.'[2] 'Just suffering', hard to accept of course in the midst of suffering, but it's not your soul; it is not you. Writing from prison, Oscar Wilde described the problem of prison thus: 'The most terrible thing about it is not that it breaks one's heart – hearts are made to be broken – but that it turns one's heart to stone.'[3] Fr Bernard Lynch, speaking about his forty years of ministry with those with HIV and AIDS, during the time when everyone including the Church excluded gay people and turned away, said: 'God's love breaks our hearts as it were, to make them bigger ... Broken heartedness is part of all love ... In the army of Lovers only the wounded may serve.' Somehow in the struggles and suffering of our lives we have to rediscover the heart of flesh. Not the victim heart; not 'Did I get what I wanted?' or 'Did I win or take for me?' – but 'Did I love well, did I live fully, was I fully alive to others, did I live with integrity and truth, did I see, hear, care? Was it a life worth living? How then shall I live today?' Mother Teresa wrote, 'We can't always do great things in life but we can do small things with great love.'[4]

Abraham came to the Nazareth Community yesterday. Until a few weeks ago, he was blind. Several weeks ago, he had the cataracts removed from his eyes, first one eye and then the other, and now his whole being seems filled with light. 'Now I can see you with my eyes,' he told me. 'But what about before, when you were still blind?' I asked him. 'Oh then,' he said, 'I could see with my heart.' 'What could you see with your heart?' I asked. 'Kindness,' he said.

In the Gospels, Jesus meets suffering face to face – those with leprosy, the woman haemorrhaging blood, the woman taken in adultery and the man possessed by demons in the country of the Gerasenes. In a few words, Luke's Gospel captures this man's suffering – he has no clothes, he has no home, he is walking among the tombs, the unclean spirit within him would seize him. People had tried to imprison him and bind him with chains and shackles, but he would break free and be driven by the demons into the wilds. It's a terrifying description of a broken, tormented life. It's the life I fear when I hear the woman shouting in the street, while everyone walks past or when I avert my eyes from the man lying down on the pavement, raw flesh against concrete in the rain. It's the chaos of paranoia; it's the poverty of neglect; it's suffering that we can't handle because we can't instantly solve it or answer it with a donation; it's the haunted face of the man trying to raise money for his next fix. It's the pile of supermarket flowers in plastic on a street, marking another tragic waste of a young life, and it's a weeping mother and sister. It's the poverty of the outcast, but it's also my own mother with dementia who I love now with the dementia, not just as she was. It's your own family breaking down. It's the friend who tells you they've done something terribly wrong. It's the ghost of a family suicide. It's suffering that says I am your brother or sister or friend or neighbour; I could be you. Or perhaps I am you beneath your façade and what are you going to do about me? Nothing? Call yourself a Christian? What are you going to do, Jesus Son of the Most High God? Are you going to torment me in my chaos with your righteousness? And what does Jesus do? He asks the man his name. He sees the man beneath, separates the human being from the legions of demons that possess him. He names the demons, drives them out – the demons that are so destructive. He sets the man free in the way that only God can. Freed from all that has tormented him, he has found a stillness and a peace. He is clothed and sitting in the same way we will also later see Mary Magdalene – sitting at the feet of Christ and in his right mind. 'Peace, be still.'

We are not the sin or the demons that possess us; we are not the sickness or the fear, or the violence that cannot be contained, or the evil that binds us in its chains. We are human beings made in God's image, and when we too are broken open, we rediscover the broken heart of God.

At the very centre of the storm the realization of a truth, Christ setting free, a greater reality, a deeper forgiveness, an eternal hope – above us, beyond, us beneath us. As Julian of Norwich wrote during a time of plague and suffering in her *Revelations of Divine Love*:

'These words, "You shall not be overcome", were said very loudly and clearly ... God did not say, "You shall not be tormented, you shall not be troubled, you shall not be grieved", but God said, "You shall not be overcome."'[5] How then shall you live?

Helen Ireland after Thomas Bewick

Staying faithful in death

You may think this staying is about this life only, but it's also about the life to come and the transition between the two.

I knew I must go to visit Sibyl Allen. She was well over ninety and I had heard she had not been well and had arranged to go the following day – the Wednesday. But something in my guts spoke to me and kept saying – no, go today. I had an important meeting and a lunchtime group with those who are homeless at the Connection. But still this inner prompting – 'No, go today.' So I listened to the intuition and reorganized. 'I will be back for the group but may be a bit late,' I told Kaz, the Deputy Day Centre Manager from the Connection. But Kaz had a greater wisdom: 'Just cancel the group this week so you can be with Sibyl and not have to rush.' At the station there were no trains. I waited for ages, getting more frustrated. Finally, I got a train to Lewisham and then a 176 bus to Bromley. The journey seemed interminable. But I got there, and Sibyl's son Martin was waiting. 'So sorry it's taken so long, I had to come on the 176 from Lewisham,' I told him.

'Well,' said Martin, 'all I can say is that my mum must have been guiding you. Every day when she came to St Martin's she always took the 176 to Lewisham. We couldn't persuade her to take the train.' Living by faith. I sat down with Martin at Sibyl's bedside; they had made a bed up for her in the front room. Sibyl was breathing deeply. Martin told me how she had refused to go to hospital when the ambulance was called. She spent hours telling the ambulance crew quite clearly that she wanted to die in her own home. There is no arguing with Sibyl. And here she was in her own room – with the piano that Alastair Anson had had tuned for our carol service held here with her last December, the stained-glass window of St Martin in the hallway, teacups and cake on the table. I said a prayer with her and anointed her. We said the Lord's Prayer together, the Nigerian carer joining in. We held her hand. Her breathing became more difficult. 'I think she is leaving us,' I said to Martin. It was like I was breathing with her. 'She has with her,' Martin said, 'the two things she loves most – her family and her church.' It is these times when you know that we are indeed just walking in faith. I said the twenty-third Psalm. 'Goodness and mercy shall follow me all the days of my life, and I will dwell in the house of the Lord forever.' And we realized that Sibyl's breathing had become almost imperceptible and then stopped completely.

'All things work together for good for those who love God'.

VI

Staying with love

Love waits for you at the station

Filled with joy at your coming
Or outside the doctor's surgery
In the car to drive you home
It frustrates, irritates, gets in the way, longs, hopes,
    worries, wants to do it for you, knows jealousy, protects,
    confronts, defends, flashes with anger at your selfishness
    or neglect
Longs for your successes
And yet loves you exactly as you are
Through years of imperfections
Love waits at the door for your return
Under the hanging basket of flowers you gave them years
    before
And welcomes the whole of you
The bed is already prepared with towel
The endless cooking of the food you like
The room which you painted is waiting
The photo by the bedside from twenty years ago
And the thousand memories that pierce your heart
with affection and concern
and fear of loss
This love is home
To which you will return in search again and again
For this one who is watching and waiting
Whose eyes you know better than your own
And clothes you with the carefully folded clothes they have
    kept in your drawer for your return
The pyjamas smelling of washing powder
And the clock on the wall already aching with the tick of
    departure.

Steadfast friendship

She phones and she listens
And understands the whole of my life
There is no demand, no further expectation, no ownership,
just this generous offering
Held together across the world by this unseen chain of love
Our lives are redeemed and cherished
We have known each other through storms,
despair, achievements, celebrations and grief
We have shared our deepest failings and inadequacies in the
    knowledge of our affection
We have known an unconditional friendship
that can laugh in the valleys and on the mountains
A laughter that cherishes the other and understands the
    story told and left untold
Without invasion or judgement
We nourish all that is good in each other
We face our demons together in the knowledge that another
    understands
Generously she gives me the gift of a friendship
Longer than the years
Broader than my strengths or failings
Deeper than my deserving
More expansive than my dreams.

The guest

He visits me from the past
And brings such blessing into my home
His being is light
And his energy and kindness shine in his face
His spirit is alive
After all these years
There is no division
Just an easy generous open presence
There is nothing draining in welcoming this guest

Rather a spring of joy and healing
As though the past has returned as blessing
My guest offers me back the gift of hospitality in my own
    home
We share our inner goodness
Closer even than we were
Recognizing in one another
All we feared we may lose
And all which through one another we have become.

Laughter

She radiates joy
Bubbles with it
Her delight in others is as irrepressible as her laughter
With us she is like a fountain of refreshment in sunshine
    that soaks everyone in the vicinity
You could pick out her laughter in a crowded restaurant – it
    overflows
And there she is – lit up with delight and love for her friends
Longing for those around the table to shine as brightly for
    each other as they do for her
And we in our formality and stiffness are melted by her
    warmth
Made generous by her friendship
Liberated by the whoop of her laughter
She transforms us from our day jobs into human beings
Releases us from our suits, dog collars and ties
To become the people we once were
After dinner she runs after a woman in the train station
    to find out where she bought her shoes that one of her
    friends admired in the theatre queue
And, of course, that woman in the shoes becomes her friend
    too
Then in the wake of her enthusiasm and joy,
I direct her onto the platform to catch her last train, which
    she would otherwise miss

I can still hear her laughter as
I return to my emails
And even they seem warmed by her summer sunshine.

The grace of love

I wish I could revisit the past
And tell you how much I love you
You are the one who untangled me
Untied my very sinews and the knots in my heart
You brought me inner healing – rehydrating my parched soul
You stayed with me
Let's go! We did not move or move away
You held me
But I did not hold on to you.

I saw us come alive when we were together
I prayed at your side
Felt you through the pores of my skin
I saw you laugh and love
I reread your many letters now, and long for you
I saw you sow my garden with your generous goodness
A felt you share my inner soul
A poetry of words and laughter
You welcomed me from sleep with sunlight
You held me on the bridge
And whispered my name in the darkness and kissed me in
    the trees
Strong and unashamed of our love
Again and again, you told me, 'I love you'
And I did not realize you were the treasure beyond price
For which it would be worth selling everything
A love which held me so naturally, so gently
that I did not recognize it was the most beautiful gift I have
    ever been given,
until I turned away.

You will always hold my heart
You are never far from me
And I pray you will be waiting for me when I at last return
To wake me in love and light
With the warmth and beauty of your body
And your kiss of peace.

My brother

I saw, suddenly, that you were growing older
And I feared for you
Even more for me losing you, or being parted ...
I still love you more than my own life
Long for you to win
To be acknowledged
To shine
With your brilliance
Your perfectionism in all things
Your eccentric genius
Your perceptive humour
Your tough fear and dangerous talk
Your love of the familiar and
Your originality and generosity
The traditions that you have created to save you from
    imagining too much
That insightful mind
watching life, exposing, filleting, laughing, inventing
the most vivid pantomimes and jokes of our past
forgetting nothing
Holding the pike you have caught in your hands with both
    pride and trepidation
And letting it go unharmed
You always know without being told
I see the dissecting honesty in your eye, that in achievement
    could be cruel

yet now softened by pain, tenderness and knowledge of
    your own frailty
In the broken bits of all our lives I see both your fear and
    your love
There is a loyalty, an extra mile, a generous dinner cooked,
    a wisdom, an unspoken knowing, a card which arrives in
    the post with your familiar handwriting
Disdaining the internet, here is a relationship as indelible as
    ink, going back to my birth
That holds us all together
A weakness, that is loving, steadfast and strong
And makes us all long to be with you.

Staying when full of doubt

In the place of longing, a dried-up heart
In the place of beauty, your own tired reflection in the
    mirror
In place of God
Nothing
Did you love me?
Or did I imagine it?

We are removed
Detached from human interaction
Our anxiety is for the process
We screen ourselves behind screens
We talk of the poor but not to them
We are the poor
They have moved carers into offices to write endless emails
Ministry in measurables
Love with an invoice
Relationships in an agenda
Quantifiable concern
Creation in plastic
No time to gaze upon the mystery.

The earth covered the moon tonight with its shadow
I saw a large tennis ball looking down on our world
Out there in the dusky sky
The moon hanging
In silence and space
Waiting, as I wait
For the shadow to peel back
So that the light will come back again
From the thin slice of the moon's crescent
To the white gold of the full moon
I stay watching and waiting.

Helen Ireland after Thomas Bewick

Staying faithful when lost

He is here, at the bottom of the fall
A peace below the waves and currents
An easy stillness
A stillness where birds land
Where rain falls
And where the ground drinks
Listen, the wind is moving through the trees
A stillness within too
Where we can move freely
Possessing nothing
And connected with all
Come, Lord
Take us home to the centre of the pattern
So that we may belong and yet be free
An easy love
To walk with no hands tied
But with you forever.[6]

VII

Abiding

Take me home to the love that stretches forever
To your prayer that has become my prayer
To the revelation in the dark night when I knelt at the altar
  with my father
To a cross, lost and found
Which tells my story
From my childhood with my brothers
where I ran down the hill from an ancient church
with its smell of mystery and awe
Those laughing days of heroes and discovery
Take me home to a gospel which came alive in darkness
To the community that centred and held my heart
To the Christ I saw in others

To the discoveries I made in vast seas and far-away places
In the theatres of your creation
Take me through the pain and beauty and touch of love
Where we long never to be parted and yet are ...
Hold fast to me in the places of poverty and desolation
The bleak bus stop, the windy road
In the cold damp fear
And the darkness that nearly drowned me
Forgive me seventy times seven
For in the wounds of my loneliness and sin you planted the
    seeds of my redemption
Take me to your tomb and yet beyond it
Take me home across shallow water and low tide and white
    morning sun
Take me to the parting and yet the finding
The seed dying and yet rising
Take me home to a grace which came when I never believed
    it possible
But flooded me with your mercy
Take me through the landscape of your love
Through each encounter of your presence in the face of
    others
Take me back to the family I will always love
To the Christ who goes ahead of me and yet waits to
    welcome me
And sends me out
In the stream of his Spirit
Take me beyond human understanding
To the centre of this city
In the uniqueness of every human life and the wonder of
    each encounter
May I be a bearer and a witness of your risen life
This city is my monastery
For this city is your home.

Vicky Howard

Notes

1 'Christ before the High Priest', The National Gallery, London, www.nationalgallery.org.uk/paintings/gerrit-van-honthorst-christ-before-the-high-priest.

2 Jack Kornfield, *The Wise Heart*, Random House, 2008, p. 199.

3 Oscar Wilde, De Profundis, Philosophical Library, 1951, p. 91.

4 Mother Teresa of Calcutta, *A Gift for God*, Collins, 1975, p. 83.

5 Julian of Norwich, *Revelations of Divine Love*, Penguin Classics, 1966, Chapter 68, Revelation 16.

6 Richard Carter, *In Search of the Lost*, Canterbury Press, 2006, p. 183.

8

When the Me Becomes Us

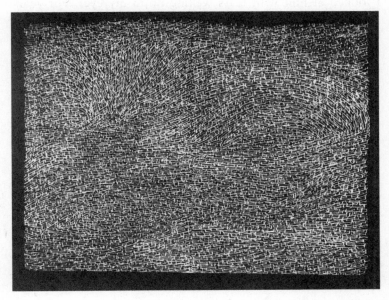

Vicky Howard

I

The community we begin on earth is continued in heaven

They phoned me from the monastery at Mirfield to tell me Fr Simon had been diagnosed with leukaemia and been given only a few weeks to live. We had shared so much of our lives for twenty years.

I entered a bedroom filled with winter light
Simon was sitting up alert and full of joy
'I feel as if I am in a ship's cabin on a vast ocean,' he said
We talked about going home. What is home?
Simon said, 'Home – is making a space for God in yourself
     for other people.'

I looked at him with tears welling up in my eyes. For years
I had been coming and sitting in his room, and he has made
space for me, a safe life-giving space. And we had talked about
the meaning of our lives. This monastery was my sanctuary,
but I was acutely aware that Simon was being called to leave it
behind. 'Are you frightened?' I asked.

'I am walking into something beyond human understanding
Under
Standing
I am standing under a mystery
God is surprise
Understanding is about control
But God's peace passes all understanding
The Church tries to represent something that is under our
     control
It's a load of bollocks.' His eyes twinkled with the adventure.

He spoke of how we led the retreat together a few months
     before:
'It was like a song, sung through us
And those who were with us recognized the song
And tuned in
God is the song
I feel so thankful to say that which I truly believe
I have no desire to say that which I ought to say
Nothing stood in the way of God's song.'

We talked about his diagnosis:
'I am not frightened of illness
As though illness were an enemy

I am me
I am part of creation
There is no me and the illness – just me.'

We talked about the nature of love:
'Everyone who God has given to me, has given more of God
    to me
I have never been given people who prevent me from loving
    God
What I am sharing with you now is truth
I don't have much more time, so I want to share it with you
Love taught me that loving someone was not loving them
    for yourself
But sharing the love God has for that person
The love was not mine it was God's
God's love.'

'Will you pray for me in heaven?' I asked
'Of course I shall still pray for you, what else would I be
    doing?
That's what you do in heaven. Being in heaven will be a
    prayer for you.'

And then he said
'I think of the pain and misery some people suffer, if only
    they realized they were part of us. You just have to know
    you are loved by God to be part of the us
You cannot talk about God and us as separate things they
    are not
God dwells in us
We dwell in him.'

We talked about the difference between this inner knowing
    and all the explanations we try to give:
'Talking about God is impossible
The peace of God beyond my understanding
The piece of God I carry within me.'

'What is your prayer now?' I ask
'What is my prayer?
It is to be unafraid of the truth
The truth that sets you free
If you are afraid then you have not been freed
If you think truth is this room, then you are not free to go
    beyond this room
But you do know the truth, you know it in your heart, you
    carry it with you.'

I then spoke about the realization in me of how I have held back parts in my life. I will love God but keep this part from God in the hope of keeping an alternative alive in me, keeping the 'if' alive. Costing not less than everything, but not yet. Even after many years of following Christ, I had still been holding something back, wanting something in addition to his love. My conversion continues. Do you turn to Christ? I have realized I cannot be turned to Christ and look away. It is everything. It had come to me like an epiphany: 'My grace is sufficient for you, for power is made perfect in weakness. I will boast all the more gladly of my weakness, so that the power of Christ may dwell in me.' (2 Corinthians 12.9) There was nothing more I wanted apart from this love in which all other love moves and has its being.

Simon understood. He said to me:
'Delight in that discovery
Delight in God
You cannot love Jesus and ...
As though the *and* were something different or alternative.'

He talked about his fading memory:
'Memory is a strange thing,
the older I get, the more difficult it is to remember the
    narrative
It's the now that matters
I want to sing God's song now
I want to dance now

Like Mary, I want to sing now
Sarah laughed, I want to laugh now
Yes, God surprises us
People talk about God as if they are talking about God, but
    they are not
They are beset by the instinct to want to control
But God, thank God, is uncontrollable
All that matters is God.'

'What advice would you give me?' I ask and he is silent
'Distrust self
Jesus said "I AM"
Put your trust in God
The Passion of Christ is a complete oneness in God
There is great struggle but in the end a truth that is met
And this truth sets you free
Father into your hands I commend my Spirit
And when your spirit and the Spirit of God are one
It is complete
You have come home.'

Of all this conversation, the words that I struggle with are:
'Distrust self.' Had I misheard? 'Trust yourself.' I tried to get
him to clarify, to take away the struggle those words were
causing. But he did not seem to take them away only to say
that those were the words that he had said and that perhaps I
was not ready to hear them.

As I pondered this, I realized how much I dwell in myself
– depend on affirmation and achievement. But this calling of
God is not a trusting in self, it is a trusting in Christ. It is a
calling to dwell in God. 'It is no longer I that live. It is Christ
who lives in me.' You cannot half invite. You cannot half
dwell, you can only fully dwell and each time you turn away
from Christ it's as though you want to make a separate dwelling. I thought of Peter. He wanted to dwell in the light on the
mountain of transfiguration, but he had been called to dwell
with Christ who now was on the road to Calvary. 'I will never
betray you, Lord' – but then I thought of those three betrayals.

Do not trust yourself. Trust in Christ. There is an unfathomable humility in this admission; there is a letting go of pride and reputation and the belief that we are saved by our own goodness or righteousness or ability. There is simply a turning to Christ. Fully turning, unreserved, not held back, allowing all of ourselves to come into the light and stay with Christ. And in the fullness of this turning there is a love that passes all understanding. I remember the words of the Morning Office in the Melanesian Brotherhood – a prayer I had said so many times I knew it by heart:

> Trust in the Lord with all your heart,
> And do not trust in your own understanding.
> Trust in the Lord with all your heart,
> And he will make straight your path.

Bernard of Clairvaux spoke of loving God for God's own sake, freed from self-interest. But beyond that was an even higher stage of love and that was loving self for God's own sake. That is when there is no separation, and we know that we have come home to the Father and the Father has run to meet us and lifted us up and God and his child are one:

> As a drop of water poured into wine loses itself, and takes the colour and savour of wine; or as a bar of iron, heated red-hot, becomes like fire itself, forgetting its own nature; or as the air, radiant with sun-beams, seems not so much to be illuminated as to be light itself; so in the one who loves self for God's sake all self-will and demands melt away through some inexpressible transmutation into the will of God.[1]

Much to think about.

I go to the Church of the Resurrection for the Eucharist, and these are the words that are read in the Gospel:

> Jesus said to them, 'Come and have breakfast.' Now none of the disciples dared to ask him, 'Who are you?' because they knew it was the Lord. Jesus came and took the bread and

gave it to them, and did the same with the fish. This was now the third time that Jesus appeared to the disciples after he was raised from the dead.

When they had finished breakfast, Jesus said to Simon Peter, 'Simon son of John, do you love me more than these?' He said to him, 'Yes, Lord; you know that I love you.' Jesus said to him, 'Feed my lambs.' A second time he said to him, 'Simon son of John, do you love me?' He said to him, 'Yes, Lord; you know that I love you.' Jesus said to him, 'Tend my sheep.' He said to him the third time, 'Simon son of John, do you love me?' Peter felt hurt because he said to him the third time, 'Do you love me?' And he said to him, 'Lord, you know everything; you know that I love you.' Jesus said to him, 'Feed my sheep.' (John 21.12–20)

In the Reconciliation Chapel, the angels on the engraved window are pointing beyond the grave as if to say, 'He is not here, he is risen. He has gone on ahead of you.' And I feel a rush of joy and hope.

I go to say goodbye. 'Did you hear the Gospel?' I ask.
'That's our calling now,' says Simon, 'to feed the sheep. You
    will have to do it for us.'
I make my confession
As I hear the words of absolution, I think of Peter
Three times forgiven, three times the call to love
Forgiven the past to live forgiveness now
I leave the monastery
But the monastery does not leave me
The city is also my monastery
And so is heaven.

Fr Simon Holden CR died two weeks later, on Thursday 6 February 2019. I can still hear him speaking to me. 'I want to disappear into God's love. I want the me to become us.'

The kingdom of God

You look through the window
And see the wild beauty beyond
You see and long, but you are not fully part of it
You try to open the window, but it is locked
And you feel the separation
The iron frame and rusted lattice you cannot open
But then you find the key
And ease open a window used to being closed
And the wind comes through
No glass now, just this opening
And you gulp the air
and feel the softness of the rain in your face
and the greens and the blues calling you to be part of them
to go beyond the spectator stand
And enter in
So you climb through the window
You feel the ground
You taste the sky
You hold the wind in open hands
And find that your heart has opened too
And there is no longer any division
No in
No out
Just God.

Vicky Howard

The Nazareth Community

In March 2018 the Nazareth Community was formed at St Martin-in-the-Fields and forty-eight people became members. In September of that year and then the following March more joined them. Our community had begun.

As he received his simple wooden Lampedusa Cross
Placed around his neck
He wept
And his weeping was like a movement along the line
As we knelt to receive God's calling
It was like the Spirit
Moving through the trees
It was like tears on dry ground
It was like witnessing the soft crack
Of the shell of a seed breaking open
And a green shoot
Emerging
Tender and good
And I wept too, in hope.

What is the purpose of the Nazareth Community Rule of Life?

During a clergy course on ministry and discernment I was invited to attend, we were asked to choose three verbs from a list of hundreds that we felt were at the heart of our ministry and calling. We had to choose spontaneously – from our guts rather than our heads – the words that spoke to us most deeply. I found it impossible to choose just three but found myself arriving at seven verbs, each of which I felt was somehow very close to my heart. There were many words like to lead, to organize, to direct, to minister, to help, to uplift, to guide, to manage, to teach, to call, etc. But the seven verbs I arrived at were these:

1 To behold
2 To accept
3 To gather
4 To inspire
5 To enrich
6 To restore
7 To live

I was not sure why at the time I had chosen seven or why these seven, for there were many other beautiful ways of action described in other verbs. But these were the ones that spoke most immediately to my heart as I prayed. The following day, I spent an hour in the chapel praying, and it suddenly came to me like a revelation that each of these words spoke of the action of the seven parts of our life within the Nazareth Community. It was one of those revelatory moments that was a gift from God:

1 Silence – to behold
2 Service – to accept
3 Sacrament – to gather
4 Scripture – to inspire
5 Sharing – to enrich
6 Sabbath – to restore
7 Staying – to live

Since that moment these words have lived on in me, and I realize the whole of my life has led to the truths of this simple discovery. These words and their connection to the pattern of life we have been forming together filled me with hope: the sense that this rule of life was not something I had invented but a gift and these actions were the fruits of prayer as we had prayed this community into being. The words were not just mine, they belonged to all of us and I noticed the way all these verbs could be individual but also collective – the purpose of our community. I also noticed the way these verbs could be both active and passive.

We behold; we are beheld
We accept; we are accepted
We gather; we are gathered
We inspire; we are inspired
We enrich; we are enriched
We restore; we are restored
We live; we are given life

When I brought these words to the Nazareth Community one of our members, Michael, pointed out that they actually work best the other way round – beginning with God. And another member, Paul, noticed that they are words that do not end but invite us into a circle – the Trinity of God for ever taking us deeper into the life of God:

We are beheld; we behold; we are beheld
We are accepted; we accept; we are accepted
We are gathered; we gather; we are gathered
We are inspired; we inspire; we are inspired
We are enriched; we enrich; we are enriched
We are restored; we restore; we are restored
We are given life; we live; we are given life

I realize too that each of these verbs have past, present perfect, present, present continuous and future tenses. They also have a movement – from being beheld, to being accepted, to being gathered, to being inspired, and then enriched and restored and given new life – and ultimately this is eternal life.

The other important realization was that this rule of life was not a private rule or territory to be defended but a rule of life to be shared. It was porous. It invited others in. Each noun of Nazareth invites the verb which draws us into relationship with God and other.

To behold – both to be and to be held, to hold the other and let them be who they truly are. There is both immense attention and compassion in this word but also freedom. Freedom to love and yet to let be. Freedom to be held in love and to truly be who God intends you to be. In German the word is 'behalten', which means to keep – I think of us all being held in the palm of God's hand – 'the Lord bless you and keep you'.

To accept – the opposite of acceptance is rejection. I wonder how much of our pain or fear of humiliation comes from that sense that we are not accepted for who we are. Real service begins with acceptance not a sense of pity. When you know that you are accepted it will unlock your heart. When you accept others without condemnation it will unlock theirs too.

To gather – Christ gathers – in the Gospels he gathers people around him – especially those on the edge. He is the good shepherd who draws in and leads out, and who knows each by name. They recognize his voice. They are gathered by it. Our faith was never meant to be a lonely and isolated thing, rather it is a communion, and if we live this communion it will attract others for it is a beautiful and life-giving thing. We ourselves become sacrament – the sign of the one who gathers – a parable of community.

To inspire – to be Spirit-filled and to fill with Spirit, to be filled with that Pentecost fire and to share that light with others. The Scriptures are intended to do just that, not to contain or trap but to fill us with the one who is our inspiration. The more attentive we are to him, the more we too will reflect his Spirit using words only when we have to. Inspire is not about outward appearance; it is about Christ with*in* us.

To enrich – we often think it is possessions that enrich us. But we are most enriched by relationship. When we face our own mortality, we will realize that it is not how much we have but how much we have loved – how much we shared ourselves with others and allowed others to share their lives with us that is the treasure beyond price. I wonder who enriches you and how you can you enrich another.

To restore – when a painting or a beautiful piece of furniture is restored, it recognizes the value that it already has and rediscovers its original beauty or authenticity so it can be seen again. We are all made in the image of God, but over the years we can easily become broken, or tarnished, and smeared by our sinfulness, or torn by pain. To restore is about healing – gently cleaning away all that has obscured and finding beneath the original beauty of the creator. To arrive at the beginning and recognize it for the first time.

To live – the Word became flesh and lived among us. Our aim is not a set of rules rather a life to be lived – to be breathed, inhabited, touched, tasted, smelt, seen, heard, within the world. What Jesus offered us was life, life in all its fullness. We were called to incarnate his life – to become the life that we received as pure gift from him. This is our Nazareth promise: 'I want to live the gospel, O Lord give us grace.' The city is **our** monastery.

Blessing of the Nazareth Community

'I Come Like a Beggar with a Gift in My Hand' *(Sung)*

During the singing of the following, those wishing to become members of the community come forward:

I come like a beggar
With a gift in my hand.
I come like a beggar
With a gift in my hand.
By the hungry I will feed you,
By the poor I make you rich,
By the broken I will mend you,
Tell me, which one is which?

The need of another
Is the gift that I bring,
The need of another
Is the gift that I bring
By the hungry I will feed you ...

Take the wine that I bring you
and the bread that I break,
Take the wine that I bring you and the bread that I break.
By the hungry I will feed you ...

(Sydney Carter)

Beloved in Christ, through prayer and discernment you have been called by God to become the members of the Nazareth Community here in the centre of London. This will be an experiment in being with – enjoying God, cherishing life and discovering God's revelation in others.
I therefore ask all of you who wish to become members of the Nazareth Community:
What do you seek?
We seek to live the gospel with the Spirit of simplicity, compassion, forgiveness and joy
What grace do you ask?
The mercy of God and the community of my sisters and brothers
From where will your help come?
Our help comes from the Lord who made heaven and earth
I invite the St Martin's community now to keep a time of silence as we pray for God's Holy Spirit to bless you and uphold you in this calling

A period of silence is held

The Blessing of the Crosses (on the altar)

Almighty God, bless these crosses as a sign of the Nazareth Community. May it become for those who wear it a sign of resurrection revealed both in the pain and hope of this cross.
Members of the Nazareth Community I invite you now to make your promise of commitment
Most high and everlasting God
accept me now as I come before you in love.
I dedicate myself to the service of my Lord Jesus Christ
with silence, with sacrament, with compassionate service,
with the study of your word

and the sharing of your love for others,
with perseverance and with thanksgiving –
I want to live the Gospel. O Lord give me grace. Amen

My beloved in Christ receive this cross as a sign of your
membership of the Nazareth Community. May it remind
you at all times of the commitment you have made this day
and encourage you at all times in this path of discipleship to
which you have been called.

(*Name*) I receive you as a member of the Nazareth
Community in the name of the Father and of the Son and of
the Holy Spirit. **Amen.**

During which the choir sing: 'Give us the Wings of Faith'
(James Whitbourn)

Go forth into the world in peace;
be of good courage;
hold fast that which is good;
render to no one evil for evil;
strengthen the fainthearted;
support the weak;
help the afflicted;
honour everyone;
love and serve the Lord, rejoicing in the power of the
Holy Spirit.
Amen
And the blessing ...
Beloved go gently,
go simply,
go joyfully,
go humbly.
And may the Spirit of God be with you.
Amen.

Note

1 Bernard of Clairvaux, *Ways of Loving*, Chapter 10.

Afterword

ROWAN WILLIAMS

My dear Richard,
What your wonderful book says to me is that I'm invited
into a shared space; so that it seems most natural to write an
afterword as a letter of thanks, not a little essay of some sort.
I warmed so much to the basic idea of exploring the 'with-
ness' of God at so many levels. One of the really strange and
fresh things about Christianity is that it says that God is never
anything other than 'with' – with God's self in eternity as the
interwoven action that is the Trinity; and then, overflowing
from that, God's free act of being with what isn't God. And
because God is completely faithful to God's own nature and
character, this being with what isn't God is the steady, dependable backdrop to everything in the universe.

You're inviting us into a style of living that is meant to share
and show this steady *being-with* in our own acts, words and
plans. You show us a variety of ways in which we might allow
ourselves to step back far enough from feverish maintenance
work on our own security and worry to be free to see and
hear and sense what every encounter with the world gives us.
Lots here about seeing and sensing, I thought. And it's not just
about some kind of aesthetic enrichment: you keep bringing us
back to the embodied reality of accompaniment, a being-with
that really requires us to put our bodies – and hearts – on the
line: standing with someone without any defence that will keep
the world at bay ...

'Running towards those you love': what an extraordinary phrase to ponder: God's own irresistible urge to be as fully *with* us as can be, and our summons to let that divine urge come alive in us. What you write here about the Eucharist makes me think of receiving Communion in terms of opening up to God's urgency of longing to be with us, and to be *in* us, with whoever we are given to meet: the mystery of seeing 'the peace of Christ carried on his father's back', where we have feared to find negation and violence. I was moved by the Eucharistic order you offered, and thought how much we clutter our celebrations to the point where we can't properly see that promise carried into our midst, into our company.

And then, the silent dance, free from self-consciousness, when we are no longer worried about the impression we make or even the 'results' we achieve. Thank you for that, for the memorable image of Molly dancing to the music in her head. Perhaps as we learn to dance like that, we make ourselves at last visible to ourselves and others – or rather, we make visible to ourselves the reality of which we are a part, so that we and those looking at us and reacting to us might pick up something of that music in the head, unheard but imperative, deeply personal but just as deeply connected and connecting.

I realize that all I'm doing is leafing through and picking up bits that have struck and moved and kindled something as I've read, and I could go on with this for a very long time indeed. But this is meant to be just a letter of thanks, in which what matters is to say that yes, this is both recognizable and startlingly new. What you've given us here is not simply another book on 'spirituality' but a workbook for living in and with meaning, Christian meaning, Jesus-shaped meaning. Wherever we are, here and now, is the centre, the ground of the soul, because this here and now is where God has chosen to be and to be with. I hope that all those who are gathered in the Nazareth family of friends, who have chosen to be where they are because *God* has chosen to be where they are, will become words of hope and affirmation to all who don't know where they are and don't yet fully see the God who is with them where they are.

Thanks so much, dear Richard. It has been a privilege to find a way to Nazareth with you in reading this book. I hope this conveys my delight in and gratitude for your book.

With much love as always,

Rowan

Appendix

The Nazareth Community was launched in March 2018, with forty-eight people joining. Since then others have joined. It brings together members of St Martin's and other churches to learn to live the Christian life more intentionally, in the midst of London. The community is an experiment in being with – with God, with one another, with ourselves and with creation. We are a dispersed community, with a commitment to seven disciplines which members incorporate into their own lives and contexts. Members renew their vows each year and there is opportunity for others to join.

1 Silence

As we enter into silence, we place ourselves inside the love of God. St Martin's offers three times of contemplative prayer a week, alongside Morning and Evening Prayer.

2 Service

In simple acts of giving, and face-to-face encounter with those in need, we discover the joy and reciprocity of service. We discover Christ in those we serve. The community serves in different ways, dependent on their own gifts.

3 Sacrament

The sacrament of Communion is central to our life together: how God in Christ is with us, and we are with one another.

Each week there is an informal Wednesday 6.30 p.m. Eucharist, *Bread for the World*, open to all, where members gather.

4 Scripture

We humbly make our experience and knowledge subject to the wisdom and understanding of theological reflection and scripturally formed imagination. Through a daily *Lectio Divina*, we reflect on who God is and who God calls us to be.

5 Sharing

We spend most of the week away from the church and community. We meet one Saturday morning a month, to discover new insights through sharing and listening to others. Meeting with a spiritual companion gives us guidance along the way.

6 Sabbath

We commit to creating a place and space in our lives each week for rest and relaxation and time to replenish our lives and spirits through beauty and creativity.

7 Staying with

We aim to create a way of life that is sustainable and life-giving, flexible enough for members of the community to integrate with the demands of their lives and yet structured and stable enough to allow for growth, depth and spiritual nourishment.

On the Sunday nearest to 19 March (St Joseph) the Nazareth Community renew their promises at the 10.00 a.m. Eucharist and admit new members. If you would like to find out more about this experience of faith and hope, or consider joining, contact: Nazareth@smitf.org.

YOU MAY ALSO BE INTERESTED IN...

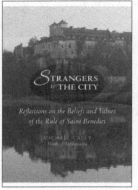

Strangers to the City

*Reflections on the Beliefs and
Values of the Rule of Saint Benedict*

Michael Casey,
Monk of Tarrawarra

ISBN 978-1-61261-397-0
Trade paperback | $17.99

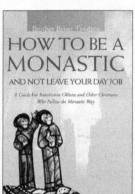

How to be a Monastic and Not Leave Your Day Job

*A Guide for Benedictine Oblates
and Other Christians Who Follow
the Monastic Way*

Brother Benet Tvedten

ISBN 978-1-61261-414-4
Trade paperback | $16.99

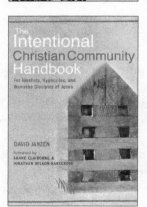

The Intentional Christian Community Handbook

*For Idealists, Hypocrites, and
Wannabe Disciples of Jesus*

David Janzen,
Foreword by Shane Claiborne
& Jonathan Wilson-Hartgrove

ISBN 978-1-61261-237-9
Trade paperback | $26.99
